CONSCIOUSNESS IN NEW ENGLAND

✳

Consciousness in New England

*From Puritanism and Ideas
to Psychoanalysis and Semiotic*

JAMES HOOPES

THE JOHNS HOPKINS UNIVERSITY PRESS
BALTIMORE AND LONDON

New Studies in American Intellectual and Cultural History
Thomas Bender, Consulting Editor

The Johns Hopkins University Press, 701 West 40th Street,
Baltimore, Maryland 21211
The Johns Hopkins Press Ltd., London

The paper used in this publication meets the minimum requirements
of American National Standard for Information Sciences—Permanence of
Paper for Printed Library Materials, ANSI Z39.48-1984

Library of Congress Cataloging-in-Publication Data

Hoopes, James, 1944–
  Consciousness in New England : from Puritanism and ideas to
psychoanalysis and semiotic / James Hoopes.
    p. cm. — (New studies in American intellectual and cultural
history)
  Bibliography: p.
  Includes index.
  ISBN 0-8018-3824-X (alk. paper)
  1. Psychology—United States—History. 2. Psychology—New
England—History. 3. Consciousness—History. 4. Subconsciousness—
History. 5. Puritans—New England—Intellectual life. 6. New
England—Intellectual life. I. Title. II. Series.
BF108.U5H66   1989
155.2'0974—dc20   89-2663
                                                                         CIP

For Carol, Johanna, and Benjamin

Contents

CONTENTS

CONSCIOUSNESS IN NEW ENGLAND

Introduction

Puritan piety, a self-interpretive process, was challenged in the late seventeenth and early eighteenth centuries by a new epistemology, the "way of ideas," or, as it was commonly referred to in the nineteenth century, the "evidence of consciousness." According to the new epistemology, all thoughts were ideas, all ideas occurred in full view of the knowing self, and therefore all thoughts were immediately, empirically known by the self. Desire, being a thought, was an idea empirically known within the self, and no interpretation was needed to comprehend it.

As opposed to this new concept of consciousness, the Puritan theory and practice of religion employed the traditional faculty psychology in which there was a distinction between two fundamentally different kinds of thinking, between willing and understanding, between desiring and knowing. The distinction allowed for the possibility of subjective conflict with regard to an object of perception. A saint might desire holiness without knowing that he or she did so. The reconciliation of such inward conflict—conversion—could be attained through a self-interpretive act. Doubt, interpreted as religious scrupulosity, became a sign of grace. But this dynamic psychology was challenged by the consciousness concept, with its insistence that the self enjoyed complete knowledge of its thoughts, including its desires.

The clash between conversion and consciousness would help bring, in time, the rejection of the consciousness concept's insistence on the immediate and total availability of self-knowledge. Neither did traditional piety escape unscathed from its encounter with consciousness. But the long dying of the consciousness concept—the notion that the self enjoys complete knowledge of its thoughts—is the subject of this book.

For most of the twentieth century it has been fashionable to consider the notion that some thought is unconscious as one of the fundamentally radical and innovative concepts that created and characterizes the "modern" era. But one argument of this book is that the notion that some thought is unconscious was a conservative compromise aimed at preserving as large a role as possible for consciousness and for the self. The chapters entitled "The Self Sign" tell of the development of this conservative insistence that even unconscious thought is action by the self. In the chapters entitled "The Thought Sign," I relate the little-understood story of a more radical if far less influential development, the rise of the notion that *no* thought is subjective, the notion that no thought is created by or in a self but rather that the self is created by and contained in thought.

This book is written from a reconstructionist rather than deconstructionist perspective, and my use of the word "sign" in chapter titles and in the text indicates nothing more than my view that my subjects were engaged, whether wittingly or not, in a process best understood as interpretation rather than "experience." That is, it seems to me that in at least one respect the proponents of the thought sign had the better argument and that thought is not correctly viewed as an immediate experience within a self, though I have occasionally been forced by the absence of alternative terminology to use words and phrases like "subjectivity" and "inner life." Nevertheless, I view subjective "experience" as interpretation of external signs. I do not, however, subscribe to the deconstructionist notion of the liberty with which signs may be interpreted, and I object to the present tendency to grant deconstructionism a monopoly on semiotic method. The "Afterword" at the end of this book explores the way in which the history of the concept of consciousness sheds light on the fallacies of deconstructionism.

The consciousness concept related two signs—self and thought—and described the latter as action by and in the former. In the seventeenth and eighteenth centuries, as the consciousness concept came to dominate mental philosophy and epistemology in the West, it conflicted, in New England and no doubt elsewhere, with the conventional description of religious conversion. Holding that all thought was immediately intuited—that is, occurred as ideas in the full view of the knowing self—the consciousness concept stood in the way of the humility that was crucial to piety; one knew whether one desired God, and there was no need for abasing self-examination. Yet the New England religious establishment was too proud of, or too insecure in, its learning to reject the new mental philosophy and retreat into a mindless fundamentalism. The result was a dialogue in which New Englanders resisted, with varying degrees of intensity, the consciousness concept and helped, as logically as they could, to shape new interpretations of self and thought.

✼

CHAPTER ONE

Conversion

Two Conversions Interpreted

In old England in the late 1620s or early 1630s, while Jane Holmes was still a girl, God took her mother and gave her a stepmother "which was an affliction to me. And [I] thought to make good use of it. Hence began to read the word. . . . I thought I could not live holily in father's house and hence thought to live in a minister's house better." While ensconced with the town vicar, "one . . . opposing openly Puritans," a friend "told me of a new birth and she spake of her misery" and urged Jane "to hear but one and not the vicar." Listening to that Puritan preacher, her "heart was so endeared to that man to live with him." But there, her "heart cross to command," she rebelled against God and "found I was not humbled, yet feared night and day to hell because not humbled. . . . and Lord making way for New England I thought I should find feelings." On board ship she met an antinomian and was so "taken with joy with his delusions that I knew not how to renounce it." He suggested that like another woman he had known, who could only be driven "by a gross act" to depend on faith rather than works for grace, Jane similarly would be done to by God. The antinomian "by insinuation got within me and I would not leave him which I speak it to horror of that which it left me."[1]

In Boston Jane found her heart still drawn to the lascivious antinomian, but orthodox friends "entreated me to refrain his company." Hearing Thomas Weld preach on Jeremiah 3:14—"Turn, O

1. Thomas Shepard, *Thomas Shepard's Confessions*, ed. George Selement and Bruce C. Wooley (Boston: Colonial Society of Massachusetts, 1981), 76–79.

4

backsliding children"—Jane recognized her lapse as well as the way out of the morass. She told the pastor of her "ship entanglements yet by him I was encouraged to go to the Lord. . . . Yet troubled so I followed God in days of humiliation. . . . But my heart at last was struck with admiration at God's mercy to deliver one from such a wretch [the antinomian] and errors. . . . Yet I fearing I was a hypocrite and that appeared the more because I was ready to take comfort. So going to hear Mr. Wells [Weld] . . . [who] showed [that the difference between] a false reliance and true [was] that nothing could content [a] soul that truly relied [on the Lord] but the Lord. . . . by many trials I found Lord in me . . . and I found that my grief was that sin parted between me and God. And on Sabbath Day morning . . . in prayer I found Lord persuaded my heart of His love. . . . yet since [then I have had] fears, seeing [the] greatness of the sin I am turned from."[2]

But such doubts were no more than were to be expected in regard to the self-knowledge of fallible human beings. Jane was able to stand before Thomas Shepard's congregation in Cambridge in the late 1630s and offer the above confession as evidence of visible sanctity and of suitability for church membership.

In Beverly, Massachusetts, in 1873, Clara Fowler was born to unhappily married parents, and her resemblance to her father cost her her mother's affection.[3] As a child she idealized her mother, whose coldness she attributed to her own imperfections. If she could only improve herself, she felt, she would earn her mother's love, so she became extraordinarily conscientious. Thirteen years old when her mother died, she was delirious with grief for weeks.

At age twenty Clara takes up nursing in Fall River. Perhaps she goes to work less out of financial need than out of a combination of idealism and the opportunity of living apart from her ill-tempered father. One night in Fall River she suffers deep psychological

---

2. Ibid., 79–80.
3. This account of her life is based on Morton Prince, *The Dissociation of a Personality: A Biographical Study in Abnormal Psychology* (New York: Longmans, Green, 1906) and Michael G. Kenny, *The Passion of Ansel Bourne: Multiple Personality in American Culture* (Washington, D.C.: Smithsonian Institution Press, 1986), chap. 4.

trauma from a sexually charged encounter with "William Jones," whom she has long admired and idealized. But she represses the painful memory of this encounter for six years.

Forgetfulness is not new to her, but from the time of the incident with Jones it becomes a severe problem. Her unhappy childhood has accustomed her to introspection and daydreams, and her friends have accepted a quality of abstraction in her. Now she becomes even more estranged, slipping out of the hospital dormitory to walk alone when she should be sleeping. She is excitable but at the same time develops "aboulia," a strange lassitude in which she is conscious of desires that she cannot fulfill, not because of external constraint but because of an inner feebleness, an inability to enact her wishes.

Yet in some activities she is capable of great effort. She ceases nursing to attend college on a scholarship, which promotes a sense of indebtedness and leads her, against the advice of teachers and friends, to study night and day. She eats poorly, dissipates what health remains, suffers from persistent neuralgia, insomnia, and fatigue. Her alienation worsens. Ordinarily prim, reserved, and abstinent, she sometimes emerges from a trance to find herself drinking wine at a dinner party or even smoking a cigarette.

Clara leaves college to be treated by Morton Prince, one of Boston's leading neurologists, but the periods of abstraction continue. Sometimes she takes two baths in a row, having forgotten the first. Dressing is another struggle; she often goes through two or three costumes before she is ready for the day. Worst of all is the strain of hiding her problem. She finds herself in the middle of a conversation but has no idea what it is about and must guess or evade. She feels as if her self is withering away.

And she grows more religious. From childhood on she has been subject to visions of Christ and the madonna. Now she indulges in the fashionable turn-of-the-century interest in Roman Catholicism, considers entering a convent, and fantasizes life as a religious. One winter day in 1900 she enters a church and, staring fixedly at some brass ornaments, despairingly ponders her fate. Suddenly, there is a great change. Joyousness and feelings of well-being surge through her. At the same time she is more restful than in years, is "light as air." She believes herself to have been the subject of a "visitation" and considers herself cured: "I want you," she writes to Doctor Prince, "to be the very first to hear my glad tidings of peace and joy. They have come to me . . . despite my little faith, my much sinning."[4]

There are obvious similarities between the experiences of these two young women. Both are vulnerable, needy, and lacking in self-confidence and self-esteem. Both lose their mothers and leave their fathers at relatively early ages to begin adult life pretty much alone. Both suffer on account of youthful relations with men they mistakenly trusted. Each turns to an older, male healer whose essential teaching is that self-knowledge is a difficult study.

But just as the similarities between these two young women's crises of selfhood are great, so too are the differences.

Jane ultimately derives comfort from her encounter with despair, for she has sat in the rude, seventeenth-century meetinghouse and heard Thomas Shepard bluntly preach to the effect that the experience of a broken heart is infinitely preferable to the blithe wretches who "know not their misery." The sincere penitent will therefore ask how "to get mine heart affected with my misery," and the answer is that one must work at being miserable with all one's strength. Jesus Christ is not got with half-efforts: "It is not shedding a teare at a Sermon, or blubbering now and then in a corner [that] . . . will save thee." True, a rebirth in the spirit is an unconditioned gift of God, but effort and will cannot be separated from the enjoyment of this gift. Conversely, if people "perish everlastingly, [it] is because they *will;* every man that perisheth is his owne Butcher."[5]

Shepard's confidence that a person's desire is consistent with his or her spiritual estate implies that the way to fathom one's estate is to examine the quality of one's desire. The question for Jane is, does she genuinely desire God? She fears that she might be a hypocrite because of her readiness "to take comfort." But those fears can also be interpreted reassuringly as a graceful scrupulousness, a desire to be satisfied by nothing but the Lord. It is not by abandoning

4. Prince, *Dissociation of a Personality,* 347, 344.
5. Thomas Shepard, *The Sincere Convert* (London, 1641), 157, 225, 144, 155.

her fear but by interpreting it as a desire for holiness that she be-comes convinced of the presence of an Other within.

Clara, on the other hand, gets her counsel in the plush Beacon Street office of Morton Prince, who, unlike Thomas Shepard, finds no compensating comfort in misery. Happiness is to be had by be-ing happy. Clara needs not Jesus Christ but a "normal self" in place of her "sick self."[6] His treatment, so far as she is aware, consists mainly of hypnosis. Doctor Prince views her as a capable young woman, but he sees no reason for her to make a willful effort. Her illness has originated, he believes, in a part of her mind that is not part of her self. So a self-prompted effort, no matter how strong and willful, could hardly solve her problem. By Clara's time the notion that the conscious self represents only a part of normal men-tal life is becoming an article of faith in New England's official cul-ture. According to Clara's counselor, then, her problem is not to interpret her feelings but to find out her feelings.

Clara's joyous feeling of conversion in church is obviously known, but does she know it or is it known by some part of her mind outside her "true" self? Doctor Prince thinks that the latter is the case and views her conversion as "an abnormal condition, and one that could not last."[7] He does not quite say that its not lasting is proof of its abnormality. But neither does he offer any reason, as Thomas Shepard and others did to Jane Holmes, to interpret subse-quent fears that she was not saved as evidence to the contrary. In-stead, Prince promptly hypnotizes her and places her in one of the psychological states that she considers unhealthy. Evidently she ac-cepts his rather violent treatment and his view that she is not cured. For she allows him to continue the search for four more years, not for the right interpretation to place on her feelings but rather to discover what feelings are hers.

Puritan and Modern Notions of the Self

The question of whether the similarities between Jane's and Clara's experiences outweigh the differences strikes at some of the most important issues in history, especially intellectual history as it is

6. Prince, *Dissociation of a Personality*, 233.
7. Ibid., 346.

written today. History, the platitude once went, is about change
over time. But some of the best-received recent scholarship on Puritan New England deals with seventeenth-century religious conversion as if it is best understood by studying it in the light of twentieth-century psychological theory. Consider two statements, each by
a respected scholar, on the central event of Puritan life—conversion. Sacvan Bercovitch skeptically writes that the Puritan's self had
first to destroy itself and then reconstitute itself—the latter act of
reconstitution being clearly impossible for the self to accomplish if
it was annihilated in the former act of self-destruction. The
Puritan

> tried to explain away the contradictions by claiming that in this case,
> the will was not his own but the action of the Holy Spirit in him.
> The printed results of his efforts belie his claim.[8]

On the other hand, Charles E. Hambrick-Stowe affirms the Puritan
faith:

> Those who took seriously the charge to prepare for meeting God on
> the Sabbath, in the Sacrament, and in death were perforce brought
> into contact with the ultimate realities of the soul and God."[9]

Bercovitch has studied the Puritans out of a desire to locate the
origins of the American self, a self which he finds aggressive and
deceitful, not in spite of, but because of, the Puritan rhetoric of
self-examination and humiliation. Hambrick-Stowe speaks for
many contemporary pietists who affirm a faith something like the
Puritans' and believe in the reality and truth of sanctity. Beneath
the disagreement, each scholar assumes it appropriate to judge the
Puritans by the standard of his own, contemporary understanding
of the process of self-knowledge. Hambrick-Stowe and Bercovitch
are hardly alone in their propensity to ascribe their own psychological views to the Puritans,[10] whose psychological intensity and acuity
do give them a contemporary flavor and probably are part of the

8. Sacvan Bercovitch, *The Puritan Origins of the American Self* (New Haven: Yale
University Press, 1975), 23.
9. Charles E. Hambrick-Stowe, *The Practice of Piety: Puritan Devotional Disciplines in Seventeenth-Century New England* (Chapel Hill: University of North Carolina Press, 1982), 287.
10. See, for example, Howard Feinstein, "The Prepared Heart: A Comparative
Study of Puritan Theology and Psychoanalysis," *American Quarterly* (Summer 1970):

reason for the enormous amount of scholarly attention devoted to them in this century.

Moreover, the insistence of many twentieth-century psychologists on the universal applicability of their theories seems to sanction a degree of ahistoricism in the study of past subjective life, the Puritans' included. A leading historian, John Demos, recently asserted that the biological and chemical bases of mental life give it an element of "invariance" that justifies the application of modern psychiatric theory to seventeenth-century people.[11] On the other hand, Norman Fiering and others have suggested that the inner life has developed over time, with new theories of the mind leading to a more complex subjective life, which in turn leads to more sophisticated theory.[12]

The advocates of change in subjective life have the better case. Demos himself points to evidence that the type of symptoms reported by victims of conversion reaction depends on the sophistication of the patient and his or her culture, with those from "backward, rural" regions suffering the classical hysteria, whereas more "sophisticated" patients "expertly simulate complicated disease entities."[13] With regard to changes in concepts of self and thought, it is easily conceivable that increasingly sophisticated concepts would lead to increasingly complex self-interpretations, even if "invariable" biological processes underlay them. And since self-interpretation is itself part of subjective life, a change in self-interpretation amounts to a change in the inner life. So even if psychological processes do rest in invariable chemical processes, it is mistaken to assume that twentieth-century psychological theory can adequately explain seventeenth-century self-interpretation. The assumption that twentieth-century psychological theory can compre-

---

166–76, and Perry Miller, *Jonathan Edwards,* intro. Donald Weber (1949; rpt. Amherst: University of Massachusetts Press, 1981), 183.

11. John Demos, *Entertaining Satan: Witchcraft and the Culture of Early New England* (New York: Oxford University Press, 1982), 158. For reservations to Demos's approach, see David D. Hall, "Witchcraft and the Limits of Interpretation," *New England Quarterly* (June 1985): 270–71.

12. Norman Fiering, *Moral Philosophy at Seventeenth-Century Harvard: A Discipline in Transition* (Chapel Hill: University of North Carolina Press, 1981), 182–84.

13. Demos, *Entertaining Satan,* 442n.

hend seventeenth-century inner life would be justified only if the self was interpreted through the same language and concepts in the seventeenth century as in the twentieth.

The argument of this study is that the meaning of the word "self," its relationship to "thought," and consequently human self-interpretation have been significantly transformed over the last several centuries of Western, or at least New England, history. It is difficult to imagine a Puritan stopping to define what may have seemed the clearest word in his or her vocabulary. Forced to do so, the Puritan would have said something to the effect that "self" is the person named "I." If asked what would have seemed a puzzling question—whether part of the self is unconscious—the Puritan would have answered yes and located the unconscious part in the body. "Mind" and "consciousness" were as synonymous to Puritans as to John Locke, who objected to Descartes's assertion that the mind always thinks with what he considered the devastating riposte that then the mind must sometimes think unconsciously, must think without knowing that it thinks.[14] Despite all the Puritan emphasis on the difficulty of "knowing" the self and especially the "heart," the difficulty, as in the case of Jane Holmes, was with interpretation of feelings known rather than unknown. As the New Englander Samuel Willard put it, the ability "to reflect upon it self, and read its own Knowledge" was a crucial distinction between the human and animal souls.[15] Difficult to interpret it might be, but the self and its contents were available for inspection.

Puritans little suspected the mysteries often connoted by the word "self" today. In modern, psychoanalytic "self psychology," the self is not synonymous with mind but is "a content of the mind. . . . we recognize the simultaneous existence of contradictory selves: of different selves of various degrees of stability and of various degrees of importance. There are conscious, preconscious, and unconscious selves; there are selves in the ego, the id, and the superego; and we may discover in some of our patients contradictory selves, side by side, in the same psychic agency."[16] The psy-

14. John Locke, *An Essay Concerning Human Understanding,* ed. Peter H. Nidditch (London: Oxford University Press, 1975), 115.

15. Samuel Willard, *A Compleat Body of Divinity* (Boston, 1726), 124.

16. Heinz Kohut, *The Search for the Self: Selected Writings* (New York: Interna-

choanalytic complexities are reflected in popular terminology, which if it does not allow for a multiplicity of selves as a normal state, does posit a self that is at least partly unconscious. In the popular view, the problem of self-knowledge is not a problem of interpreting known feelings, as it was to the Puritans. Rather, the problem of self-knowledge is to gain knowledge of the self's presently unknown feelings. To do so is important because pain and conflict are understood to result if external behavior and conscious personality are not in harmony with the underlying self. Therefore sensitive, well-educated, upper middle-class youths and adults devote time and energy to enlarging their acquaintance with their selves, in some cases possibly about as much time as their Puritan forebears spent in examining their souls for the activity of the Holy Ghost.

This popular notion of unconscious selfhood is scarcely hegemonic in twentieth-century culture. For while the seventeenth-century meaning of "self" has been abandoned by some groups, others, especially fundamentalist Christians, have retained it to some degree. The words "modern" and "modernist" will be used in this study to designate only a part, possibly the less numerous part, of twentieth-century American society. How the "modern" element and its complex view of the self came to exist is a principal theme of this study. But the story told here would have been quite different had there not been, in addition to the modernizers, traditionalists

---

tional Universities Press, 1978), II, 660. "Self psychology" should not be confused with Erik Erikson's better-known "identity psychology" which has enormously influenced historians and biographers for the past twenty years. The self psychologists' central revision of Freudian theory is their positing that the self is not composed through a "coalescence of self-nuclei" (Kohut, *Search*, II, 747) but rather that an individuated self exists from the beginning or at least nearly the beginning of infancy and that it gradually incorporates other experiences and functions: "the parts, in other words do not build up the self, they become built into it" (Kohut, *Search*, II, 749). The self psychologists object to Erikson's use of "ego-identity" to designate the problem of adolescent selfhood in modern society. In their view this confuses questions of social psychology with questions pertinent to basic ego development that occurs much earlier in life than adolescence. See John E. Gedo and Arnold Goldberg, *Models of Mind: A Psychoanalytic Theory* (Chicago: University of Chicago Press, 1973), 64. Possibly, it is Erikson's raising of the broader social situation to greater psychological significance than many analysts would accord it that has made his work so appealing to a generation of historians concerned principally with social history.

who clung to the old view. The new theory did not eclipse the old theory but developed out of and alongside the old. The attempt of the modernizers to placate traditionalists, or even to convince themselves that they were traditional, accounts for some of the more convoluted aspects of modernist thought on the self. The absence of such placatory efforts by the least-compromising theorists, such as Emerson and Peirce, accounts for their failure to exercise, at least so far, as much influence on modern thought on the self as did the less well-known, more compromising modernists such as Nathaniel W. Taylor, Horace Bushnell, and James Jackson Putnam.

Hambrick-Stowe is right, then, to apply his contemporary theory to the Puritans, but only because he shares their view of the self. He is right, not necessarily that the Puritans were brought into contact with the realities of the soul and God, but right to respect the thoroughness and integrity of their soul searching. There was no self-delusion in their belief that they were in touch with something profoundly Other. They understood and encouraged the active role of the self in achieving selflessness, but that does not mean, as the modernist critique of Puritanism has it, that a selfless self had to "reconstitute" itself and simultaneously explain away the "contradictions."[17] Such a view blends modern and traditional notions in a way that is at odds with them both. Such a critique of Puritanism rejects the seventeenth-century view that feelings that did not seem to originate in the self were attributable to God or the devil. At the same time it implies a rejection of the twentieth-century view that feelings of otherness have their origin in the person but *out* of the conscious self. The psychological theories of both centuries teach us to respect the genuineness of feelings of otherness. If we will listen to the converts' own words, not merely for their rhetorical devices but also for their meaning, we will find little delusion in the many available accounts they gave of their religious lives.[18]

17. Bercovitch, *Puritan Origins of the American Self*, 23.
18. In addition to the numerous published spiritual autobiographies of illustrious New Englanders, those of more ordinary converts are recorded in *Thomas Shepard's Confessions; The Notebook of the Reverend John Fiske, 1644-1675*, ed. Robert G. Pope (Boston: Colonial Society of Massachusetts, 1974), passim; *Edward Taylor's "Church Records" and Related Sermons*, ed. Thomas M. and Virginia L. Davis (Boston: Twayne, 1981), 97–117; *The Diary of Michael Wigglesworth, 1653-1657: The*

The Puritan Interpretation of Religious Conversion

Undoubtedly the most famous spiritual autobiography of a New Englander was that of David Brainerd, to whom it pleased God, on a Sabbath morning in the winter of 1738 when the Yale undergraduate was walking alone in the woods, to give such a sense of the danger of Almighty wrath that the young man "begrudged the birds and beasts their happiness because they were not exposed to eternal misery." For more than a year afterward he harbored secret hopes of pleasing God by works and, alternately, resentment that faith alone was the basis of salvation, till at last he was exhausted and truly humbled. Then he understood and accepted his utter dependence on God. Gradually, his spiritual tumult subsided. Sabbath evening, July 12, 1739, "walking again in the same solitary place . . . in a dark thick grove, unspeakable glory seemed to open to the view and apprehension of my soul." With conversion came such enthusiasm and arrogance that he was heard to say that Tutor Whittelsey "has no more grace than this chair." For thus subverting the peace of the college, the rector expelled Brainerd, which provided an opportunity for him to recover his lost humility: "Oh, how much mercy have I received the year past!"[19] Returning to New Haven on commencement day in 1743, he expected to be tormented at the sight of his classmates receiving their degrees but instead found peace and resignation to the will of the Lord. He wrote out a Christian apology to the rector after taking counsel with Jonathan Edwards, another of Yale's returning sons.

Brainerd may not have been able to find and eventually did not want an ordinary, settled pastorate. Instead, he carried the faith to Indians at Stockbridge and then in New Jersey, which obliged him to ride horseback four thousand miles a year "and oftentimes over hideous rocks, mountains and swamps—frequently to lie out in the

---

Conscience of a Puritan, ed. Edmund S. Morgan (Gloucester, Mass.: Peter Smith, 1970), 107–25. There are also some as yet unpublished accounts, at least for the eighteenth century, fifty-three in the John Cleaveland Papers, Essex Institute, Salem, Massachusetts, and sixty in the Parkman Family Papers, American Antiquarian Society, Worcester, Massachusetts.

19. Jonathan Edwards, *The Life of David Brainerd,* ed. Norman Pettit (New Haven: Yale University Press, 1985), 106.

open woods" or gasp for breath in a smoky wigwam. Subsisting on bread or meal baked in ashes, and sometimes not even that, he longed for nothing but God even when, as happened more than once in winter, he fell into a river and spent the day "without much sense of divine and heavenly things." Although a successful revival attended his efforts with the Indians, his extraordinary missionary zeal was merely cause for further humiliation; eventually he had his own Indian congregation, among whom he found it difficult to settle down and contrary to "my disposition, which has been and still is, at times especially, to go forth and spend my life in preaching the gospel from place to place, and gathering souls afar off to Jesus the great redeemer." Yet that very evening brought him into a new relation with his flock, for whom "blessed be God, I enjoyed liberty in prayer . . . and was enabled to pour out my soul. . . . Oh, how sweet! I knew not how to go to bed."[20]

The cycle of humiliation and exultation continued to the end. Surely few readers of the hardships Brainerd recorded in his diary have been surprised that eventually he complained of fatigue and weakness, of protracted coughing, of spitting up blood, and of course of wanting more spirituality. Edwards, to whose home Brainerd had come to die, found no affectation of holiness in him, but rather, he seemed "to nauseate all such things." As the young missionary reviewed his life to find if his had been true religion, he saw corruption in even his most holy acts, but he was reassured by his longing "earnestly to be in that world where holiness dwells in perfection . . . not so much for the sake of my own happiness . . . as that I might please God." Great agony lay between him and the Kingdom. With swollen limbs and diarrhea, with breaking of ulcers in his lungs and spitting up mouthfuls of pus, with alternately clear and distempered mind, he lingered for months and learned it was, as Edwards reported him saying, "another thing to die than people imagined."[21] He tried not to dishonor God with impatience for an end to his suffering, till finally it came on October 9, 1747, in his thirtieth year.

Brainerd's narrative shows that whatever initial indications re-

---

20. David Brainerd, *Mirabilia Dei inter Indicos* (Philadelphia, 1746), 237; Edwards, *Life of David Brainerd*, 231, 397.
21. Edwards, *Life of David Brainerd*, 445, 476.

generate Christians had of the saving work of the Holy Ghost, they marked not the end but the beginning of a rigorous spiritual life, replete with defeats as well as victories. Hambrick-Stowe and Charles Lloyd Cohen recently reminded us that the order of redemption, in which the soul's humiliation for sin preceded its salvation from sin, characterized spiritual life after conversion as well as before.[22] That was why a lay Christian, Francis Moore, cited waywardness in support of his application for church membership and confessed to Thomas Shepard's Cambridge congregation that *after* "the spirit of God did seal to his soul that he was . . . received to mercy" he fell to "loose company and so to drunkenness." Yet "the Lord recalling him usually back again, . . . it did more endear his heart to the Lord and to walk more humbly." By 1764, when Elizabeth Beals applied for admission to Ebenezer Parkman's congregation in Westborough, the required statement seems to have become more doctrinal and less narrational than a century earlier. But Elizabeth nevertheless begged "of God that I may be deeply humbled for the sins which I have been guilty of in times past."[23] All such statements were formulaic to a degree, possibly a great degree. But the formula indicated not only what aspiring Christians were expected to say but also what they were expected to expect, and the latter scarcely amounted to continual bliss.

Advice of eminent ministers and accounts of spiritual life by more illustrious saints indicate that salvation resulted in disappointment as well as delight. Thomas Shepard's journal records frequent bouts with "darkness and atheism." Edward Taylor, presenting himself as a candidate for the ministry, told his future flock that he had some confidence of faith yet knew not how to be pleased with himself "on the account of Sin." Anne Bradstreet, formerly perplexed "that I have not found that constant joy . . . which I

22. Hambrick-Stowe, *Practice of Piety*, ix; Charles Lloyd Cohen, *God's Caress: The Psychology of Puritan Religious Experience* (New York: Oxford University Press, 1986), 234–35; cf. Thomas Shepard, *God's Plot: The Paradoxes of Puritan Piety; Being the Autobiography and Journal of Thomas Shepard*, intro. Michael McGiffert (Amherst: University of Massachusetts Press, 1972), 15; John Owen King, III, *The Iron of Melancholy: Structures of Spiritual Conversion in America from the Puritan Conscience to Victorian Neurosis* (Middletown, Conn.: Wesleyan University Press, 1983), 29.
23. Shepard, *Confessions*, 36–37; Parkman Family Papers, Box 2, Folder 2.

supposed most of the servants of God have," alerted her children against such unreasonable expectations and may never have been as naive as she made herself appear for their benefit. John Winthrop suffered "many falls," and the antinomian crisis caught him "in as drowsy a condition, as I had been in (to my remembrance) these twenty yeares, and brought me as low (in my owne apprehension) as if the whole work [of conversion] had been to begin anew."[24] Any adequate interpretation of Puritan spiritual life must make it possible to understand both the Puritans' belief in the genuineness of their conversions and also the subsequent cycle of fallings off and renewals of spirituality that they themselves acknowledged and expected.

Psychoanalysis Applied to Puritan Conversion

Psychoanalysis, the more or less official doctrine of the inner life in our time, is an aid to such understanding precisely because it respects the conscious self's report of mental, or, in seventeenth-century terminology, "spiritual," experiences that do not seem to originate in the self. Perhaps the best application of psychoanalytic theory to Puritan materials is John Demos's analysis of witchcraft victims, whose torments he interprets as symptoms of "conversion."[25] In psychoanalytic terminology, conversion is a displacement from psyche to soma, a physical expression (or conversion) of a repressed wish. In the case of witchcraft, the victim's repressed wish is projected. Rage and hate too fearful to be acknowledged as part of the self are attributed to the witch. The rage and hate then find their somatic expressions in feelings of being bitten, pinched, poked, and otherwise tormented. Coming from outside the conscious self, these torments are attributed to another, to the witch, and add to the agony and helplessness expressed in the fits and shrieks of the victims.

It is a reasonable surmise that the same underlying process, the

24. Shepard, *God's Plot*, 135; Edward Taylor, "Spiritual Relation," *American Literature* (January 1964): 472; Anne Bradstreet, *Works*, ed. Jeannine Hensley (Cambridge: Harvard University Press, 1967), 243; John Winthrop, *The Winthrop Papers* (Boston: Massachusetts Historical Society, 1929), I, 160.
25. Demos, *Entertaining Satan*, 117.

same conversion of hate and rage, was at work in the awakened sinner as in the bewitched.[26] That the Puritan character contained a good deal of hate and rage is quite likely in view of the Puritan emphasis on "governing" or "breaking" the will of children. Philip Greven, the most thorough student of evangelical parenting in the United States from the seventeenth through the nineteenth centuries, reports only a few references to the "rod" and one account of denial of food to a willful infant. The sources, he finds, are "curiously silent about the actual practices by parents in their conquest of their children's wills."[27] This silence suggests that although corporal punishment and denial of food were sometimes used, more frequent recourse may have been had to less notable "moral" means such as frowns, admonitions, scolding, and shaming. Cotton Mather reserved corporal punishment for "gross Enormity" and taught his children that it was a "*shameful* thing to do amiss." For an "ordinary Fault," his first response was "to lett the Child see and hear me in an Astonishment, and hardly able to beleeve that the Child could do so *base* a Thing."[28] Esther Edwards Burr, a daughter of Jonathan Edwards, said that her ten-month-old daughter "knows the difference between a Smile and a frown as well as I do. . . . and if I only knit my brow, She will cry till I Smile." Edwards himself, according to Samuel Hopkins who lived for a few months in the great theologian's house, waited to govern his children until they first showed "any considerable degree of will and stubborness, [and then] he would attend to them till he had thoroughly subdued them and brought them to submit . . . with the greatest calmness, and commonly without striking a blow."[29]

26. Interesting parallels between the witchcraft tragedy in Salem in 1692 and the "Little Awakening" in Northampton in 1734 are pointed out by Paul Boyer and Stephen Nissenbaum, *Salem Possessed: The Social Origins of Witchcraft* (Cambridge: Harvard University Press, 1974), 27–30.

27. Philip J. Greven, *The Protestant Temperament: Patterns of Child Rearing, Religious Experience, and the Self in Early America* (New York: Knopf, 1977), 38.

28. Cotton Mather, "Some Special Points Relating to the Education of My Children," in *The Puritans*, ed. Perry Miller and Thomas H. Johnson (New York: Harper and Row, 1963), II, 725–26; cf. Mather's report that John Ward advised that in treating the young, "whatever you do, be sure to maintain shame in them." *Magnalia Christi Americana* (Hartford, Conn.: Silas Andrus and Son, 1853), I, 522.

29. Esther Edwards Burr quoted in Greven, *Protestant Temperament*, 35; Samuel Hopkins, *The Life and Character of the Late Reverend, Learned, and Pious Mr.*

With regard to the spiritual needs of both Puritan child and Puritan parent, such moral discipline would have been far more functional than physical force. Refraining from force and acting calmly in dealing with refractory children would have been, for parents, an exercise in the self-denial that was at the heart of their piety. And inculcation of that self-denying principle in children would have been best accomplished through moral discipline, which, far more than physical force, offered a way to develop the sensitive conscience so crucial later in religious life.

Demos's analysis of "conversion" in witchcraft as a physiological expression of repressed hate and rage becomes all the more helpful in understanding positive Puritan encounters with the supernatural if crucial differences between bewitchment and conversion are kept in mind. Whereas the bewitched projected their hate and rage onto another human being, albeit a witch, normal Puritan converts projected their malevolence onto God. The bewitched were not truly helpless but had recourse to the use of countermagic, to community support, to a learned ministry, to prayer, and ultimately to the courts, which might hang the witch. Against God, none of these resources would avail, and people who perceived themselves the object of God's wrath must well expect to be destroyed. Lending weight to God's anger, moreover, was shame, for where the witch's victim was entitled to self-righteousness, the awakened sinners viewed themselves as vile and added their own damning conscience to the accusatory weight. Groan and writhe as it might, the self must indeed be destroyed or at least permanently subdued.

Puritan Theory as Puritan "Experience"

Yet psychoanalysis offers an account of conversion as an unconscious process—a historical shortcoming in dealing with a process that was at least partly conscious[30] and self-motivated. To the Puri-

---

Jonathan Edwards (Northampton, 1804), 47. For a psychoanalytic interpretation of Edwards's own youthful experiences with humility, see Richard Bushman, "Jonathan Edwards and Puritan Consciousness," *Journal for the Scientific Study of Religion,* 5 (Fall 1966): esp. 393–95.

30. The words "conscious" and "unconscious" are used here in the sense in which

tan, conversion was not a rationalization but a self-interpretation. The meaning of conversion and therefore conversion itself were determined by the interpretation placed upon them by conscious thought. We will come closest to understanding the Puritans' religiosity if we approach it not with our theory but with theirs.

In describing religious life to the unredeemed, Puritans explained conversion in language comprehensible not only by their unbelieving contemporaries but by modern, secular thinkers. A psychoanalyst may interpret inward signs of otherness as "unconscious thoughts," whereas a Christian calls them "emanations of the Spirit," but both agree that the conscious self seems to be influenced by something other than consciousness. To a Puritan convert like Jane Holmes, it was clear enough that the conscious self lacks control not only of events in the outer world, such as the death of her mother, but of inner events as well. Her inability to subdue her emotional conflicts revealed to her the foolishness of her father's vicar, "an Arminian, one that taught free will." To her, the Calvinist ideology of determinism and the abject helplessness of the self to live righteously without the grace of God was proved by her own life. Accordingly, the most sensible behavior was a self-conscious attempt at selflessness, at accepting the dominion of otherness. "In times of greatest and smallest fears," her pastor preached, "remember to be humble and vile in thine own eyes, worthy never to be beloved. And let the Lord have his will of thee, and this will give you peace."[31]

The escape from self that was the essence of conversion was facilitated by self-humiliation because conversion was, in large part, that very humiliation at its greatest intensity. The more deeply a pietist despaired of himself or herself, the more reasonable it was to *believe* in the absolute sovereignty of God. Since salvation depended on *faith* in divine sovereignty, the soul's blackest experience of self-despair could be interpreted as a sign of grace. This new

---

they are defined in the first section of chapter 8. That is, the distinction is not between thoughts immediately known in the self and thoughts that are not. Rather, the assumption is that no thought is immediately known in the self. "Conscious" thoughts are signs and attain meaning through an act of sign interpretation.

31. Shepard, *Confessions*, 76; idem, *The Parable of the Ten Virgins Opened and Applied* (London, 1660), I, 146.

self-interpretation, this new meaning, can be understood only as a conscious, not unconscious, process. The conscious self's inability to live up to the injunction to love God rather than oneself was shameful and humiliating in the extreme. But shameful defeat was unavoidable to the truly awakened; since self was attempting to escape self, failure was built into the system. If the regimen of self-loathing was carried forward with sufficient sincerity and tenacity, the self was humiliated and humiliated until in exhaustion it inertly recognized both the futility of the attempt to escape self and the truth of the doctrine of the self's own helplessness. In such a moment of self-despair, it was possible to *believe* in the absolute sovereignty of God and to interpret that belief as saving faith. Out of abject surrender emerged a triumphant identification with the Other. There *was* a contradiction in the attempt of the self to escape the self, but the contradiction, far from showing conversion to have been a delusion, was the hinge on which conversion swung.[32]

The modern reader of conversion accounts must resist the temptation to say that conversion was self-humiliation in its extremest form, but that statement would fall only slightly short of the fact. The best recent studies of conversion find that for Puritans, "faith changed how they regarded their behavior rather than the behavior itself,"[33] an assertion that needs qualification in that a change in

32. William Bouwsma points out that Calvin accepted a similar paradox, the "interdependence" of "fear and hope." *John Calvin: A Sixteenth-Century Portrait* (New York: Oxford University Press, 1988), 44.

33. Cohen, *God's Caress*, 17. Only after formulating by myself the view of conversion as self-interpretation did I find the same point argued at greater length in Charles Lloyd Cohen's recent, fine study. I differ with Cohen, though, because of what seems to me his unduly sunny emphasis on the positive aspects of Puritan religiosity. He is undoubtedly right that "by incessantly going 'out of themselves' to God, Saints grow in faith, assurance, and strength" (108) and even in "self-reliance" and "self-confidence" (109). But these positive elements depended for renewal on the Saint's prowess in self-abasement, as Cohen himself shows in his discussion of John Winthrop's self-conscious attempts at spiritual renewal (270). Conversion, Cohen says, was not "thralldom" (46), but he admits it was "submission" (109). Saints drew satisfaction and strength from conversion, but they were not cheerful prophets of the contemporary theology of "self-realization." Cf. E. Brooks Holifield, *A History of Pastoral Care in America: From Salvation to Self-Realization* (Nashville: Abingdon Press, 1983), esp. chap. 7. Cohen's thorough critique of Max Weber (113–19) shows how poorly informed Weber was about Puritan religiosity, yet I tend to think Weber right, even if for the wrong reasons, about the loneliness of the convert's spiritual life, with only occasional moments of union with the Other achieved through renewals of self-despair.

self-regard *is* a change in behavior and may affect other aspects of behavior. Unless it is emphasized that self-interpretation is behavior that influences the rest of a person's behavior, including the person's relation with others, there is danger of glibness and ahistoricism in saying that conversion depended on a new self-interpretation born of humiliation. For Puritans supposed that their satisfaction in sanctification was drawn from their renewed relationship with God and other people, not from within the self. My point is not to question that view or, for that matter, the agency of the Holy Spirit in the process. But whether it was divine or human agency that lay behind the transformation, what renewed the saint's relations with others was a change in self-interpretation.

Understood as an interpretation rather than a religious "experience," conversion becomes comprehensible to modern readers. Many historians, burdened by the description in the consciousness concept of conscious thought as undeniable self-knowledge, have assumed that Puritan conversion must have been a dramatic, undeniable inward "experience." This view makes conversion literally unimaginable to modern secular historians, who, though not denying its phenomenality, assume that they must approach it on a different level than the phenomenal. Since the "experience" is unattainable to moderns, they must explain it with methodologies such as linguistic analysis and psychoanalysis that were unknown to the Puritans. The inevitable result of explaining conversion by methodologies unknown to the Puritans is to suggest that they did not understand the true basis of conversion. The implicit, sometimes explicit, conclusion is that conversion was a delusion. There is nothing wrong with calling Puritan conversion a delusion if that was indeed what it was. But the historical record supports a quite different conclusion. It suggests that Puritans viewed conversion not as an undeniable "experience" but as a self-interpretation and that they were well aware of what they were doing.

Despite their emphasis on selflessness, Puritans saw that to a significant degree grace was a matter of self-interpretation. Thomas Shepard said succinctly, "at first conversion it is much self," and it was out of self-humiliation that his parishioner, Jane Holmes, longed after otherness and joyously recognized that her greatest grief was "that sin parted between me and God."[34] She could then reasonably believe that she had come as close to the divine as humans ever do. Humiliation like Jane's was what the modern prophet of the self, Nietzsche, had in mind when he called Christianity a slave religion, but Jane interpreted her humiliation as a result of mistaken self-assertion. Having attempted and failed to save herself, she knew that true freedom was to be had not by defying the Other but by identifying with it.

That at least some Puritans understood the crucial role of humiliation in achieving identification with the Other is indicated by their numerous statements, both prescriptive and descriptive, that came close to saying that humiliation and faith were the same thing. William Perkins, possibly the most widely read of early seventeenth-century Puritan divines, counseled that "if you will go to heaven, the right way is to saile by hell." Brainerd believed that "much more of true religion consists in deep humility, brokenness of heart, and an abasing sense of barrenness and want of grace and holiness, than most who are called Christians imagine." Brainerd's spiritual teacher, Jonathan Edwards, reported that "after the greatest mortifications, I always find the greatest comfort." Of humiliation, Edward Taylor cried, "oh that I had more of it," a passionate acknowledgment of the interrelation of misery and grace. That God, "when he shows mercy to any of his, it is in . . . letting them feel much corruption," was meditated by Thomas Shepard. "But what is this Humiliation of heart?" Thomas Hooker asked rhetorically: "It is thus much. When the soule upon search made despaires of all help from it selfe: he . . . submits himself wholly to God."[35]

Humiliation, after all, occurred on account of sin, so that the very fact of humiliation indicated that something was right with the soul, that it abhorred sin and desired God. This "Puritan para-

---

34. Shepard, *Parable of the Ten Virgins*, II, 167; Shepard, *Confessions*, 80.
35. William Perkins, *A Treatise Tending unto a Declaration . . . estate of Grace* (London, 1658), 437; Edwards, *Life of David Brainerd*, 445; Edwards, "Personal Narrative," *Works*, ed. Sereno Dwight (New York, 1830), I, 81; Taylor, "Spiritual Relation," 472; Shepard, *God's Plot*, 198; Thomas Hooker, *Soules Humiliation* (London, 1638), 7.

dox," as it has been well named by Michael McGiffert, was central
to piety and could be expressed with lovely succinctness. Shepard
noted in his journal that "the greatest part of a Christian's grace lies
in mourning for the want of it." Years earlier, Perkins had polished
the same thought for publication: "To see and feel in ourselves the
want of any grace pertaining to salvation, and to be grieved therefore, is the grace itself."[36]

The almost coextensive relation between humiliation and grace
suggests an explanation for the saintly cycle of despair and exultation noted earlier. Only the rarest saints could continuously humiliate themselves. New saints seldom possessed personalities so completely renovated that the joys of submission could totally change
their lifetime habits. Backsliding was inevitable, but just as before
conversion, so afterward, the humiliation caused by sin could be
interpreted positively. Roger Clap assumed that sanctity and postconversion humiliation were intimately related: "when I had most
assurance of God's love, I could most mourn for my sins." Increase
Mather quite self-consciously associated humility with salvation,
the former leading to the latter: "I desire to be more broken
hearted, more humble, more fervent, God knows it. Therefore he
has heard me." Into Thomas Shepard the "Lord dropped this meditation. . . . Be not discouraged therefore because thou art so vile,
but . . . loathe thyself the more. . . . and this I found of wonder-
ful use . . . whereby I was kept from sinkings of heart and did beat
Satan as it were with his own weapons."[37]

Yet modern students err if they assume that humility was all
there was to grace, for one could possess humility without grace. So
taught Thomas Hooker, the master psychologist of his generation,
who preached the necessity of recognizing that "a wounded soul is
the gift of God." Hooker had made his reputation as a pastor in
England through skillful comfort of overly fastidious souls, and in
New England his essential teaching continued to be that humiliation was only part of the preparation for conversion. Too much hu-

36. Shepard quoted by Michael McGiffert, Introduction to Shepard, *God's Plot*,
20; William Perkins, *Works*, ed. Ian Breward (Appleford, England: Sutton Courtenay,
1970), 402.
37. Roger Clap, *Memoirs* (Boston, 1844), 26; Increase Mather, "Autobiography,"
Proceedings of the American Antiquarian Society (Part 2, 1961): 298; Shepard, *God's
Plot*, 44–45.

mility might work against faith. The well-prepared soul must also practice positive thinking: "be sure to take thy soul at the best: Do not always pore upon the worst that is in it."[38] For exactly the same reasons, Cotton Mather advised ministers that "it is of the last importance that you be a good casuist." He urged them to read William Ames, Richard Baxter, and others on the conscience, which "whill abundantly qualify you to . . . distinguish the clean from the unclean." The point was not only to weed out false professors but also to enable true Christians to take comfort from their religion rather than indulge exclusively in humiliation. Ames had warned against the same perversity a century earlier, calling conscience of sins the "causes why beleevers, and godly men, oft-times do not conclude for their own consolation."[39]

The best strategy to ensure that humility resulted in grace was to keep the object in view. Cotton Mather rightly insisted on the necessity of Christ: "the first thing whereto you are to be directed is to . . . humble your selves. . . . secondly, this repentance is to be accompanied with . . . a continual endeavor to converse with your savior."[40] Humility alone was not and could not be grace. There was no self-delusion involved. The soul genuinely had to seek and find something Other if it was to transpose humiliation into salvation. As Murray Murphey has written, "Puritan conversions involved interaction with God, Christ, and the Holy Spirit conceived as real persons; these were *inter*psychic relationships, not *intra*psychic ones. Unless it is clearly understood that for the Puritans these beings were real, and that interactions with them were just as real and just as truly experienced as interactions with human persons, Puritan religious experience makes no sense."[41] Thus even from the standpoint of modernist secular psychology, the doctrinal distinction between humility and grace cannot be counted a delusion.

But if the Puritan account was satisfactory, why was there ever

38. Thomas Hooker, *The Poor Doubting Christian Drawn to Christ* (London, 1700), 350. For Hooker's English career, see John Hart, *The Firebrand Taken Out of the Fire* (London, 1654), 117–32.

39. Cotton Mather, *Manuductio ad Ministerium* (Boston, 1726), 87; William Ames, *Conscience with the Power and Cases Thereof* (London, 1643), 3.

40. Cotton Mather, *The Case of a Troubled Mind* (Boston, 1717), 17–18.

41. Murray Murphey, "The Psychodynamics of Puritan Conversion," *American Quarterly* (Summer 1979): 137.

felt to be a need for a change? Why did modernist, secular interpretations arise? Why was psychoanalysis ever received positively by
significant parts of the New England establishment? The entire answer to that question is doubtless as complex as the entire history of
the three centuries treated in this study, though some elements of
the answer are very obvious. Part of the story involves social, economic, and institutional history. Another important aspect of a
complete answer would be the history of medicine, on which this
book touches. But the indispensable parts of the story on which
this narrative focuses are changing interpretations of thought and
self.

A Conversion Thwarted by Consciousness

The process of self-interpretation, on which Puritan conversion depended, was eventually challenged by a new epistemology, the
"way of ideas," according to which all thoughts were ideas, and all
ideas occurred in the immediate presence and full view of the conscious self. Desire, being a thought, was an idea empirically known
by the self, and no interpretation was needed to comprehend it. As
opposed to this new concept of consciousness, the Puritan theory of
conversion employed the traditional faculty psychology in which
the distinction between willing and understanding allowed for the
possibility of subjective conflict with regard to an object of perception. A saint might desire or will holiness without knowing or understanding it. The reconciliation of such inward conflict—conversion—could be attained through self-interpretative acts. But this
dynamic psychology was challenged by the consciousness concept,
with its insistence that the self enjoyed complete knowledge of its
thoughts, including its desires.

As a broad gauge of the possibility that a conflict between the
concepts of consciousness and conversion may help account for the
differences between the self-interpretations of Jane Holmes and
Clara Fowler, consider the case of Catharine Beecher (1800–1878).
Like Jane and Clara, she lost a beloved mother in adolescence, experienced a mental crisis caused in part by romantic disappointment, and was counseled during that crisis by an older male, in her
case her father, the stumpy, stubborn, jaunty, and zealous Lyman

Beecher, one of the great revivalists of the early nineteenth century. On her mother's side, Catharine was descended from small-town, Connecticut aristocracy, but her father had the impoverished backcountry origins typical of the evangelical ministry in his time. Lyman had courted Catharine's mother with Calvinist tenets and converted her from Episcopacy by guiding her through a spiritual crisis so severe that her family believed he was driving her mad. Although she had willingly abandoned her family's church, she struggled vainly to maintain a superior life-style, and Lyman eventually feared that life on a minister's meager salary had helped her toward consumption and early death in 1816. He remarried the next year, which was a "trial"[42] to Catharine, age seventeen, who as the eldest and favorite daughter had briefly filled the maternal role for Beecher's numerous other children. Catharine felt increasingly rejected as her domineering father thrust her outward from the family circle and toward adulthood. Outwardly submissive and accepting of Lyman's values and views, Catharine covertly rebelled against her revivalist father by failing in the work of conversion.

Lyman had already begun to urge Catharine toward conversion when, in 1821, he was delighted at the attention shown her by Alexander Fisher, a brilliant and prayerful professor of mathematics at Yale. Catharine, after initial misgivings as to the intensity of Fisher's ardor, was won to him but not to Christ. Lyman, at the height of his success as a revivalist, was anguished by the inactivity of the Spirit among his "children at home all stupid."[43] Catharine's impending marriage made hers an especially pressing case since women were thought to be usually converted before matrimony or not at all.[44] Lyman began "addressing her conscience," and, to his satisfaction, she experienced "acute distress" and "agonizing pain. I hope it will be sanctified."[45]

Soon, however, came the news that young Fisher, who had embarked on a year of European study prior to his marriage, had been

42. Lyman Beecher, *Autobiography*, ed. Barbara Cross (Cambridge: Harvard University Press, 1961), I, 270.

43. Ibid., 353.

44. Kathryn Kish Sklar, *Catharine Beecher: A Study in American Domesticity* (New Haven: Yale University Press, 1973), 29.

45. Beecher, *Autobiography*, I, 353.

shipwrecked and drowned in a storm off the coast of Ireland. Lyman held out to Catharine kind hope, but no more than hope, that the young man, hitherto unconverted, had received divine grace at the last moment. Then Lyman tried to put his daughter's emotional distress to her spiritual advantage: "And now, my dear child, what will you do? . . . Will you send your thoughts to heaven and find peace, or to the cliffs, and winds, and waves of Ireland, to be afflicted, tossed with tempest, and not comforted?" Catharine tried with all her might, even to the point of accepting her father's tactless metaphor for a lost soul as "tossed with tempest":

> I weep not that my youthful hopes
> All wrecked beneath the billows rest,
>
> . . . .
> I mourn that, tempest-toss'd on earth,
> I have in heaven no peaceful home.[46]

Unluckily for Lyman, Catharine went to visit Fisher's family at Franklin, Massachusetts, where she heard and rebelled against the harsh preaching of Nathanael Emmons, who clung rigidly to orthodox doctrines like infant damnation and original sin. She admitted to being a sinner with a selfish heart, but she could not achieve the humility, the feeling of "entire guilt," on which she knew grace depended. Her difficulty was with the doctrine of original sin: "I feel that I am guilty, but not as guilty as if I had received a nature pure and uncontaminated." It was easier to "doubt the truth of these doctrines than the rectitude of God." Within a few months she was ready to abandon hope of ever achieving regeneration and told her father she would have to find some other path to happiness in God. As an experienced revivalist, Lyman easily diagnosed Catharine's condition and responded with the traditional evangelical strategy of self-interpretation. Her defeat was not final and must be interpreted not as despair of God but as "self-despair," an indication that God "has advanced His work in your mind." Much depended on a positive interpretation. She must not give up but rather "attempt daily to give yourself away to him," for he requires us "with humble boldness to come to him." Dutifully, she depre-

46. Ibid., 356–57.

cated her "insubmission and murmuring" and for several more months struggled in her slough.[47]

Catharine eventually found her way out of despond, but in an untraditional way, through the philosophy of "consciousness." Had she labored long enough, she might have come round to a traditional interpretation of her self as converted, for evangelical history included famous cases more protracted than hers. But during her time in Franklin with Fisher's family, she tutored his younger sisters in their studies, including philosophy, and planned the "female school" in Hartford that would eventually make her a leading educator. In the same letter to her father in which she reported studying philosophy and broached the idea of founding a school, she brought into their theological dispute, for the first time, the concept of consciousness, or "the certain knowledge which the mind has of its own faculties and operations." Her father's arguments that she had the power to obey and love God were useless in the face of the "certain knowledge" of her own mind offered by consciousness. Having consciously examined herself and finding no ability to love God as He demanded, she considered her father's arguments as to her guilt to be pointless:

> I do feel as certain that I have not present ability to realize the being and presence of God, and to awaken emotions of love toward him, as I do of the existence or non-existence of any faculty of the mind; and it is not strange, nor do I think it wrong, while this consciousness exists, that a conviction that God does require these impossibilities should awaken hard feeling toward him, for we ought not to experience other feelings than those of aversion toward what seems cruel and unjust in any being.[48]

Not so easily stifled, Lyman tried to disabuse her of her faith in consciousness, but Catharine believed that she had finally found good reason to ignore his blandishments. Her state of mind did not require interpretation but was fully and certainly observable: "Should arguments equally powerful with those advanced by you, . . . and ten thousand times more so, be advanced to prove that I had physical strength to move the everlasting hills, it would

47. Ibid., 358–68.
48. Ibid., 377–78.

be to no purpose. Consciousness would be that brow of iron that would resist them all." The question "can never be settled, even to the conviction of my understanding, unless by supernatural interference." The ball was in God's court, she as much as said, and unless He acted soon, "unless in a few weeks all things become new," the world would "engross my thoughts."[49] Since she had already given up the humble guilt that made grace desirable and had also ceased the futile attempt to escape self that led to surrender to the Other, it is not surprising that God forsook her in those next few weeks. Within a year Lyman gave up and allowed her to join his church without benefit of conversion.

The conflict between Lyman and Catharine was also a clash between the conversion and consciousness concepts. He had hoped to bring her to the religious self-interpretation of Jane Holmes and numerous other Puritans. Catharine resisted out of a complex tangle of personal and social motivations. But her motives included her confidence that she could observe within herself a genuine desire for holiness and therefore need not guiltily humble herself before God. Her confidence in her lack of guilt was based on "consciousness," on the "certain knowledge which the mind has of its own faculties and operations." This concept of consciousness was unknown to Jane, who, although she had been utterly certain that she knew what she thought, had been humbled by lack of certainty as to what she desired or willed. Only after anguished soul searching did Jane reach the self-interpretation that "my grief was that sin parted between me and God." Out of the clash between consciousness and conversion was to come, in New England, the modern signs of self and thought that informed Clara Fowler's despair so differently from Jane's and Catharine's.

49. Ibid., 376–77.

CHAPTER TWO

Consciousness

The Consciousness Concept

By the time Jane Holmes was converted in the early seventeenth century, human beings had possessed for at least several thousand years, and probably much longer, the capacity for self-reflection, which had come, by her time, to be associated with the word "consciousness."[1] Belief in a knowing self that existed apart from the objective world required an explanation of how knowledge of the world was possible, required a description of the relationship between the self and the objects of which it has knowledge. For at least two millennia before Jane's time, the predominant explanation was that objects either physically impressed themselves upon the bodily senses or were presented to the senses intermediately, through the emission of immaterial "species" by objects. This theory of knowledge probably did not so much inspire as reflect confidence in the accuracy of human knowledge of the external world. But in the seventeenth century Western philosophers paid increasing attention to the distinction between sensation and perception, the latter being an activity that included the mind's synthesis and

1. This book is not concerned with the much vexed question of when and how self-consciousness or the reflexive ego developed. There is a widespread but mistaken notion that Darwin's remarks on the question in *The Descent of Man,* Part I, chap. iii sparked the flood of modern interest, though Darwin did inspire Chauncy Wright's brilliant essay, "The Evolution of Self-Consciousness," *North American Review* (April 1873): 245–310. But the question was widely discussed in the early nineteenth century, and one can find in romantics like Jones Very (see below, chap. 6) adumbrations of Julian Jaynes's fascinating argument placing the origin of self-consciousness within recent millennia. In my view, Jaynes's argument is weakened by his assumption that metaphorical representation or substitutive reasoning depends on the acquisition of language rather than language on it. Jaynes, *The Origins of Consciousness in the Breakdown of the Bicameral Mind* (Boston: Houghton Mifflin, 1976), 66.

interpretation of sensations. The image of an external object in the mind's eye began to be understood not merely as a mechanical replication of the object but also as an ideal representation of it. Thus even if sensations resulted from a mechanical process, the perceptive activity of the mind in synthesizing and interpreting sensations allowed for the possibility of representational error.

Much has been made of how the "way of ideas," as this perceptual theory came to be called, gave rise to skepticism about the accuracy of knowledge of external objects, but for the purpose of this study the far more important and seldom noticed fact is that the theory greatly heightened confidence in the accuracy of subjective knowledge. Even if an idea of an external object was mistaken, the self's knowledge of the idea was accurate, complete, and unmediated or directly intuited. In this model, the accuracy of self-knowledge was unquestionable. It may have been impossible to attain certain knowledge of external objects, but internal objects—ideas—were experienced as in themselves they really were. This belief in the immediacy of the self's knowledge of its thoughts held sway long after the way of ideas began to be questioned. In this book I have called by the name "consciousness concept" this notion that the self is the creator and container of thought and that it therefore has privileged, completely accurate knowledge of its own actions in thinking.

Belief in the immediate availability and accuracy of self-knowledge threatened the Puritans' dynamic notion of human spiritual life, according to which self-understanding was laborious self-interpretation rather than immediate self-perception. Puritans to some extent underestimated the threat because of the synergy between their concept of conscience and the new concept of consciousness, both of which employed a model of the self as self-reflective. But the Puritan concept of conscience had been articulated within the framework of faculty psychology, which allowed for subjective conflict between thoughts resulting from the faculties of willing and understanding. An object might be understood as evil but, in another thought, desired as good. Conversely the thought might be understood as good but, in a second thought, nilled as evil. Although many proponents of the consciousness concept, such as Locke, continued to allow for subjective conflict between faculties, their notion that every thought was completely and immediately known in the self would eventually make it difficult for potential converts in need of humility to doubt that their desire for God was anything other than it appeared to be. Failure by seventeenth-century Puritans to recognize these fundamental problems made it possible for them to attempt to accommodate their religion to the new "way of ideas," especially by emphasizing the traditional use of sensory metaphors for the gift of divine grace. In doing so they lent unintentional assistance to the weakening of traditional forms of piety and to the intellectualization of religion and indeed of all emotion.

Ideas

An *"Idea"* is an "Object of the Understanding when a Man thinks,"[2] wrote John Locke in the most famous seventeenth-century formulation of the "way of ideas," the epistemological system that dominated Anglo-American philosophy for the next two hundred years. The word "idea" had been a major philosophical term since Plato, but its meaning had changed radically by Locke's time. Plato, by "idea," had meant an eternal "form" rather than a momentary perception. An "idea" was "that which always is and has no becoming" and "is apprehended by intelligence and reason." In contrast to the ideal, the merely perceptual was received "with the help of sensation" and in Plato's view was always "becoming and perishing and never really is."[3] Locke used "idea" in exactly the opposite sense of Plato by limiting it to a momentary perception. And then, by applying the word "idea" to every thought, Locke implied that all thought is perception: "Consciousness is the perception of what passes in a man's own mind."[4]

The long, tortuous transition of "idea" from Plato's eternal form to Locke's momentary perception can only be highlighted here with references to a few major contributors to a developmental pro-

2. John Locke, *An Essay Concerning Human Understanding*, ed. Peter H. Nidditch (London: Oxford University Press, 1975), 47.
3. Plato, *Timaeus* in *Collected Dialogues*, ed. Edith Hamilton and Huntington Cairns (New York: Pantheon, 1961), 1161.
4. Locke, *Essay*, 115.

cess in which hundreds or even thousands of thinkers participated.

In Plato's writings ideas were the model on which a divine agent was forming the world, which raised the possibility to which Plotinus later objected, the possibility that God, or "the Intellectual-Principle," possesses "the Ideal realm as something outside of itself." Skeptical horrors lay implicit in such a view, since it meant that the Intellectual-Principle "possesses images and not the realities" which would lie in an "Intellectual Realm" separate from God. "No," said Plotinus, "these two constitute one substance—though in a unity admitting that distinction" between Intellectual-Principle and "Intellectual Object."[5] Although speculation and debate on this question continued for more than a millennium, the general tendency of Christian Platonists was to follow the unchristian Plotinus in ensconcing ideas within the mind of God.[6] This use of "idea" as a mental pattern in God's mind was eventually extended to human minds, as when Aquinas defined "idea" as a model for an external work "in the mind of the maker."[7]

The next step in the march of "idea" from eternal form to momentary perception was to reverse the locations of the copy and the model by using "idea" in the sense of an internal, mental copy of an external object. When Hero is spurned in *Much Ado about Nothing*, Friar Francis counsels her father to let Claudio believe that she is dead: "The idea of her life shall sweetly creep . . . Into the eye and prospect of his soul."[8] This representational use of "idea," though new in the sixteenth century, had been implied all along by the Plotinian notion that ideas were in God's mind before they were in humanity's. Alexander Richardson made the connection clear in the middle of the seventeenth century when he wrote that since an "idea . . . is in God as in the fountaine," it can only

5. Plotinus, *The Enneads*, trans. Stephen MacKenna (London: Faber and Faber, 1956), 251.

6. Norman Fiering, *Moral Philosophy at Seventeenth-Century Harvard: A Discipline in Transition* (Chapel Hill: University of North Carolina Press, 1981), 249–50; cf. Augustine, *Eighty-three Different Questions*, trans. David L. Mosher (Washington, D.C.: Catholic University of America Press, 1982), 79–81.

7. Thomas Aquinas, *Philosophical Texts*, trans. Thomas Gilby (London: Oxford University Press, 1951), 44.

8. Act 4, scene 1, lines 235–43.

be in human beings as "by a refraction."[9] By the time Richardson wrote those words, "ideas" had become, in the philosophy of Descartes, the only means of knowledge of external objects. It is not the immediate sensation of sight, "not immediately the movements which occur in the eye, but those that occur in the brain which represent these objects to the soul."[10]

The term "idea" was evidently still esoteric to Puritans in 1643, when the glossary "for the unlearned" that was appended to William Ames's *Marrow of Sacred Divinity* defined "idea" as "a forme or image of a thing in a man's mind." But by the end of the century, in New England, Samuel Willard could apparently count on lay congregants to understand the word in the context of a sermon: "To know a thing, is to conceive of the Image of it. Knowledge is made by an assimilation between the Knower, and the thing known. He conceives an Idea of it in his mind."[11]

It is noteworthy, however, that Willard's use of "idea" was influenced by scholastic physics. An idea was not a representation but an "assimilation" between an object and its perceiver. The use of "idea" as a representation of an object would soon bring the same skepticism of humanity's grasp of external reality that Plotinus had feared it would bring of God's, but neither Descartes nor Willard saw the danger because of their confidence that the nervous system was an accurate mirror of nature, their confidence that, as Willard put it, there was a "wondrous harmony between the senses and their objects."[12]

So long as an "idea" was an image of an external object, the language of "ideas" meshed nicely with scholastic physics, which guaranteed the accuracy of people's images, or, in scholastic terminology, "phantasms." External objects, the schoolmen thought, impress themselves upon the body's sensory organs through imme-

9. Alexander Richardson, *Logicians School-Master* (London, 1657), 16; cf. William Ames, *The Marrow of Sacred Divinity* (London, 1643), 24–25.

10. René Descartes, *The Passions of the Soul,* in *Philosophical Works,* trans. Elizabeth S. Haldane and G. R. T. Ross (Cambridge: Cambridge University Press, 1931), I, 338.

11. Samuel Willard, *A Compleat Body of Divinity* (Boston, 1726), 41.

12. Ibid., 120.

diate contact or through immaterial "species" emitted by the objects. These intermediate species were the first part of the scholastic theory to fall, apparently because they threatened the reliability of sensation by the possibility of their being, as the New Englander Charles Morton put it, "not Substances . . . but only a representation of them. . . . indeed all this doctrine of Species seams to be a mistake; for that which affects the outward sence is reall, and [material] body."[13] Morton apparently preferred that if the contact between object and sense was not a direct impression, it should at least be considered an impression by an intermediate body rather than a mere "representation." By insisting on a mechanical process all the way along the line between object and sensory organ, Morton hoped to guarantee the accuracy of the final impressions on the senses.

These impressions on the senses are then carried to the brain by a similarly mechanical process in the nerves, of which Descartes offered a fairly standard description as a system of "tubes" enclosing "little filaments [extending] from the brain . . . to the extremities." Contained in the same tubes are the "animal spirits," a fine fluid of "rarefied" blood which also fills the brain and provides, as Increase Mather conventionally put it, "the tye of union between the soul and body."[14] Whereas the principal function of the animal spirits is to move the muscles at the behest of either the soul or the brain, the spirits also exquisitely suspend the nervous "filaments" and thus keep them, in Descartes's words, "perfectly free" of interference from the "tubes" enclosing them. Consequently, movement at the external sense is exactly duplicated in the brain, at the other end of the nervous filament, "just as when one draws one end of a cord the other is made to move."[15] Morton used the term "pith" rather than "filament," but his description of sight was otherwise consistent with Cartesian neurology. The "pith of the Optick nerve" divaricates into the "retina where the picture is made" by the entrance of light through the pupil, and the optic nerve is "so

13. Charles Morton, "Compendium Physicae," *Publications of the Colonial Society of Massachusetts*, 33 (1940): 150–51.

14. Descartes, *Passions of the Soul*, 337; Increase Mather, *Remarkable Providences*, ed. George Offor (London, 1856), 83.

15. Descartes, *Passions of the Soul*, 335–37; cf. Descartes, *Meditations on First Philosophy*, in *Philosophical Works*, I, 197.

moved, Pressed, or Affected as to Convey the Sentiment into the part of the brain where the Common Sense is Lodged."[16]

This interpretation of perception as a mechanical process guaranteed accurate understanding of the external world and appealed greatly to even the most spiritually minded philosophers, who especially resisted Pierre Gassendi's skeptical view that it is impossible to achieve any certain knowledge of external things. Descartes may have removed the source of the soul's ideas from sensory organ to brain, but through a mechanical description of perception he guaranteed the correspondence of object, sensory organ, and brain state. There was no obvious threat in Descartes's writings to the belief of a Puritan like Edward Reynolds that "as the beams of the Sunne shining on a glasse, do there work the Image of the Sun; so the species and resemblances of things being conveighed on the Understanding, do there work their own Image." Only "Atomical Physiology," said the Cambridge Platonist Ralph Cudworth, "renders the Corporeal World Intelligible to us." Only in an external body's "Mechanical Dispositions" can it reasonably be conceived of as acting on the senses and the brain. The likenesses, or "phantasms," thus mechanically produced in the brain possessed, of course, an identity distinct from that of the object, but as Descartes said, they were as accurate as the impression of a seal in wax.[17] New Englanders like Charles Morton and Samuel Willard were scarcely alone in the seventeenth century in celebrating the harmony of the senses and their objects. But despite the confidence that this mechanical theory inspired in human perception, other considerations weighed against it.

Although a mechanical interpretation of perception guaranteed the accuracy of ideas of external objects, it did not guarantee the truth of innate ideas, such as the idea of God, a dangerous opening to skepticism that forced Descartes to insist that unimaged thought also possessed form. In order to mark a unique quality of undeniable truth in images, Descartes had insisted that to "images . . .

16. Morton, "Compendium Physicae," 155, 161.

17. Pierre Gassendi, "Objections" to Descartes's *Meditations* in Descartes, *Philosophical Works*, II, 184; Edward Reynolds, *A Treatise of the Passions and Faculties of the Soule of Man* (London, 1656), 445–46; Ralph Cudworth, *The True Intellectual System of the Universe* (London, 1678), 48; Descartes, "Rules for the Direction of the Mind" in *Philosophical Works*, I, 38.

alone is the title 'idea' properly applied; examples are my thought of a man or of a chimera, . . . or [even] of God." Ideas, considered "only in themselves, . . . cannot properly speaking be false," for even if "I imagine a . . . chimera, it is not less true that I imagine [it]." Although the fact that Descartes had an innate idea of God was, at least in his view, undeniable, the idea might have been chimerical. To accept an innate idea as true was to make a judgment, and judgments, as acts of the mind, could not be formally verified unless they possessed form. Descartes therefore asserted that not only ideas but also the mind's unimaged "other thoughts," as in judging, willing, fearing, approving, and denying, "possess other forms as well."[18] This assertion enabled him to maintain that his idea of God could be verified, for then the form not merely of images but also of mental actions might be judged to be or not to be clear and distinct in the light of reason. But the assertion also led, eventually, to use of the term "idea" to include unimaged thoughts as well as images.

Descartes maintained that although the mind can exercise no control over its perceptions, it can develop sound procedures for judging their truth and their goodness, including the idea of God. Human error derives "from the sole fact that . . . the will is much wider in its range and compass than the understanding." If people "always precede the determination of the will" by "the knowledge of the understanding" and refuse to judge whenever this condition cannot be met, they will not err, Descartes said. Since the faculty of understanding can perceive clearly and distinctly that something cannot be derived from nothing, no "idea derives its origin from nothing."[19] Similarly, a cause must be equal to its effect; otherwise something in the effect would be derived from nothing. And since Descartes possessed an idea of a perfect being, the idea must have been caused by a perfect being, who therefore must exist.

But Thomas Hobbes revealed the problem in Descartes's reliance on unimaged thought or "reason" to confirm the truth of his ideas: "But what shall we now say, if reasoning chance to be nothing more than the uniting and stringing together of names or designations by the word is? It will be a consequence of this that reason

18. Descartes, *Meditations on First Philosophy*, 159.
19. Ibid., 175, 176, 163.

gives us no conclusion about the nature of things, but only about the terms that designate them." Reason indicates nothing more than whether or not in thinking we obey some "convention (arbitrarily made about their meanings) according to which we join these names together. If this be so, . . . reasoning will depend on names, names on the imagination, and imagination, perchance, as I think, on the motion of the corporeal organs. Thus mind will be nothing but the motions in certain parts of an organic body."[20] Hobbes thus sought to locate the source of all thought in the mechanical brain processes that produced images. Acts of reason, resulting from the same physiological processes as images or ideas, could claim no special privilege or capacity for judging the truth of ideas. Hobbes's view also denied, at least by implication, the immortality of the soul, as Cartesians quickly pointed out.

Cartesian and other Christian defenders of the soul responded to Hobbes's challenge by applying the perceptual model and therefore the word "idea" to all thought, unimaged as well as imaged. Antoine Arnauld, whose *Logique, ou l'Art de penser* was translated into English and used as a logic primer by eighteenth-century American college students, withdrew Descartes's restriction of "idea" to image. It is "impossible to *imagine* a *thought,* nor to delineate any form of it in the brain," Arnauld pointed out, yet "what do we apprehend more clearly, then [sic] our *thought* when we *think?*" It was appropriate, therefore, to apply the term "idea" not only to "those Images that present themselves to the Fancy, but whatever offers itself to our *thoughts.*" Similarly, in New England at the end of the seventeenth century, Charles Morton sought to maintain the existence of disembodied minds like angels by asserting that they could possess "the species of material things otherwise than by phansy [image]."[21] By enlarging the rubric "idea" to include not only images but also judgments, Christians sought to deny that the soul was dependent on mechanical brain processes for all its thoughts. If they thereby opened the possibility of ideas being viewed as representations rather than replications, they pre-

20. Thomas Hobbes, "Objections" to Descartes's *Meditations* in Descartes, *Philosophical Works,* II, 65.

21. Antoine Arnauld, *The Art of Thinking* (London, 1685), 48; Charles Morton, "Pneumaticks," manuscript, Houghton Library, Harvard University, 98.

ferred that sort of potential skepticism to the Hobbesian variety, where a mechanical interpretation of thought led to the conclusion that minds were machines. Rather than permit the reduction of reason to a mechanical process like imagination in traditional neurology, Christians would raise imagination to the level of reason.[22] By the time Locke wrote, "idea" had been so broadened that he was only following standard usage in applying the word to unimaged thoughts and regarding all thought as perception.

Locke, however, extended Descartes's point that the human mind could more easily know itself than its body[23] into an argument for greater confidence in the accuracy of unimaged thought than of images. Locke asserted that the mind derived all its ideas from two processes—"sensation" and "reflection." By "sensation," he meant external sense, and here he worked out the famous distinction between "simple" and "complex" ideas that put in question the representational accuracy of images of external objects. An image of a ruby, for example, is not the result of a single sensation delivered intact from stone to mind via the body. Rather, the eyes deliver the simple idea "red"; the sense of touch delivers the simple idea "hard"; and the mind compounds them into the complex idea "ruby," which consequently does not necessarily totally or accurately represent the stone as it is in itself.[24] But "reflection," according to Locke, gives people *Perception of the Operations of our own Minds* within us," not with regard to the formation of images, but with regard to unimaged thought as in reasoning, judging, desiring, fearing, and so on.[25] Even though Locke put in question the representational accuracy of people's ideas or images of external objects, he lent unqualified support to belief in the accuracy of human knowledge of internal objects—ideas themselves.

At this late date it is not necessary to protest that in some respects Locke's contribution to "British empiricism" was not empirical, but it is necessary to emphasize that Locke was a proponent of empiricism. Too much of our current opinion of Locke is colored by

22. This process would eventually allow the term "idealism" to connote opposition to materialism even though Hobbesian materialism had been based partly on the way of ideas.

23. Descartes, *Meditations on First Philosophy*, 149.

24. Locke, *Essay*, 299.

25. Ibid., 105.

late nineteenth-century empiricists like William James who accused Locke of being insufficiently empirical, of arriving at his conclusions by inference rather than observation. The difference between Locke and James lay merely in their assessment of what was revealed by immediate experience. James believed immediate experience revealed thought to be a continuity rather than Locke's view that thinking was a process of associating atomistic ideas.[26] To describe the emphasis on "immediate experience" by late nineteenth-century empiricists like James as a "radical theory of knowledge"[27] is something of an overstatement, for Locke's writings contained the same emphasis. Locke agreed with James that thought was directly, immediately experienced within the perceiving self. When late nineteenth-century empiricists cited the "immediate experience" of continuity in consciousness in order to attack Locke's associationism, they were merely extending a still more fundamental principle to which Locke also subscribed, the belief that consciousness was privileged or immediate self-knowledge.

Although there has been voluminous commentary on the way in which Locke jeopardized confidence in the accuracy of images of external objects, it has not been sufficiently noticed that his emphasis on the immediate knowledge of internal mental operations greatly increased confidence in self-understanding, or, as Catharine Beecher would eventually put it, "the certain knowledge which the mind has of its own faculties and operations."[28] Ideas of sensation, though immediately and accurately apprehended, might or might not be accurate representations of external objects. But ideas of reflection, such as desire, were undeniably accurate, not only in the mind's apprehension of them but also in their quality, since they were not representations but mental things in themselves, as they really were. Once the soul's actions in desiring came to be conceived of in the perceptual model that had formerly applied only to

26. This notion was at least as questionable as Locke's. The disagreement amounts to circumstantial evidence for Charles Sanders Peirce's conclusion that there is no such thing as immediate experience within a self. See below, chap. 7.

27. James T. Kloppenberg, *Uncertain Victory: Social Democracy and Progressivism in European and American Thought, 1870–1920* (New York: Oxford University Press, 1986), 77.

28. Lyman Beecher, *Autobiography,* ed. Barbara Cross (Cambridge: Harvard University Press, 1961), I, 377.

images, some of the usefulness was lost in the distinction that earlier thinkers had drawn between, on the one hand, understanding as passive perception and, on the other hand, willing and judging as active powers of the mind. To Locke, will or desire was the perception of "an *uneasiness* in the want of an absent good."[29]

This change from the notion of desire as an action whose quality had to be interpreted to the notion of desire as a direct and undeniable perception of a quality of uneasiness owing to an absent good eventually challenged piety. The new notion made it difficult for potential converts to experience humiliating doubts as to the genuineness of their desire for holiness. Consciousness of a desire for holiness was, as Catharine Beecher would assert, a perception of uneasiness in the want of God as an absent good. Denial of the genuineness of this idea was no more reasonable than denial of any other idea when it was actually present to the mind. No wonder Catharine waited vainly for conversion when she already possessed what conversion was supposed to bring—confidence that she desired God, at least to the degree that it was possible for her to do. The confidence in human self-understanding that was inspired by the perceptual model in the way of ideas would eventually have severe consequences for traditional piety.

The Self

In addition to ideas, there was a second, less widely discussed, but equally important element in the concept of consciousness—the perceiving self, or soul. Consciousness, as it was conceived in the seventeenth century, involved not only an object but also a subject, a thinking thing to create and perceive ideas within itself. Descartes, religiously inclined, naturally presumed the soul to be that thinking thing and made thought the proof of the existence of the soul. Beginning with universal doubt and refusing to accept anything not clear and distinct in the light of reason, Descartes found it impossible to deny "that whilst I thus wished to think all things false, it was absolutely essential that the 'I' who thought this should be somewhat, and remarking that this truth '*I think, there-*

29. Locke, *Essay*, 251; cf. 372–74.

fore I am' was so certain and so assured, . . . I came to the conclusion that I could receive it without scruple as the first principle of the Philosophy for which I was seeking." Since thought was the proof of the self's existence, Descartes concluded that the self was composed of a mental or spiritual substance that differed fundamentally from the material substance composing the external world. Descartes's division of the created universe into two substances—mind whose essence was thought and matter whose essence was extension—was based on what he believed, as he tirelessly repeated, could be "seen clearly and distinctly." Any thought, even an image of a physical body, can be conceived of as unextended in itself. On the other hand, perception of everything external—figure, motion, or mass—involves extension. On the basis of this difference between internal and external phenomena, Descartes asserted that external qualities are attributes of matter, or a "substance different from me," whereas qualities that "cannot be . . . conceived apart from me" reside in intelligent substance, in mind or soul.[30]

Less religiously inclined writers, like Hobbes, accepted the existence of a self ("we can conceive no . . . thinking without a thinker") but challenged Descartes's argument that the self was composed of a distinct substance whose essence was the act of thinking: "For in the same way I might say, I am walking; hence I am the walking."[31] Logical though Hobbes was, majority opinion followed Descartes, for his distinction between mind and matter rested on a commonsense view of people and machines that must have been difficult to resist in the seventeenth century and that is familiar to the artificial-intelligence controversies of our own time.[32] A mechanist interpretation of human thought such as Hobbes's implies the possibility of constructing a machine able to

30. Descartes, "Discourse on Method" in *Philosophical Works*, I, 101; Descartes, *Meditations on First Philosophy*, I, 190–91.

31. Hobbes, "Objections," 62, 61.

32. For a broader discussion, see John W. Yolton, *Thinking Matter: Materialism in Eighteenth-Century Britain* (Minneapolis: University of Minnesota Press, 1983). A useful selection from twentieth-century writings on this question is Douglas R. Hofstadter and Daniel C. Dennett, eds., *The Mind's I: Fantasies and Reflections on Self and Soul* (New York: Basic Books, 1981). See especially A. M. Turing, "Computing Machinery and Intelligence," 53–66.

think like human beings and consequently able to deceive human beings into believing that the machine is human. Descartes conceded that a machine could be made to bark whenever it saw a cat and do everything else necessary to convincingly imitate a dog. But human language is so complex and human reason so universally applicable that a machine could never "reply appropriately to everything that may be said in its presence, as even the lowest type of man can do."[33]

As to the nature of the soul, Descartes maintained that it operates as a unity, possesses innate ideas, and thinks continuously. He rejected the hypostatization of faculties engaged in by some of the schoolmen whereby the soul was made to "play the part of various personages" as when "the understanding" conflicts with "the will." Descartes admitted that psychological conflict was real but maintained that it was not a conflict among the soul's faculties. Rather, the conflict was between the soul and the animal spirits. The soul or the animal spirits or both could exert force on the brain, or, more precisely, the pituitary gland, a fact that explained feelings of inner conflict. But the soul itself could contain no conflict, for the "soul has not in itself any diversity of parts; the same part that is subject to sense impressions is rational; and all the soul's appetites are acts of will." Since the soul is composed of a spiritual substance whose essence is thought and since a substance exists continuously, the soul always thinks. And since some ideas—God for one example and the self for another—never present themselves unexpectedly to the soul in the way that ideas of external objects often do, these ideas must be "innate in me."[34]

Descartes's commitment to innatism was shared by his English contemporaries, nearly all of whom held that innate ideas or at least innate principles in the self were essential to ethics and religion. The most famous example, multipliable by the dozen, was Robert Burton's *Anatomy of Melancholy*, which held that "the purer part of the *Conscience*, is an innate Habit, and doth signifie *a conservation of the knowledge of the Law of God and Nature, to know good or evill.*" This "naive" version of innatism, as John W.

33. Descartes, "Discourse on Method," 116.

34. Descartes, *Passions of the Soul*, 353; Descartes, *Meditations on First Philosophy*, 170.

Yolton has aptly called it, held that both moral axioms and an idea of God were present in the soul at birth. Quite popular at the beginning of the century, naive innatism was gradually tempered by more sophisticated thinkers, such as the Cambridge Platonists Henry More and Nathanael Culverwel. "Had you such notions as these when you first peep't into being . . . and were they rock't asleep with you?" asked Culverwel. But both Culverwel and More remained loyal to innatism and attacked the naive view only in order to save innatism from becoming indefensible. Hoping to preserve the doctrine of innatism, More argued for a more sophisticated view: "But the mind of man . . . cannot but discover, that there is an active and *actuall Knowledge* in a man, of which these outward objects are rather the reminders than the first begetters or implanters. And when I say *actuall Knowledge,* I doe not mean that there is a certaine number of *Ideas* . . . legibly writ there like the *Red Letters* . . . in an *Almanack;* but I understand thereby an active sagacity in the Soul. . . . So the *Mind of Man* being jogg'd and awakened by the impulses of outward objects is stirred up into a more full and cleare conception of what was but imperfectly hinted to her from externall occasions; and this faculty I venture to call *actuall Knowledge* in such a sense as the sleeping Musicians skill might be called *actuall skill* when [in sleep] he thought nothing of it."[35]

But as became clear when Locke denied the possibility of any innate idea—including the idea of God—the insistence in the consciousness concept that all thought is immediate self-perception worked against the doctrine of innateness that More and others considered essential to orthodoxy. Locke was willing to concede to More that the mind must possess some sort of innate structure or disposition prior to perception, but he would not grant the name knowledge to anything that fell short of an actual perception, an actual idea. Accordingly, Locke asserted that a newborn infant's mind is as devoid of ideas, including ideas of God and self, as the

35. Robert Burton, *The Anatomy of Melancholy* (Oxford, 1621), 42; John W. Yolton, *John Locke and the Way of Ideas* (London: Oxford University Press, 1956), 39; Nathanael Culverwel, *An Elegant and Learned Discourse of the Light of Nature* (London, 1654), 58; Henry More, *Antidote against Atheisme, or an Appeal to the Natural Faculties of the Minde of Man, Whether there Be Not a God* (London, 1653), 13–14.

infant's senses are lacking in experience of the external world. The heart of Locke's argument was that he had examined both his own ideas and others', and as far as he could perceive or "observe," he could find "none" not attributable to external sensation or internal reflection, not even the idea of God. He pointed to voyagers' accounts of peoples who had no idea of a deity and asked of those peoples who did, how their ideas of God could be innate when "in the same country . . . men have far different, nay, often contrary and inconsistent ideas, and conceptions of him?" Since the "wise and considerate" always attain an idea of God, whereas the "lazy and inconsiderate" sometimes do not, it seemed evident that the idea of God was arrived at by "thought and meditation." So, too, Locke challenged Descartes's conclusion that the idea of self or personal identity was innate, holding instead that it was a perception: "When we see, hear, smell, taste, feel, meditate, or will any thing, we know that we do so. . . . And by this, everyone is to himself, that which he calls *self*."[36]

Like everyone else in the seventeenth century, Locke believed that there was a thinking thing, a self, but he took the radical step of basing the self's feeling of personal identity on consciousness rather than attributing it to any underlying substance: "For since consciousness always accompanies thinking, and 'tis that, that makes everyone to be, what he calls *self* . . . in this alone consists *personal Identity*." Even Hobbes had assumed it was a substance, albeit matter, that was the subject of thought, but Locke followed the representationalism of the way of ideas to its logical conclusion, defining "*substance*" as "an uncertain supposition of we know not what." He admitted the possible substantiality of the soul and even of disembodied spirits like angels, but he also maintained that knowledge of spiritual substance was impossible to attain. Human knowledge of even material substance was so limited that not reason but only "faith and probability" could exclude the possibility of God's adding a thinking faculty to matter.[37]

Descartes had erred, Locke believed, in supposing thought to be the essence of spiritual substance, for the supposition implied un-

36. Locke, *Essay*, 92–95, 335.
37. Ibid., 335, 95.

conscious thought. A substance exists continuously, so if thought is the essence of spiritual substance, the mind must think continuously. But how was continuous thought reconcilable with the common experience of interrupted consciousness? "Wake a man out of a sound sleep, and ask him, what he was that moment thinking on." True, the roused slumberer might say he was dreaming, but dreams are often "*extravagant* and incoherent" and, in any case, people do not seem to have them constantly when they sleep. Locke could see only one last retreat for the Cartesians; they might say that a person always thinks "but is not always conscious of it." But that would be as unreasonable as saying "that a Man is always hungry, but that he does not always feel it." Just as hunger includes the self-perception that I am hungry, "thinking consists in being conscious that one thinks."[38] Believing that all thought is perception and that it is impossible to perceive without knowing that one perceives, Locke believed it impossible to think without knowing that one thinks. For Locke, thought was not the essence of the soul, but self-consciousness was the essence of thought, a view that ruled out any possibility of unconscious thought or even of unknown qualities in passions and desires.

Surely a large part of the appeal, in the era of the scientific revolution, of the notion of mental life as a self's or soul's perception of its own ideas was that the model was analogous to the relation between the bodily self and the material world. The body receives sense impressions; the soul perceives ideas. The body and external matter are composed of atoms; ideas are similarly atomistic, i.e., originally separate from each other and only subsequently compounded into more complex thoughts. The soul stands in relation to ideas as the senses do to external matter. This perceptual model of mental life helped inspire confidence that the human psyche and morals could be studied scientifically. If both external reality and subjective thought are known by the soul in the form of ideas, introspective psychology is on ground at least as firm as mechanics or any other branch of physics. Locke represented a broad stream of seventeenth-century thought when he asserted that "the *Idea* of a supreme Being . . . and the *Idea* of ourselves . . . being such as are

38. Ibid., 113–15.

clear in us, would, I suppose, if duly considered . . . place Morality amongst the Sciences capable of Demonstration."[39] At a time when immense gains in knowledge were being made through observation and induction, Western philosophers committed themselves to a theory of the self's action in thinking as fully self-observed.

The Puritan Affinity for the Consciousness Concept

Puritan piety had fed into and helped create the consciousness concept. In pietist usage, the seared "conscience" on which religion depended was nearly synonymous with the self-knowledge implied by "consciousness" as the word came to be understood in the late seventeenth century. "Conscience," in the late sixteenth-century formulation of a Puritan like William Perkins, resembled Locke's late seventeenth-century definition of "consciousness" as the perception of what passes in a man's own mind. According to Perkins, there were "two actions of the understanding, the one is simple, which barely conceiveth or thinketh this or that: the other is a reflecting or doubling of the former, whereby a man conceives and thinks with himself what he thinks." The latter action, the doubling back of thought upon itself, occurred with regard to every thought, for this self-reflection was "conscience," which "beares witness what the wills and affections of men be in every matter." Infallibly if often dimly, a sinner's conscience perceived his or her iniquity. Conversion, too, was self-reflection, for God "hath bound us in conscience, to beleeve in the remission of our owne sinnes."[40] The Puritan theory of "conscience" therefore blended easily if not quite consistently with the theory of "consciousness" as perception of the self's contents. It was easy to miss an important difference: in the Lockean theory of consciousness every thought was, from the start, completely perceived by the self, whereas for Perkins a thought first occurred simply or unself-consciously before being reflexively judged or interpreted in conscience.

The dynamic spiritual life in which Puritans believed was more

39. Ibid., 549.
40. William Perkins, *A Discourse of Conscience* (London, 1597), 77, 89; cf. William Ames, *Conscience, with the Power and Cases Thereof* (London, 1643), II, 2–3.

difficult to describe in a model of all thought as immediate perception of the self's contents than in the medieval model of mind as divided between willing and understanding. In Perkins's view, for instance, conscience was located in the understanding, where, by its action of "reflecting," it passed judgment on will and desire. Other Puritans, like William Ames, thinking that conscience contained an element of desire, divided it between willing and understanding. But in either case the important point was that the medieval model of mind as divided between fundamentally different kinds of thinking required interpretation of the genuineness of the soul's desire for holiness, which, once interpreted as genuine, was evidence of holiness: "if men . . . endeavour to please God in all things," Perkins wrote, "God will . . . accept their little and weak endeavour . . . as if they had perfectly fulfilled the law." For those human beings who were attempting to assess the state of their souls and who were knowledgeable of their feeble performance, everything depended on judging the genuineness of their endeavors. Faith was not an idea clear and distinct in the light of reason but, as Ian Breward has well described it, a "leap beyond the doubts of reason."[41] Puritans had, in medieval faculties, a psychological system much better suited than the concept of consciousness to describe their dynamic conception of human spiritual life.

Medieval faculty psychology is often unfairly maligned in our time when the consciousness concept is widely but mistakenly assumed to have obliterated discussion of faculties and to have been a logical step toward twentieth-century philosophy of mind. But many of the strongest advocates of the way of ideas in the seventeenth and eighteenth centuries continued to discuss faculties, and much nineteenth-century philosophical psychology, especially in New England, was conducted within the intellectual framework provided by medieval faculties.[42] Proponents of the "self sign," as I have called them below, were especially given to continuing discussion of faculty psychology. They used the terminology of faculty psychology to effect their cautious challenge and modification of

41. William Perkins, *Works,* ed. Ian Breward (Appleford, England: Sutton, Courtenay, 1970), 402. Ian Breward, Introduction to ibid., 94.
42. Daniel Walker Howe, *The Unitarian Conscience: Harvard Moral Philosophy, 1805–1861* (Cambridge: Harvard University Press, 1970), 41.

the consciousness concept. In order to maintain that the self is not as good as it sometimes seems to itself, they concluded that the self is not conscious of all that it thinks. Faculty psychology, in New England at least, helped create modern depth psychology. As an early twentieth-century scholar observed of faculty psychology, "The doctrine loses every battle—so to speak—but always wins the war. It will bend to the slightest breath of criticism; but not the most violent storm can break it. The attacks made long ago . . . appeared to be irresistible; no serious defence was even attempted. Yet the sole permanent effect of these attacks was only to banish the word 'faculty,' leaving the doctrine represented by this word to escape scot free."[43]

Nowhere is this unacknowledged persistence of faculty psychology more evident than in modern psychoanalysis, whose division of the mind into conscious and unconscious has the same basis as the medieval division of the mind into faculties of understanding and willing. Both psychoanalytical and medieval models of mind are based on the fact that human beings experience psychological conflict which they would not experience if the conscious self alone— or, as the schoolmen put it in a not quite parallel word, the understanding alone—were in control of thinking: "I see and approve the better course; I follow the worse,"[44] lamented Medea in Ovid's rendition of Euripides' great tragedy—widely quoted by Puritans—when she resolved to revenge Jason's unfaithfulness by murdering the children she had borne him. Interposed between medieval and modern theories was the consciousness concept's two-hundred-year challenge to traditional doubt of self-knowledge. The consciousness concept inspired confidence in self-knowledge by describing an idea as the self's immediate perception of both the emotional and intellectual content of a mental state. In that model, conflict over any single idea was impossible. The evangelical need for such conflict, in New England at least, eventually provoked resistance to the concept of consciousness, and the resistance leaned heavily on faculty psychology.

43. C. Spearman, *The Abilities of Man* (New York: Macmillan, 1927), 38–39; for a recent defense, see Jerry A. Fodor, *The Modularity of Mind: An Essay on Faculty Psychology* (Cambridge: Massachusetts Institute of Technology, 1983).
44. Quoted in Fiering, *Moral Philosophy*, 115.

In the seventeenth century, however, it was not easy to see that the shift from "conscience" as an after-the-fact interpretation of thought to "consciousness" as immediate perception of thought posed a threat to traditional religion. If the consciousness concept challenged the dynamic model of mind in the faculty psychology, its emphasis on sensation as the source of most ideas seemed to offer an equally satisfactory way of describing the inner conflict on which Puritan spiritual life depended. Instead of an interior conflict between willing and understanding, there might be a conflict between different ideas resulting from different senses, including a sense of virtue or even of holiness. Pietists had long used sensory metaphors like "new light" and "new taste" to describe religious life. At least partly because of the challenge of the consciousness concept, they began to literalize those metaphors, a process, as Fiering has shown, that fed into eighteenth-century sentimentalist ethics and contributed enormously to modern psychological theory. But by this same accommodation to the consciousness concept, the Puritans also contributed to the subtle intellectualization, or perhaps the right word is "alienation," of subjective life that took place once a feeling or desire became something to perceive rather than something to interpret. John Locke made clear the tendency of his perceptual model of mind to objectify the inward life when he wrote that it was only because he had reserved the term "sensation" for external experience that he called the mind's perception of its own operations "Reflection," which "though it be not Sense . . . yet it is very like it, and might properly enough be called internal Sense."[45]

Puritans were concerned about excessive intellectualism, but they were on guard against explicit intellectualism of the traditional scholastic sort rather than the implicit intellectualism of the consciousness concept. The conflict between piety and scholastic intellectualism is especially clear in the Puritans' most formidable scholar, William Ames, whose untimely death in 1633 prevented his planned immigration to New England. He was, nonetheless, the leading theological mentor of the first generation of Massachusetts Bay clergy, and he made clear why pietists found it difficult to

45. Locke, *Essay*, 105.

believe that the willing faculty was subordinate to the understanding. Helplessness and dependence were central to the humility on which religion depended, but human beings would be neither helpless nor dependent on the Holy Spirit for setting straight their spiritual lives if right willing always followed right understanding. For then the mere "inlightening of the Understanding would be sufficient" for grace, a conclusion "repugnant to Faith and godliness." No, said Ames, the will is not dominated by, but rather dominates, the understanding. The will can "turn away the understanding" from consideration of any object, and "by reason of this commanding power, the *Will* is the first cause of unadvisednesse, and blame-worthy error in the Understanding."[46] Challenging a deeply scholasticized and intellectualized Protestantism, seventeenth-century pietists like Ames rejected the Thomist view that understanding was the dominant faculty in favor of an Augustinian emphasis on willing.

Ironically, the pietist emphasis on right willing and desiring, which was intended to guard against the explicit intellectualism of scholasticism, only facilitated the implicit intellectualism of the consciousness concept. The very strength of pietists' emphasis on the renovation of a person's willing as the characteristic quality of grace could easily slip into a complete separation of willing from understanding, so that it became all the more easy to conceive of mind strictly as intellect or the perception of ideas.[47] Traditional emphasis on willing as a mental faculty was due to a voluntarist tradition within scholasticism. Duns Scotus, for instance, subordinated understanding to willing, but that was because he conceived

---

46. Ames, *Conscience*, 23–25; cf. *idem, Marrow of Sacred Divinity*, 5.

47. Pietist enhancement of the importance of right willing thus helped set the willing faculty on its course to extinction as a useful concept in formal psychology. By the end of the eighteenth century much philosophical psychology in the West was carried on with little or no discussion of "will," as the word had been used in the seventeenth and earlier centuries. A formidable eighteenth-century thinker like Jonathan Edwards used "will" as a synonym for temperament or disposition rather than rational appetite. Many Victorian thinkers, on the other hand, were inspired by nineteenth-century popular emphasis on consciousness to use "will" as a synonym for an *intellectual* domination of mind over body. The pietist reduction of will to temperament violated the traditional conception of will as a *mental* faculty, and the Victorian intellectualization of will violated the traditional conception of will as a mental faculty distinct from the understanding faculty.

of the two faculties as joint functions of the soul's highest attribute—reason. Human beings, alone among the creatures, were blessed with a mental life. Being able to understand the truth, people must be able to will it as good. Otherwise people might see the truth but nevertheless be unable to enact it when it conflicted with bodily appetites. Willing, according to Scotus, did not occur independently of reason but was a "rational faculty," the conative aspect of reason.[48] But pietists, in order to explain the unruliness of the unregenerate will, tended to dissociate willing from reason and to locate its determinants in some substratum of personality such as a "frame," "disposition," "habit," or, most prominent of all in Puritan writings, the "heart." But once separated from reason, willing could not be distinguished from the passions, and the concept of willing as a mental faculty was left with no support but academic tradition.

And academic tradition, even in Puritan New England, tended toward intellectualism. Skillful evangelists like Thomas Shepard may have held that "the main wound of men is their Will,"[49] but Harvard academicians as represented by a fair number of commencement theses defended the intellectualist position that "the will is determined by the last practical judgment of the intellect." At Yale, too, the scholastic view of the will as rational appetite was evidently propagated, if we may judge by a student's notebook.[50] Even William Ames, despite his avowed Augustinianism, sometimes spoke of will as rational appetite. Despite the fact that Ames was trying to support piety by breaking free of scholasticism, his own education was scholastic. When his intellectual heritage did not conflict with his piety, he paid his respects to the schoolmen.[51]

Not piety alone, then, determined psychological theory in New England, and it is scarcely surprising that the tension between intellectualism and voluntarism was greatest in academic centers. Pu-

48. Duns Scotus, *Duns Scotus on the Will and Morality*, trans. Allan B. Wolter (Washington, D.C.: Catholic University of America Press, 1986), 145; cf. 163–65, 171–75.

49. Thomas Shepard, *The Parable of the Ten Virgins Opened and Applied* (London, 1660), I, 60; cf. Thomas Hooker, *The Application of Redemption* (London, 1659), Books IX–X.

50. Fiering, *Moral Philosophy*, 113, 108–9.

51. Ibid., 59, 125.

ritans were people of the Renaissance, proud of their learning, and eager to participate in international culture and intellectual life. Confident that God's word as spoken in scripture would not be contradicted by his word as revealed in the book of nature, they believed that religion had nothing to fear from natural philosophy. Thomist intellectualism and scholastic voluntarism were weighty traditions that merited a hearing by Augustinian pietists secure in their learning as well as their faith. Pietists may have believed that their Augustinian voluntarism was confirmed by their own unruly willing, but they did not hold themselves above technical disputation with learned opponents. It is not surprising that intellectualism, which was the dominant position in the West at the beginning of the seventeenth century, had defenders in New England.

Moreover, pietists themselves left intellect a significant role in human spiritual life. The awakening process that preceded the work of the Holy Spirit in conversion had to be described in natural rather than supernatural terms, and justice required that sinners have enough knowledge of moral law to deserve condemnation. The solution to both problems was to insist that all people, even the most depraved, possessed a remnant of moral knowledge. Voluntarist that he was, William Ames tried to limit the significance of the "rules of honesty, which are within the booke of the mind," by holding that they were "almost totally overwhelmed by custome in sinning." But still, if conscience were to convict the natural man so that he might be humiliated by his sins, moral knowledge must be to some degree "written and ingraven in nature" and so preserved after the Fall.[52] Regeneration might be regarded as mainly a matter of straightening the willing faculty, but it was also a convention among the learned that "intellect and will are the soul as understanding and willing," as a 1684 Harvard thesis put it.[53] Respect for the unity of the soul made it impossible to deny some intellectual content to a renewed spiritual life: "wisdom or having of Divine Light" was essential, Thomas Shepard said, "not that it doth exclude the evil or change of the will and affection, but because they manifest themselves and are maintained in the mind. . . .

52. Ames, *Conscience*, II, 2; cf. Willard, *Compleat Body of Divinity*, 577.
53. Quoted in Fiering, *Moral Philosophy*, 107.

The heart makes the eyes blind, and the mind makes the heart fat."[54]

Because of their friendly attitude to new learning and their past tolerance for intellectualism, Puritans could initially welcome the consciousness concept. Cartesianism was influential at Harvard by the last third of the seventeenth century and perhaps one might even say victorious by 1686, when the commencement theses of that year led Nathaniel Mather to observe from the distance of Dublin that "the Cartesian philosophy begins to obteyn in New England."[55]

Henry More's *Enchiridion Ethicum,* adopted about this time as Harvard's principal text in moral philosophy, may have been the source for the Cartesianism in the theses of 1686. Despite More's optimistic assessment of the moral capacity of the natural man, the adoption of his text was a more or less logical result of the synergism between Puritan pietism and Cambridge Platonism.[56] More was an admirer of Descartes's analysis of the passions, and as with Descartes, More's tendency was toward basing moral life on feeling.

It would be a mistake, however, to suppose that More's emphasis on right feeling was anti-intellectual, for he tended to intellectualize feeling. Faculty psychology was based at least partly on introspective observation of an apparent conflict between understanding and willing. In that model, knowledge or understanding of God's moral law did not necessarily involve a willingness or desire to enact it. But More, influenced by the perceptual bias in the consciousness concept, spoke of a "Sense of Virtue." Even though this was an interior sense or feeling, it gave to the soul, just as any external sense might, a perception or "Idea of virtue." Virtue, therefore, was an "intellectual Power of the Soul" capable of subduing ideas resulting from the bodily senses, or "animal impressions."[57]

More's *Enchiridion Ethicum* shows how the perceptual model of

54. Shepard, *Parable of the Ten Virgins,* I, 147.

55. Quoted in Thomas Goddard Wright, *Literary Culture in Early New England* (New Haven: Yale University Press, 1920), 103.

56. Fiering, *Moral Philosophy,* 195, 248.

57. Henry More, *Enchiridion Ethicum* (1690; New York: Facsimile Text Society, 1930), 8–12.

thought in the consciousness concept permitted intellectualist innovations to creep into psychological theory almost unnoticed. He
used faculty terminology to describe the sense of virtue, calling it
the "Boniform Faculty," and he sometimes opposed "will" to "intellect." But his basic dichotomy was not the traditional one between understanding and willing, with both faculties conceived of
as mental or spiritual. Rather, he saw the basic division as lying
between an "*animal* part" and an "*intellectual* part of the Soul."
The "animal part" referred to the external or bodily organs, the
sensations of "which being obtruded with any sort of Violence on
the Soul, brings danger of Sin and Error, if not carefully
watched."[58] Such watching was the job of internal sense, or the "intellectual part" wherein the Boniform Faculty resided. More's tendency, even more strongly than Descartes's, was toward viewing desiring and willing as bodily, or "animal," functions, leaving
"intellect" to constitute the entire mind.

What contradicted the traditional division of the mind's activities into understanding and willing was not the Cartesian emphasis
on the unity of the soul but rather the notion that all thought was
perception. If every thought was a perception, it was reasonable to
suppose that those ideas not resulting from the external senses were
perceived or understood by an internal sense or senses. In the faculty model both willing and understanding were functions of a
unitary soul, but only one function—understanding—was perceptive. Willing and understanding could not occur simultaneously, at
least not if they disagreed, for then, as William Ames had said,
"these two judgements should bee together; namely, this ought to
be followed, and this ought not, which were absurd."[59] The important point was the potential conflict between these two qualitatively different ways of thinking—willing and understanding. In
the consciousness concept, on the other hand, an act of will or a
desire was not only a desire but also an idea immediately perceived
in the understanding faculty. Whatever conflict a person experienced with regard to that idea could not be interpreted as a strictly
mental conflict, for that would have implied, as Ames had said,

58. Ibid., 31, 12.
59. Ames, *Conscience*, I, 24.

the absurd notion of a thought's contradicting itself. Rather, the conflict was between mind and body.

The emphasis on virtue and even grace as sense or perception was pushed to the furthest point in seventeenth-century New England in the writings of Charles Morton, who had distinguished himself in England as the head of a famous dissenting academy, Newington Green. Well acquainted with leading philosophical developments in Europe, Morton became, upon his arrival in Boston in 1686, a central figure in the intellectual life of Massachusetts during the period of dramatic political events that culminated in the transformation of the Bay Colony into a crown colony. Morton was well prepared to help lead the transition to more liberal thinking, which better suited the colony's weakened political position vis-à-vis London and which in any case probably better suited the mood of local luminaries like the Mathers. Morton may have been influential in Harvard's adoption of More's *Enchiridion Ethicum,* and his own *Compendium Physicae* became, in 1687, the Harvard text in natural philosophy.[60] In 1693 he published an original work, *The Spirit of Man,* which, though written in a Puritan milieu, was in some respects more advanced than More's *Enchiridion Ethicum* in its accommodation of the inward life to the perceptual model of mind in the consciousness concept.

Morton's *Spirit of Man* is an early example of how the consciousness concept forced religious thinkers to dislocate part of what had previously been conceived of as human mental life and, in the absence of a notion of unconscious mentality, to relocate it in the body. *The Spirit of Man* was understood by the Boston intellectual establishment to be a friendly book, and its introduction—signed by Increase and Cotton Mather, Samuel Willard, John Bailey, and James Allen—called for a "Renewal of the *Divine Image* in our Spirits." Such language was scarcely revolutionary in itself, but Morton considerably broadened the traditional use of the word "spirit," which even Descartes had used more or less synonymously with soul. Morton applied "spirit" to the "whole man . . . both Soul and Body." While he also believed in the possibility of disem-

---

60. Samuel Eliot Morison, "Charles Morton," *Publications of the Colonial Society of Massachusetts* (1940): vii–ixxx.

bodied spirits like angels and demons, Morton believed "spirit," as applied to man, should be "a more *General* and comprehensive word" than did most of his contemporaries. Under "spirit" he included not only soul but also acquired habits, environmental influence, and bodily temperament. Since "souls in themselves are all equal," differences in spirit among individuals are attributable to "the other causes," the most important of which, Morton believed, was bodily temperament. Thus "many good Christians, by reason of natural infirmities" rather than lack of grace, "are not always able to manage a zealous spirit."[61] Although Morton cautioned that zealotry is no guarantee of true piety, his drift—surely partly unwitting—was toward interpreting religion as partly a bodily phenomenon.

Morton's emphasis on a bodily basis for spiritual life drew both on the emphasis placed on the "frame," "disposition," or "heart" by Augustinian pietists and on the perceptual model of the inward life implied by the consciousness concept. Locke, despite his opposition to innatism, had admitted that the predisposition with which a person responds to sensory input is a determinant of perception, and Morton similarly described religious conversion as a renovation, not of the traditional faculties, but of personal disposition. When Paul exhorted the Ephesians to "*be ye renewed in the Spirit of your Minds,*" he meant, Morton said, "not that you should have new Powers, or Faculties Natural. . . . But new Dispositions."[62] Like every other perception, holiness simultaneously illuminated the understanding and stirred the will in a manner determined not only by sensory input but also by the perceiver's inclination or temperament.

Morton unified conscience into a single perception resulting from something like More's Boniform Faculty. Ames and Perkins may have differed over the location of conscience within the faculties, but both believed that conscience was an act of self-judgment that depended on there being a qualitative difference between understanding and willing. Morton did not overtly overturn the two faculties but instead united them in the context of a sensory system. Understanding and willing, he asserted, are not the only pri-

---

61. Charles Morton, *The Spirit of Man* (Boston, 1693), 4, 5, 19, 50.
62. Ibid., 94.

mary faculties but rather "there seams to be a third Cal'd Conscience" which is a "complex" of the other two. Any one act of conscience, Morton insisted, involves both "an act of the practicall Judgment" and "a yeilding and Subjective act of the will." By subsuming the two faculties within any single act of conscience, Morton, while seeming to hold to the traditional faculties, was able to describe conscience not as self-interpretation but as inward sensation or perception: "the Complacence, Contentment, and Satisfaction, which we take in virtuous actions, . . . for w[h]en one has done wel he has contentment and satisfaction in him self."[63]

Morton's sensory emphasis spilled over from conscience to religion. Because he blurred the lines between what More had called the "animal" and "intellectual" parts of the soul, Morton found it impossible to deny some degree of conscience to animals and therefore necessary to redefine what was unique in the human spirit. When writing of disembodied spirits, Morton used the Cartesian definition of "spirit" as "thinking substance," but he rejected Descartes's notion that among earthly creatures only human beings had such spirits, for in brutes there is "immateriall spirit" and in dogs "a kind of conscience." Morton proposed to replace, as the fundamental trait distinguishing human beings from animals, the ability to think with the ability to think religiously. He was willing to extend conscience to animals because he preserved human uniqueness by denying animals any capacity for religion. But while Morton may have believed he was merely refining the notion of what was unique in the human spirit, his writings also marked a profound shift of emphasis toward salvation as an empirical perception. In Perkins the unique quality of human beings had lain in their God-given capacity for moral self-examination and interpretation. In Morton humanity's distinguishing trait was the capacity for perceiving God or achieving "sense of Deity."[64]

One may surmise that Morton's innovations, like More's, were acceptable because they seemed to allow for the dynamic inward processes understood to be involved in piety, but the consistency

63. Morton, "Compendium Physicae," 204; Morton, "A System of Ethicks," manuscript, Harvard University Archives, 4.
64. Morton, "Pneumaticks," 121–22; cf. Morton's phrase, "Sentiment of a deity," "Compendium Physicae," 204.

with piety was more apparent than real. Morton could urge self-examination in language that sounded traditional but that was quite innovative in content: "men should be well acquainted with their own Spirits, and Inclinations; so they will be better Enabled to resist Sin, and Address to Duty, in which two consists that Renovation of their Spirits, to which they are exhorted."[65] The difference was that in Morton's system spirit had ceased to be entirely mental. Subjective conflict was not within the soul but between the soul and body in the way that Descartes and More had described it. Conversion, or "Renovation" of spirit, was still a question of self-knowledge, but the self-knowledge was achieved not by an interpretation of the quality of a person's desire but through inward sensation. And Morton seemed to hold out hope of self-conscious dominion over temperament, a process perilously close to salvation through natural knowledge rather than a miraculous or gracious transformation of the soul. But since Morton left room for a reprobate to understand his inward life as conflict ridden and humiliating, his system bore a surface resemblance to traditional pietism.

It was not immediately understood that the emphasis on the clearness and distinctness of ideas—the mind's transparency to itself—would eventually make it impossible for a potential convert like Catharine Beecher to question the genuineness of her desire for holiness and therefore impossible to engage in the preparatory humiliation needed for conversion. Henry More's universalizing of the moral sense was heterodox to Puritans, but it probably did not seem a necessary consequence of a sensory description of the inward life. Sensory metaphors such as "new light" and "new taste" had long been used to describe the exclusiveness of grace. The common use of such expressions in the seventeenth century was not revolutionary but consistent with both scripture and the writings of sixteenth-century reformers.[66] Those metaphorical descriptions of religion as new knowledge had never before threatened pietist assertions of the superiority of willing to understanding in spiritual life. But in the late seventeenth century, old-fashioned descriptions of the religious life began to be used in the context of a new model

65. Morton, *Spirit of Man*, 95–96.
66. Terence Erdt, *Jonathan Edwards: Art and the Sense of the Heart* (Amherst: University of Massachusetts Press, 1980), chap. 1.

of mind that made it impossible to separate feeling from thinking or willing from knowing. The tendency, therefore, was to extend sensory psychology inward and to describe virtue and even grace as inward sensations as undeniable to the perceiver as any other of his or her perceptions.

The first alarm in New England was triggered not by any notion of conversion as immediately perceivable but only by the threat to the traditional doctrine of conscience that was implied by Locke's denial of innate ideas in the *Essay on Human Understanding*. The influence of Locke in America has usually been greatly overestimated, at least until recent salutary studies discovered a far broader range of sources than had previously been imagined for eighteenth-century theory in both politics and psychology. Those studies are supported by this book, for many of the thinkers treated here opposed Lockean empiricism. Yet it is important not to forget that Locke was greatly influential, even among those on whom, as Fiering has observed, his "main effect" was as "a prod and stimulus to the reformulation and strengthening of the most vulnerable traditional assumptions about the foundations of morality."[67] Locke was a powerful prod in New England, where his psychological empiricism threatened evangelical religion not only by raising doubt as to whether any perception of holiness could reasonably be attributed to God but by undermining the theory of conscience on which traditional piety and, ultimately, conversion depended.

Conscience as involving innate knowledge was necessary to Puritan understanding of spiritual regeneration. If conscience were not innate, there would be no inevitability of misery or humiliation on account of sin, for then conscience, like sin, was not from God but from human beings, as Locke plainly said: "but without being written on their hearts, many men may, by the same way that they come to the knowledge of other things, come to assent to several moral rules." The Puritans' renowned psychological sophistication depended on the opposite view, the view that conscience was an innate faculty which in innocence had been able to read and obey the moral law written on the human heart. This had been the common view in England in the seventeenth century, when it informed such widely read books as Burton's *Anatomy of Melancholy*. But

67. Fiering, *Moral Philosophy*, 296.

this view was dying out in England by the early eighteenth century, when, in New England, Cotton Mather defended it. Provincial and ashamed to be so, Mather was nevertheless forced into explicit reaction by the increasing popularity of Locke's views. People are born, Mather announced, with "a rich cluster of Ideas," and it is a mere pretense "that we have no Ideas in our minds, but what are introduced from abroad, by Observations." Among humanity's innate ideas are "the Principles of Reason," by which people judge "what is morally Good, or what is morally Evil."[68] It was probably the threat Mather saw to the doctrine of conscience that led him in old age to desire to "be excused from recommending an Essay of Humane Understanding which is much in vogue."[69]

The New Englanders who opposed Locke did so not merely out of contradictory doctrine but also because they were far more inward and interpretive than Locke, who was so wed to the concept of consciousness as composing all there is of the mind that he could not have appreciated, as the Puritans did, Pascal's saying that the heart has reasons the reason knows not of. Locke held that if moral rules were innate, people could not transgress them with "confidence and serenity" as an army does in sacking a town. Confidence and serenity were the last words by which Cotton Mather would have described looting and rapine. Pillage, he would have held, was performed in rage brought on by an accusing conscience. So, too, he held that belief in God was "imprinted on the hearts of all the world" and is acknowledged by an "innate faculty in the mind of man." True, "there have been horrid and filthy swine, looking like men, who have brag'd, that they did not believe a God; but even these too have ly'd. . . . These wretches undergo horrible twinges in their souls."[70] Mather made no attempt to reconcile such assertions of inner conflict with the way of ideas, whose language he sometimes employed. Had he attempted to do so, he would have found it hard going, for if the mind does possess an idea of God, the idea, as an immediately known object of consciousness,

68. Locke, *Essay*, 70; Cotton Mather, *A Man of Reason* (Boston, 1718), 3–4. For a discussion of a similar reaction to Locke by Harvard's most distinguished president in the colonial era, see Arthur Kaledin, "The Mind of John Leverett" (Ph.D. diss., Harvard University, 1965), 180–81.

69. Cotton Mather, *Manuductio ad Ministerium* (Boston, 1726), 36.

70. Locke, *Essay*, 70; Cotton Mather, *Reasonable Religion* (Boston, 1700), 11–13.

ought to be impossible to deny, ought to produce more evidence for itself than a twinge.

Only slowly would New England theologians see that their principal intellectual challenge was to reconcile the need in piety for two qualitatively different kinds of thinking with the perceptual model of the consciousness concept, which outmoded the traditional division between willing and understanding. Some would move slowly down the path blazed by Charles Morton, a trail that by the late eighteenth century brought a mere moralist and believer in natural religion such as Ezra Stiles to the presidency of Yale.[71] Although displacement of part of the source of spiritual life from mind to body might allow for inner conflict, it left open the possibility that human rather than divine conquest over sinful willing could resolve the conflict. The opposing option, a fundamentalism divorced from modern thought and culture, was also too extreme for mainstream pietists proud of their learning. Considerations of this sort, in the nineteenth century, would force some evangelical theologians toward an entirely mental division, toward the conclusion, mockingly rejected by Locke, that the mind sometimes thinks without perceiving that it does so. Before that happened, however, there would be some consideration of one other option—the enormously ambitious one of attempting not to describe religion in terms of ideas but rather to interpret ideas in terms of religion.

71. The great influence of the way of ideas on Stiles' liberal theology is discussed in Edmund S. Morgan, *The Gentle Puritan: A Life of Ezra Stiles, 1727-1795* (Chapel Hill: University of North Carolina Press, 1962), 73-76.

※

CHAPTER THREE

The Thought Sign: Edwards

Born-again Christianity and the Eighteenth-Century Problem of Personal Identity

Although Locke's opposition to an innate conscience was the first clearly seen threat to orthodoxy, his rigorous perceptualism posed another basic challenge to evangelical religion by putting in theoretical doubt the possibility that regeneration was a perceivable fact. Once all thought came to be understood as perception, the only way people could expect to know that they were saved was through a perception. New Englanders like Charles Morton accordingly moved toward a sensory description of grace, but Locke questioned whether any such sensation could be perceived to be from God. Puritans could usually subscribe to attacks on antinomianism. But Locke's famous criticisms of "Enthusiasm" were as damaging to Puritan claims that sanctification was visible as to antinomian claims of direct communication with the almighty: "These men have, they say, clear light, and they see; they have an awaken'd sense, and they feel: This cannot, they are sure, be disputed them. For when a man says he sees or he feels, no body can deny it him, that he does so. But here let me ask: This seeing is it the perception of the truth of the proposition, or of this, that it is a revelation from God? . . . These are two very different perceptions, and must be carefully distinguish'd, if we would not impose upon ourselves."[1]

If people have no direct knowledge of spiritual or material substance but only simple ideas delivered by sensation or reflection and compounded by the mind, it would seem that no idea can be

1. John Locke, *An Essay Concerning Human Understanding,* ed. Peter Nidditch (London: Oxford University Press, 1975), 700–701.

perceived to be from God. As John Toland soon said, in words very much like Morton's but with a much clearer import, ideas are "the common Stock of all our Knowledge; nor can we possibly have Ideas any other way without new Organs or Faculties." And since God's revealed word does not mention any new organs of sensation, all people have the same resources for acquiring ideas. It follows "that God should lose his End in speaking to them, if what he said did not agree with their common Notions." Samuel Clarke was only the most famous of those Englishmen who by the early eighteenth century noted that people claiming "to be convinced of the Being of Spirits by the powerful demonstration of their own senses" were not more exemplary for their conduct or even their piety than those whose faith rested merely on scriptural revelation.[2]

The eighteenth century's most thorough and philosophical defense of traditional religion against these impious implications of the consciousness concept was that of an American provincial, Jonathan Edwards. While insisting against Locke that holiness was a perceivable "idea," Edwards guarded against the consciousness concept's other threat to conversion, its tendency to make a desire for God an undeniable inward perception. Edwards's position amounted to a compromise with the consciousness concept. Holiness was a perception, but an uncertain perception requiring subsequent interpretation. Edwards thus left room for the traditional dynamic of evangelical religion whereby doubt could be interpreted as faith. But Edwards achieved this delicate balance through a metaphysical idealism not initially known to his disciples and, when known, not understood by them.

Edwards's philosophical writings were fragmentary and to a large degree unknown in his lifetime because of geography, because of his own priorities which were theological, and because of an outwardly harried life. Born in 1703 in Windsor, Connecticut where his father was pastor, Edwards was also, on his mother's side, the grandson of a minister, Solomon Stoddard of Northampton. The

2. John Toland, *Christianity not Mysterious* (London, 1696), 16–17, 128; Samuel Clarke, *A Discourse Concerning the Being and Attributes of God* (London, 1719), II, 339.

grandfather had shocked defenders of traditional Massachusetts church polity, such as Cotton Mather, by dropping, as a requirement for church membership, testimony of personal religion such as Jane Holmes had offered to Thomas Shepard's congregation. In Northampton all but the openly scandalous were accepted by the church and given the benefit of communion, which, in Stoddard's view, was not exclusively a privilege of visible saints but a means for conversion of the unregenerate.

Stoddard's innovation was momentous for the career of Edwards, who eventually succeeded his grandfather in the Northampton pulpit. After eight years of study and teaching at Yale, interrupted by a brief pastorate in New York, Edwards was installed in Northampton in 1727 as junior colleague to Stoddard. After the old man's death two years later, Edwards became the town's minister. There he led a revival in 1735 that spread through the Connecticut valley, received international attention thanks to his *Faithful Narrative* (1737) of it, and served as a model for the Great Awakening of 1740–42. The latter revival provoked such excesses of zealotry and hysteria that Edwards had to protest against them even while defending religious emotion from its numerous critics. Possibly out of desire for a guard against future excesses of fervor, Edwards attempted in 1749 to repeal his grandfather's policy of open church membership. He wanted to return to the traditional practice of restricting communion to those who could profess, not merely doctrinal knowledge, but also an acceptable account of the work of the Holy Spirit in the soul. Edwards's congregation was unwilling to tolerate the change. Alienated also by his accusation of licentiousness against children of prominent families, they dismissed him. Edwards went to Stockbridge as a missionary to the Indians and there wrote many of his greatest books. In 1757 he was called to the presidency of the College of New Jersey at Princeton and died there the next year of an inoculation against smallpox.

The most recent as well as the most thorough study of Edwards's attempt to repeal Northampton's policy of open church membership concludes that Edwards acted according to the "logic of his theology," which, by demonstrating that religious conversion was "sensible," convinced him that it was possible "to draw lines between sheep and goats."[3] What needs to be added is that Edwards's defense of traditional religious conversion as the distinguishing mark of true Christians rested on his radical interpretation of the consciousness concept and on the insolubility of the problem of personal identity for other eighteenth-century thinkers.

The seventeenth-century conquest of Western philosophy by the consciousness concept left eighteenth-century thinkers the bitter inheritance of the problem of personal identity. Descartes had based personal identity on the mental substance of which he believed the soul or self was composed. But Locke, while accepting the existence of mental substance, had focused on the personal feeling of identity, which, he concluded, was based not in mental substance but in the self-reflection that accompanied perception, "it being impossible for anyone to perceive, without perceiving, that he does perceive." Regardless of whether individual consciousness "be continued in the same, or divers Substances," in consciousness alone "consists *Personal Identity*. . . . And as far as this consciousness can be extended backwards to any past Action or Thought, so far reaches the identity of that *Person*."[4]

George Berkeley (1685–1753) backed up a step by insisting that since human beings have no direct perception of the soul, personal identity is not established by consciousness. The soul must be an occult entity or substance of the sort to which he everywhere else in his writings objected. But although people have no idea, no direct apprehension, of their own souls or anyone else's, they do have a "notion"—that is, reasoned or nonperceptual knowledge—of the existence of souls and of spiritual substance. For ideas are passive and must therefore occur in something active, must be created by a mind, a spirit, a self. Berkeley shared Hobbes's and Descartes's assumption that thought must have its existence in a thinking thing, "one simple, individual, active being."[5]

3. Patricia Tracy, *Jonathan Edwards, Pastor: Religion and Society in Eighteenth-Century Northampton* (New York: Hill and Wang, 1979), 169.

4. Locke, *Essay*, 335.

5. George Berkeley, *A Treatise Concerning the Principles of Human Knowledge* in *The Works of George Berkeley, Bishop of Cloyne* (hereafter *WGB*) (London: Thomas Nelson, 1948), II, 106, 42, 52.

David Hume (1711–76) returned to the empirical tradition by refusing to account for the self on a "notional" basis and insisting on finding a basis for it in consciousness, an insistence that led him to question the "perfect identity and simplicity" of the self. Since Hume agreed with Berkeley that people can have no simple idea, or, in his terminology, "impression," of the self, Hume held that the self was not a spiritual substance but merely an accumulation of perceptions, a "bundle" of ideas "which succeed each other with an inconceivable rapidity." The mind was therefore not a simple, unified substance but a "republic" of ideas in which the constituents and even the laws may change while the identity of the state persists.[6] Memory of this succession of ideas accounted, Hume said, for the sense of self or personal identity.

But if the self was a bundle of ideas, what was it that bundled them? Without a substantial soul in which the ideas could inhere, there seemed to be no way for one atomistic idea to be related to another in order to compose a bundle of them. If ideas create the self, the self cannot be the creator and container of ideas. In an appendix to his *Treatise of Human Nature* Hume admitted that "there are two principles, which I cannot render consistent; nor is it in my power to renounce either of them, viz. *that all our distinct perceptions are distinct existences* and *that the mind never perceives any real connexion among distinct existences.* Did our perceptions either inhere in something simple and individual, or did the mind perceive some real connexion among them, there wou'd be no difficulty in the case. For my part, I must plead the privilege of a sceptic, and confess, that this difficulty is too hard for my understanding."[7]

In the middle of the eighteenth century the consciousness concept seemed paradoxically to have triumphed at the same time that it had led to conclusions undermining its original premises. Originally, the external world was supposed to be represented to the self in the form of ideas. Berkeley reduced the external world to those ideas, and Hume similarly reduced the self. Matter and mind, rather than being related to each other through ideas, had been

6. David Hume, *A Treatise of Human Nature*, ed. L. A. Selby-Bigge, 2nd ed. rev. by P. H. Nidditch (London: Oxford University Press, 1978), 251.
7. Ibid., 636.

consumed by ideas. The weakest facet of the consciousness concept was its inability either to offer empirical evidence for the existence of the self or, in the absence of that evidence, to explain how perceptions might be bundled into a self.

The conundrum of personal identity, painful to other eighteenth-century thinkers, delighted the age's greatest theologian by making it easier to believe that, in regeneration, God might arbitrarily create a new man or a new woman. Edwards, who saw more clearly than any of his New England contemporaries the threat posed to traditional religion by the consciousness concept, aimed a brilliant counterattack at its weakest aspect. Like Berkeley, Edwards rejected as occult, as unperceivable, any substantial constitution of the universe. Unlike Berkeley, he made no exception for the soul. Like Hume, Edwards rejected as occult any attempt to constitute the self of anything but ideas. Unlike Hume, he did not run aground on the question of how, in the absence of a substantial soul, relations could be established between ideas so as to constitute a self. Rather, Edwards delighted in the absence of empirical evidence for a substantial human soul. By rejecting the notion of a substantial self, he could argue that the human soul is constituted of nothing but ideas in the mind of God, who may therefore graciously and perceptibly transform human identity.

Metaphysical Idealism Interpreted as Religious Conversion

Piety and ideas came together in Edwards one day in 1737 when, riding in the woods for his health, he dismounted to engage in prayer, was ravished by a perception of the "glory of the Son of God . . . as Mediator between God and man," wept aloud for nearly an hour, and "felt withal, an ardency of soul to be . . . emptied and annihilated; to lie in the dust, and to be full of Christ alone." The ardency of this desire for annihilation was doubly delightful to Edwards because of his general lack of religious emotion. Unlike most Christians, who would have described their conversions in emotional terms, Edwards had philosophized himself into his faith and only subsequently interpreted his philosophy as an experience of heart religion. What seemed particularly glorious to Edwards about his 1737 epiphany was the unusual intensity and ardor of his apprehension that Christ was "great enough to swallow up all thought and conception." For his own conversion had been merely a matter of reaching the philosophic conclusion that all ideas, all "thought and conception," are created by, and contained in, the mind of God.[8]

The metaphysical idealism by which Edwards refuted rationalists like Toland and Clarke was also the path by which he found personal salvation. The young Edwards, like other unregenerate sinners, had erred on the side of pride and selfishness by objecting to human helplessness and divine sovereignty: "From my Childhood up, my Mind had been wont to be full of Objections against the Doctrine of GOD's Sovereignty, in choosing whom he would to eternal Life, and rejecting whom he pleased; leaving them eternally to perish, and be everlastingly tormented in Hell. It used to appear like a horrible Doctrine to me." When Edwards added that he "never could give an Account, how, or by what Means" he changed his mind and became "convinced" of divine sovereignty, he did not mean that he had no understanding of how his objections to the doctrine had been overcome but only that he could not testify to there having been "any extraordinary Influence of God's Spirit in it." Rather, it was "only that now I saw further, and my Reason apprehended the Justice and Reasonableness of it."[9] By adopting a metaphysical idealism in which he argued that God's ideas constituted the universe, Edwards found it possible to believe that God possessed sovereignty over the world and could not be accused of injustice for thinking as he pleased about it. Edwards had probably arrived at these conclusions by February of 1721 since he seems to have dated his conversion from that time. Only after having concluded in favor of its philosophic reasonableness did Edwards begin to find holy delight in the doctrine of divine sovereignty.[10]

Beginning in 1723 to commit to paper the speculations by which he had been converted, Edwards commenced his notes on "The Mind," wherein he argued that everything that exists is perceived

8. Jonathan Edwards, "Personal Narrative," in Sereno Dwight, *The Life of President Edwards* in Edwards, *Works* (New York, 1830), I, 133.

9. Ibid., 60.

10. Edwards placed the beginning of his "sense of divine things" about a year and a half before he went to New York to preach in August 1722. Ibid., 64.

and that there must be an infinite mind to do the perceiving. Edwards believed that it was impossible for a human being to think that anything could exist without there being an idea of that thing in some consciousness somewhere. For when a person tries to think of an unidealized thing, there is inevitably an idea of the thing in the person's consciousness: "How is it possible to bring the mind to imagine? Yea, it is really impossible . . . that anything should be and nothing know it. Then you'll say, if it be so, it is because nothing has existence anywhere else but in consciousness. No, certainly nowhere else but either in created or uncreated consciousness." But finite human consciousness certainly cannot contain an infinite universe. To the question of what happens to a table and chairs when people do not perceive them "in a room shut up," Edwards answered in the only way possibly consistent with his belief that existence depends on perception. The unperceived table and chairs literally cease to exist in the human world but are still present "in God's Consciousness." Since the uncreated consciousness of God is the creator of the human world, he causes the world to behave *as if* it still contains the table and chairs. Whatever part of the universe people do not perceive does not exist in any way that human beings can comprehend, for it then exists "nowhere but in the divine mind," which indeed does swallow up all thought and conception.[11]

Edwards's insistence that the consciousness of the eternal being contains and upholds the entire physical universe led him to reject the concept of material substance on which Descartes and Locke had based the material world. Locke had believed that human beings know nothing of the external world and its objects except the properties or qualities they sense such as solidity and color. The English philosopher nevertheless assumed, with Descartes, that the causes of those sensations must inhere in some external substance. Edwards, however, objected to the claim in Cartesian physics that cohesion among the parts of a solid body resulted simply from the parts being at rest—a tautology rather than an explanation. Moreover, the Cartesian position implied that any body, no matter how

11. Jonathan Edwards, "Of Being" and "The Mind," both in *idem, Scientific and Philosophical Writings* (hereafter *SPW*), ed. Wallace E. Anderson (New Haven: Yale University Press, 1980), 204–6, 351, 377.

hard, could be broken by a force sufficient to move some of its parts. Edwards had worked out an argument, too elaborate for summary here, showing that a "perfectly solid body" or "atom" must successfully resist division by any finite force. Consequently, it could only be the infinite force of God who keeps "the parts of atoms together."[12] If the fundamental property of bodies—solidity or resistance to penetration—requires the exercise of divine power, the concept of external substance becomes a pointless superfluity: "the certain unknown substance . . . is nothing at all distinct from solidity itself." And if God rather than an external substance makes bodies resist penetration, it is evident that solidity is a phenomenon of mind. For "it is easy to conceive of resistance as a mode of an idea [an image] . . . which [in the mind's eye] may move, and stop and rebound." On the other hand, a person cannot imagine one object resisting penetration by another in a universe devoid not only of substance but also of mind, for there would be "nothing there, *ex confesso,* but resistance." That is, there would be nothing imaginable there, nothing that could be an image, for there would only be one portion of empty space resisting penetration by another portion of empty space—nothing resisting nothing—"which is exceedingly ridiculous."[13]

That no one can possess an idea of nothing was one of Edwards's most important philosophical discoveries and was the basis, among other things, of his proof of the existence of God. An idea, in Locke's phrase, is an "object of the understanding when a man thinks," and an object must be something rather than nothing. "And if any man thinks that he can think well enough how there should be nothing," wrote Edwards, "I'll engage that what he means by 'nothing' is as much something as anything that ever [he] thought of." Even a mental image of empty space is accomplished by imagining boundaries or backgrounds and therefore is an image, is something rather than nothing. Only by conceiving "of the same that the sleeping rocks dream of . . . shall we get a

---

12. Jonathan Edwards, "Of Atoms," *SPW,* 209, 214. This idea, though consistent with Edwards's mature metaphysics, was probably worked out by him prior to and independently of the development of his idealism. See Anderson, "Editor's Introduction," *SPW,* 63–64.

13. Jonathan Edwards, "Of Atoms," 215; *idem,* "The Mind," 351.

complete idea of nothing." If we base our conclusion on ideas that we can actually possess in our minds, "we see it is necessary some being should eternally be."[14]

Edwards's belief that no one can perceive an idea of nothing led him eventually to distinguish between two different kinds of knowledge—"speculative knowledge" and "ideal apprehension."[15] Edwards used the distinction between speculative knowledge and ideal apprehension to formulate his disagreement with Locke, Arnauld, and other seventeenth-century thinkers who had broadened the use of "idea" to denote all the mind's contents, whether imaged or unimaged. Several times in his notebooks Edwards jotted down plans for showing that not "all the immediate objects of the mind are properly called ideas, and what inconvenience and confusion arises from giving every subjective thought that name."[16] Speculative or nonideal knowledge is knowledge represented in the mind by a word or sign but which is not necessarily capable of existence in the mind as an idea or image. The mind may possess, on the one hand, an idea or image of a chair or, on the other hand, merely the verbal sign "chair." The latter may be an image, but if so it is an image not of a four-legged chair but only of a five letter word. The verbal sign is "speculative knowledge." The image of a chair is what Edwards called "ideal apprehension" or "sensible knowledge." "Nothing" differs from "chair" in that "nothing" can never be other than a verbal sign; "nothing" itself cannot exist in the mind as an idea or image.

Having very early attained the crucial insights that existence depends on divine perception and not every human thought is an idea, Edwards put them to use all his adult life in refuting deists and rationalists like Toland and Clarke who used Lockean empiricism to deny the possibility of there being a religious experience

14. Locke, *Essay,* 47; Edwards, "Of Being," 202, 206.

15. These particular terms may have derived from Edwards's middle age, for among his "Miscellanies" that have been published, the terms first appear in number 782. But he hit upon the distinction much earlier. See, for instance, Miscellany 123 entitled "Spiritual Sight" in *The Philosophy of Jonathan Edwards from his Private Notebooks,* ed. Harvey G. Townsend (Eugene: University of Oregon Press, 1955), 245–46.

16. Jonathan Edwards, "Subjects to Be Handled in the Treatise on the Mind," *SPW,* 392.

reserved for saints alone. Their argument was that all thought, including religious thought, originated in sensation and that therefore God must speak to humankind in "common notions" or else not at all. Edwards, in his great series of sermons on *Religious Affections* (1746), would show how the consciousness concept did not exclude the possibility of a "new spiritual sense" so that, contrary to Toland and Clarke, God could impart a special idea of holiness to the elect. But Edwards's notebooks show that even as a young man he had worked out the rough outlines of his philosophical defense of evangelical religion. If all ideas are upheld immediately in the mind of God, the almighty may deliver ideas to the human mind in some other way than through the external senses so that the Christian "knows that what he thus sees and feels is the same thing he used to call God." This was in Miscellany aa, which Edwards wrote by early 1723, and in which he also reflected that "no man can deny but that such an idea of religion may possibly be wrought by the Holy Spirit." Contrary to Locke, Toland, and Clarke, " 'Tis not unphilosophical to think so."[17]

By resting all existence in the divine mind, Edwards's philosophy offered him not only a means for accepting the absolute sovereignty of God but also the basis for his famous "mystical" sense of intimacy with God in nature. The natural world only seemed to be composed of material substance but was actually present to God in ideas of the same order out of which he also composed humanity. A regenerate Christian could interpret ideal apprehension of natural beauty not as a mere symbol of divinity but as direct contact with God's thoughts. Year after year Edwards walked alone in the woods, glorying in their beauty and filled with heartbreaking longings for still more holiness. At such times nothing seemed more natural than to pray aloud "in soliloquies with a singing voice." And the almighty was similarly uninhibited: "I felt God, if I may so speak, at the first appearance of a thunder storm; and used to take the opportunity, at such times, to fix myself in order to view the clouds, and see the lightning's play, and hear the majestic and awful voice of God's thunder, which oftentimes was exceedingly

17. Edwards, *Philosophy of Jonathan Edwards*, 244, 245. On dating, see Anderson, "Editor's Introduction," 28–29.

entertaining, leading me to sweet contemplations of my great and glorious God."[18]

Edwards versus Locke

Considerable speculation has been devoted to possible sources for the young Edwards's metaphysics. He has long been supposed to have written "The Mind" during 1717–18, his second year at Yale. This would have been an astonishing achievement and not merely because he was then fourteen years old. As a member of a dissident group of students and tutors living at Wethersfield during his first two years of undergraduate study, he had little or no access to Yale's library, which had recently acquired the kinds of sources Edwards would have needed to have been as up-to-date in philosophy and science as "The Mind" shows him to have been. That in this seeming intellectual vacuum he wrote some of the best speculative philosophy in the world in the eighteenth century therefore created puzzlement (and awe) and led to the conclusion that at least one major text must have made its way into the wilderness and been at hand to provoke his thinking. There have been many suggestions as to the identity of that master text: *The Essay on Human Understanding* by Locke; the anti-Lockean *Principles of Human Knowledge* by George Berkeley; *The Art of Thinking* by Arnauld, a Cartesian; *The Search after Truth* by Nicolas Malebranche, another Cartesian; *The Theory of the Ideal or Intelligible World* by Malebranche's English disciple, the Cambridge Platonist John Norris; *The Court of the Gentiles* by Norris's fellow Platonist, Theophilus Gale; and *The True Intellectual System of the Universe* by Ralph Cudworth, another Cambridge Platonist. This list of candidates for Edwards's master text shows that his concern with the implications of the way of ideas for questions of knowledge, perception, substance, being, and identity was not unique but common to his age. He needed no single text but could have drawn on many, if he had the opportunity to read them.

A crucial contribution to the demystification of Edwards's intellectual achievements is Wallace Anderson's recent report of

18. Edwards, "Personal Narrative," 62.

Thomas Schafer's finding that Edwards wrote the first entry of "The Mind" in 1723, rather than in the 1717–18 academic year, the long-accepted date stated by Sereno Dwight, Edwards's great grandson and first editor of "The Mind."[19] By 1723 Edwards had completed his last two years of undergraduate work in New Haven and done two years of postgraduate study there as well. He had had ample time to study Yale's recently acquired works by Locke, Newton, Boyle, Gassendi, Descartes, Malebranche, and many other important thinkers.

Moreover, metaphysical idealism was no claim to uniqueness in New England by the end of the 1720s. Rather than hitting on idealism by himself, Edwards may have learned it from other Yale men. Or perhaps he worked out his ideas first for himself and then taught them at Yale in 1724 when he began his two years as a tutor there. But by 1729 he was not the only New England idealist, for in that year Samuel Johnson, who had preceded Edwards as a Yale tutor, was himself moving toward idealism. The principal influence on Johnson's metaphysics was the great idealist George Berkeley, whose books Johnson read avidly and loaned to friends. Johnson met Berkeley in 1729, when the Irish philosopher was living in Newport, Rhode Island, and wrote to him later that year that "in these parts, several ingenious men" had already come to the position "that the *esse* of things is only their *percipi*."[20]

Though Edwards was superior to any other thinker in eighteenth-century America and the intellectual equal of any in Europe, his philosophy was not particularly distinctive, and almost every element of it can be found in one or another of his contemporaries, especially Berkeley. Like Edwards, the Bishop of Cloyne attacked the notion that mental ideas could represent material substance: "I appeal to anyone whether it be sense to assert that a colour is like something which is invisible." Metaphysical idealism was no more a skeptical philosophy to Edwards than to Berkeley, who made "not the least question" that "the things I see with mine

19. Dwight, *Life of President Edwards*, 30, 34.
20. Samuel Johnson, *Samuel Johnson, President of King's College: His Career and Writings*, ed. Herbert Schneider (New York: Columbia University Press, 1929), II, 263; cf. Edwin S. Gaustad, *George Berkeley in America* (New Haven: Yale University Press, 1979), chap. 3.

eyes and touch with my hands do exist," for they were real ideas. Both thinkers challenged not the existence of reality but the reality of matter. The "groundless and absurd" hypothesis of material substance, Berkeley said, "is the very root of *skepticism*."[21]

The skepticism to which Berkeley referred was religious as well as epistemological, for "how great a friend material substance hath been to *atheists* in all ages, were needless to relate." The great stress laid on "unthinking matter" by "your Epicureans, Hobbists, and the like" ought to suffice to put people of good principles on guard. Once done with matter, said Berkeley, philosophy would be done with such questions as how matter can operate on the soul and vice versa. "Matter being once expelled out of Nature, drags with it so many sceptical and impious notions . . . which have been thorns in the sides of divines, as well as philosophers" that even if his arguments against matter were not convincing, Berkeley was nevertheless "sure all friends to knowledge, peace and religion, have reason to wish they were."[22] As long as people think reality lies outside their minds, they will be uncertain that they possess any real knowledge at all. Once reality and knowledge are both understood to exist only in the mind, there can be no doubt of the existence of either to the mind that experiences ideas of them.

Even in the particular theological and evangelical use to which Edwards put his idealism, he differed only in degree from Berkeley. While living in Rhode Island, Berkeley wrote his dialogue, *Alciphron,* which defended the concept of divine grace against the deists' charge that it contained no "ideas" and was therefore an "empty name."[23] Countering that grace was indeed a meaningless abstraction to deists who had no perception of it, Berkeley held that believers do have an idea of grace and consequently know it to be real. Edwards had begun to think along these lines much earlier, but he read *Alciphron* within a year of its publication in 1732[24] and was probably influenced by it as he developed his distinction between speculative knowledge and ideal apprehension into a defense of religious experience. Edwards, however, would go into a

21. Berkeley, *Treatise*, 44, 55, 78.
22. Ibid., 81–82.
23. Berkeley, *Alciphron or the Minute Philosopher* in *WGB*, III, 290.
24. Schaefer's dating, reported by Gaustad, *George Berkeley in America*, 159n.

great deal more detail in *Religious Affections* than Berkeley had in *Alciphron* as to the nature of both the idea of holiness and the "sense" which delivered it to the mind.

In defending humiliation and saving grace as necessary and authentic events in Christian life, Edwards's strategy was not, as has often been asserted, primarily to describe religion in a new fashion consistent with Lockean empiricism. Instead, he mainly attacked the metaphysical assumptions underlying empiricism in order to make *it* consistent with the old view of religion. Perhaps one reason scholars have often missed Edwards's assault on empiricism is that to a significant degree his attack was based on the same consciousness concept on which Locke had rested his psychological empiricism. Indeed, given the traditional Anglo-American prejudice that Locke more or less alone initiated discussion of "ideas," the mistaken notion of Edwards's singular indebtedness to Locke might have got under way without Samuel Hopkins's anecdote of the young Edwards studying *An Essay Concerning Human Understanding* with more pleasure "than the most greedy miser in gathering up handfulls of silver and gold."[25] Moreover, Locke was one of the few influences Edwards acknowledged by name in "The Mind," and he sometimes referred to Locke elsewhere. But in religion and theology Edwards was an antagonist of Locke. For unlike Locke, who used the way of ideas to address epistemological issues about human knowledge of matter, Edwards used the way of ideas to question the existence of matter and thus to give conversion the same metaphysical basis of credibility as any external event.

Not only the physical universe but also the spiritual world and the human soul are composed solely of ideas, according to Edwards. For if existence depends on perception, the removal of human thought can leave only divine perception or else nothing, the latter of which reveals the illogic of Descartes's concept of spiritual substance: "If the removal of all properties . . . leaves nothing, it seems to me that no substance is anything besides them." Thought being the essence of mind, "a mind or spirit is nothing else but consciousness, and what is included in it."[26] The mind's existence,

25. Samuel Hopkins, *The Life of the Late Reverend, Learned, and Pious Mr. Jonathan Edwards* (Boston, 1765), 4.

26. Edwards, *Philosophy of Jonathan Edwards*, 78; *idem*, "The Mind," 342.

like the body's, is ideal, deriving immediately from the mind of God.

Therefore a disembodied mind or spirit is capable of sensory perception. Reason indicates that "the soul in a separate state must depend on sensation." Otherwise, how could it converse with other minds or know anything at all? Scripture indicates that angels have witnessed some of the same providential works as human beings. Like people, angels are not omniscient, and they seem to exist in a place, for example, when they descend from heaven to earth. Their perceptions being thus limited, it is obvious that angels are related in some sensory way to matter. But since they lack bodies, their sensations, unlike humanity's, cannot seem to them to be caused by bodily organs. For both angels and humanity, then, a sensation is not due to any bodily organ and can only be defined as an impression "wherein the mind is passive."[27] The mind's passivity in the receipt of external ideas is an orthodox Lockean concept, but Edwards's metaphysical idealism permitted him to subvert the premises of sensory psychology while employing the fashionable terminology of "ideas." For if angels can receive ideas of sensation in their disembodied state, so may the passive human soul *before* it is embodied, which means that, contrary to Locke, ideas may be innate.

Locke had put conversion on trial not only by questioning the perceivability of sanctity but also by opposing innate ideas. A reprobate will not necessarily be humiliated by sin if the human mind begins as a blank slate whose subsequent knowledge is determined by the mere happenstance of whatever ideas are provoked by its encounters with the natural world. And the orthodox doctrine of a merciful, saving change of human nature requires some supernatural influx rather than a chance encounter between the right ideas and a person willing to attend to them.

Edwards was therefore an innatist, an opponent of Lockean empiricism. As examples of the mind's "innate ideas," Edwards cited the mind's "natural inclination . . . to excellence and order" and the belief of the soul when it suffers injustice that a superior being will punish the evildoer. Edwards also rejected Locke's notion that

---

27. Edwards, "Treatise on the Mind," 390.

all universals are formed by abstracting particular ideas from objects of sensation, by abstracting, in Locke's words, the idea of "white . . . which the mind yesterday received from milk" and applying it to "the same Colour being observed today in Chalk or Snow." That will do for "white," but the idea of "color" itself cannot be formed by such a process of abstraction, for colors are—and here Edwards used Locke's phrase—"simple ideas" from which nothing can be removed. Abstract white from white and no other qualities are left. In a planned but never written treatise Edwards would have challenged Locke by arguing that universals are innate ideas without which the human mind would rarely function.[28] Although Edwards did not elaborate on this point, he perhaps intended to argue that the mind could not associate its simple ideas of red and white under the general idea of color unless the mind had the general idea prior to the simple ideas. Evidently, then, the general idea is not derived from simple ideas or external sensory perceptions but is innate. Edwards believed that a person born blind, if given the faculty of sight, would instantly and without ratiocination know that "red" and "white" fall under a general principle from which "sour" is excluded.[29]

Therefore Edwards rejected Locke's definition of "knowledge" as "the perception of the connexion and the agreement, or disagreement and repugnancy of any of our ideas." Locke's definition accounts for a person's knowing that white is not red, but since these two ideas are simple, their disagreement must be total. How then could the mind perceive that red and white do have a relation to each other in that they are both colors? Knowledge, Edwards insisted, "is not the perception of the agreement or disagreement of ideas, but rather the perception of the union or disunion of ideas." Some ideas are innately united to others in the human mind, so that one idea, "yea, against our wills, excites the thought of other things that are like it." Humanity's inability to believe arbitrarily that red is a color and white is not indicates that God made "the soul of such a nature that those particulars which he thus made to agree are unavoidably together in the mind." If to know is

28. Edwards, *Philosophy of Jonathan Edwards*, 78–79; Locke, *Essay*, 159; Edwards, "The Mind," 361–62; Edwards, "Treatise on the Mind," 392.
29. Edwards, "The Mind," 362.

to recognize the way God associates one idea with another so that they "belong to one another," then, as Anderson notes, the evidence of religious faith is as compelling to the saint as the evidence for scientific truth. Both rest on innate principles or "dispositions of the mind."[30]

The Uniqueness of Religious Sensation

Edwards was a fundamentalist in the sense that he believed in the literal truth of the Puritan teaching that genuine religion was due to an influx of the Holy Spirit into the human soul. Locke's view that people have no empirically verifiable knowledge of anything divine was his most obvious and direct challenge to fundamentalist belief in conversion. Edwards's metaphysics, by establishing God's arbitrary control of, sovereignty over, and predestined determination of human affairs, opened the possibility of showing that human knowledge need not be based only on ideas acquired through the five external senses but might also involve ideas derived from a "new spiritual sense."

Scholars have interpreted Edwards's phrases "new spiritual sense" and "sense of the heart" as if they are interchangeable in his writings, but these two phrases had quite different meanings for him. "Sense of the heart" was a broad category that included various sensations of both saints and sinners. Edwards's fundamental meaning in the phrase "sense of the heart" was that human beings are willful or emotional in their perception of all ideas, moving toward or away from an idea depending on whether the mind is predisposed to be pleased or displeased by the idea. He called such emotion a "sense of the heart" for physiological reasons; God has so joined soul and body that as the soul experiences pleasure or displeasure in its ideas it stirs the blood and causes "some bodily sensation, especially about the heart."[31] Edwards's purpose was not so much to locate the uniqueness of religious experience in the sense of the heart as it was to establish that genuine spiritual per-

30. Locke, *Essay*, 525; Edwards, "The Mind," 385, 361, 362; Anderson, "Editor's Introduction," 128.
31. Jonathan Edwards, *Religious Affections*, ed. John E. Smith (New Haven: Yale University Press, 1959), 96.

ceptions, *in common* with ordinary external sensations, involve the will or emotions. This lent philosophical support to his defense of the pietist belief that true religion is heart religion. But since both sinners and saints possess senses of the heart, it is crucial to recognize that only one special and unique sense of heart constitutes the "new spiritual sense" given in grace, a point Edwards emphasized in *Religious Affections,* where he devoted possibly as much space to showing that strong affections alone do not make an experience religious as he did to emphasizing that genuine religion is emotional.

Strangely, perhaps partly because of the book's title, *Religious Affections* has often been misinterpreted as solely a defense of heart religion when it actually based the uniqueness of religious experience on its intellectual content. Redemption, for Edwards, was not a matter merely of achieving ideal apprehension generally but rather particularly with respect to a single new idea—holiness—which was perceivable thanks to a divine influx. In attacking reasonable religion Edwards drew on his distinction between "ideal" and "speculative" knowledge, the latter being the unemotional sort that "consists in mere speculation or understanding of the head," i.e., mere words or signs of ideas rather than ideas themselves. But Edwards could just as well have applied the adjective "mere" to emotional or "sensible" knowledge since he maintained that a heart feeling void of new intellectual knowledge is not redemptive. For instance, an awakened sinner looks anew at the world and, achieving an "ideal view of God's natural perfections," realizes that nature's creator must be a very great being. But this powerful feeling of the heart is not redemptive since it contains no new intellectual or speculative knowledge; the sinner has been told since childhood that God is great. The sinner's experience in awakening is an "ordinary influence of God's Spirit," that is, the communication of "a sensible knowledge of those things that the mind had a speculative knowledge of before." In redemption, on the other hand, the "extraordinary influence of the Spirit of God . . . imparts speculative knowledge to the soul."[32]

---

32. Jonathan Edwards, "782. Ideas, Sense of the Heart, Spiritual Knowledge or Conviction. Faith," in Perry Miller, "Jonathan Edwards on the Sense of the Heart," *Harvard Theological Review* (April 1948): 136, 141, 139–40.

Holiness is an intellectual illumination of the soul. Holiness brings light as well as pleasure, for understanding and willing can no more be separated from each other in regard to this ideal apprehension than in regard to any other. The perception of holiness supplied by the new sense is no more restricted to mere emotion than is the delightful taste of honey. Like any other idea supplied by any other sense, the perception of holiness constitutes new understanding: "there is the nature of instruction in it; as he that has perceived the sweet taste of honey, knows much more about it, than he who has only looked upon and felt of it." Emotional apprehension or a sense of the heart is necessarily involved in conversion since the saint's new knowledge is ideal or "sensible knowledge of the things of religion with respect to their spiritual good or evil."[33] But this new sense of heart is distinguished from all other new senses of heart by its unique speculative or intellectual content since it is derived from a new idea.

Expounding in *Religious Affections* the doctrine that religious knowledge is entirely new knowledge, Edwards used the terminology of the way of ideas in order to distinguish natural perceptions from religious perceptions on the basis of their new intellectual content. Like numerous previous theologians, he cited sensory metaphors in the Bible, suggesting that grace gives a "new light" to the elect. But Edwards differed from those earlier theologians in the rigor of his insistence that utterly new knowledge requires a new sense. If, as scripture indicates, almighty God produces something new in the saint's mind, it will indeed be new and not a "compounding of . . . sensations which the mind had before." Therefore, "there is what some metaphysicians call a new simple idea." But Edwards could not stop there, since natural human beings can experience new simple ideas—new odors, colors, textures, tastes, or sounds. Besides being simple, the new idea must be completely different "from everything that natural men experience . . . in kind." The new idea can differ "in kind" from all ideas produced by the natural senses only if it results from a new sense, "a new spiritual sense." In conversion human beings become able to perceive spiritually because the Holy Spirit enters into their

33. Edwards, *Religious Affections*, 272; *idem*, "782," 142.

souls, enabling them to perceive at least partly as he does. The convert's newly disposed soul finds unprecedented pleasure in the Promise and the Promiser, causing the soul willingly, desiringly, to embrace them both. Out of this sort of response to particular objects, the saint begins to perceive, intellectually as well as emotionally, what holiness itself is and that it dwells within. Like any other idea supplied by any other sense, the perception of holiness constitutes new understanding: "There is the nature of instruction in it; as he that has perceived the sweet taste of honey, knows much more about it, than he who has only looked upon and felt of it."[34]

Yet the idea of holiness is neither certain nor undeniable to the consciousness that perceives it, for it requires interpretation. Edwards believed that the saint's newly disposed soul might believe that it perceived holiness in some particular object yet be mistaken because the mind did not view the object in a suitably broad context. An extreme example would be a saint who mistakenly honored the holiness of the Sabbath by refusing to work to save a neighbor's house from fire. Edwards insisted that the possibility of error did not make holiness less perceivable than any other quality perceived by any other sense. The natural external senses also often result in mistaken perceptions, as in optical illusions or, as Edwards pointed out, in the case of poison berries, which, though they taste undeniably good to the palate, yet the "palate itself must be judged of . . . by certain rules and reasons."[35]

"Sense" is a precise word for the mind's willful relation to a mental phenomenon such as holiness. For one cannot have ideal apprehension "of mental things without having those very things in the mind." To have ideal apprehension of "thought" the mind must then be thinking. So, too, to have ideal apprehension of "holiness" means that at that instant the mind is thinking holily—an assertion well suited to rebut the tendency in the way of ideas to make desire for holiness more a static perception than an interpretive action of the soul. And since holy thoughts are pleasurable, holiness is not merely speculative knowledge but also "a sense or feeling of the heart."[36] The new spiritual sense thus resembles the

34. Edwards, *Religious Affections*, 205, 272.
35. Ibid., 284–285.
36. Edwards, "782," 136.

natural external senses in every possible way. Although the phenomenological reference of the new sense is in the mind rather than outside the body, that has no bearing in a metaphysical system in which ideas seemingly derived from the external senses are actually created immediately in the mind by God. Sweetness is no more "in" honey than holiness is "in" the paper, ink, and words that compose the scripture that delights the saint's heart. In both cases—honey and scripture—the objects are not causes but merely occasions when God produces pleasurable ideas in people's minds. Contrary to Toland and Clarke, some people possess a new, exclusive sense. The five external senses are not God's sole means of communicating with human beings, and therefore God need not speak in common notions.

That Edwards interpreted the working out of this metaphysical defense of conversion as the process by which he himself was saved is supported by the fact that his postconversion doubt differed from that of other new converts. Doubt, for traditional converts, was caused mainly by backsliding sinfulness, which, because it humbled the soul, could be interpreted as a renewed sign of grace, a renewed awareness that God was all. But Edwards, in his "Diary" entry for December 18, 1722, nearly two years after his conversion, was troubled by his lack of humility, his lack of "experience of that preparatory work, of which divines speak. . . . I do not remember that I experienced regeneration, exactly in those steps, in which divines say it is generally wrought. . . . I do not feel the Christian graces sensibly enough, particularly faith."[37] Edwards's conversion had not consisted of humility interpreted as grace. Rather, his conversion was exactly the opposite of the traditional dynamic. Traditionally, inability humbled the soul and revealed that God was all. For Edwards, on the other hand, the philosophical reasonableness of the doctrine of divine sovereignty and free grace made humility delightful, albeit difficult to obtain.

Edwards sought humility with a ferocity nearly as frightening as Brainerd's physical self-destructiveness. In 1722 and 1723 Edwards regularly added to a list of elaborate resolutions for Christian be-

37. Edwards, "Diary" in Dwight, *Life of President Edwards,* 76.

havior, not so much because he hoped to fulfill them as because he hoped to humiliate himself by his failings. Totaling his infractions weekly, he delighted in any increase, not because he wanted an increase in sin but because he wanted an increase in humility. Other weeks, "unhappily low" in his sum of infractions, he attributed the shortfall to "listlessness and sloth" in self-examination and mortification. Vowing to expect no ease, he pursued humiliation relentlessly, though others cautioned that he might thus injure his health: "I will plainly feel it [ill health] . . . before I cease, on this account." Yet soon falling "exceedingly low in the weekly account," he found a new explanation, a "heart so deceitful, that I am almost discouraged from making any more resolutions." Soon reflecting that "I am fallen from my former sense of the pleasantness of religion," he pondered the question whether forcing "myself to think of religion at all times, has exceedingly distracted my mind and made me altogether unfit for that, and everything else. . . . I think that I stretched myself farther than I could bear, and so broke." Soon, however, he was at it again, trying narrowly to search out "all the subtle subterfuges of my thoughts, . . . that I may know what are the very first originals of my defect, as with respect to . . . loathing of myself."[38]

In rare moments, like that in 1737 when he dismounted in the woods, Edwards was able to follow the traditional morphology of conversion and attain spiritual pleasure in humiliation. Then he was given not the "speculative knowledge" of holiness to which he was well accustomed but an overwhelmingly "ideal apprehension" of it. His enormous sin and pride could be atoned for only by a holiness sufficient to swallow up all thought. For likewise, "My Wickedness, as I am in my self, has long appear'd to me perfectly ineffable and infinitely swallowing up all Thought and Imagination." To wish humbly to lie in the dust, to have some ideal apprehension of one's own vileness, was not merely the obverse of the idea of holiness but also its basis. The modern critic ahistorically ponders the question whether the Holy Spirit or the human self produced conversion, but like many other Puritans, Edwards knew that there was an intimate relation between self and humility in the redeemed heart, a relation analogous to that in God between maj-

38. Ibid., 77, 80, 82, 91.

esty and meekness, glory and grace: "And as I was walking there, and looked up on the Sky and Clouds; there came into my Mind, a sweet Sense of the glorious Majesty and Grace of GOD. . . . I seemed to see them both in a sweet Conjunction. . . . it was a sweet and gentle, and holy Majesty; and also a majestick Meekness."[39]

Orthodoxy: Free Will and Original Sin

In retrospect it is possible to see, as Edwards's contemporaries and near successors could not have done, that *Freedom of Will* (1754) and *Original Sin* (1757) were coda to his great achievement in *Religious Affections* (1746), where, owing to his metaphysical idealism, he succeeded in reconciling the perceptualism in the consciousness concept with religious conversion. Had he been unable to uphold the possibility of religious conversion, maintaining orthodox doctrines on will and sin would have been to no purpose to an evangelical like Edwards. On the other hand, once it was established that modern philosophy did not contradict the possibility of conversion, it made all the more sense to push on to a defense of orthodox doctrines on will and sin. Conversion depended not only on fending off philosophical challenges but also on maintaining doctrinal orthodoxy, for if people are not convinced of their original sinfulness they will have no reason to turn to God. If people do not believe in their inability to will the good, they will not achieve the humiliation that leads to surrender to an Other. Edwards, an effective preacher and revivalist, understood from experiences like Brainerd's and his own that for sinners in search of Christ "nothing is more necessary . . . than thorough conviction and humiliation; than that their consciences should be convinced of their real guilt and sinfulness." But in the Arminian scheme "truly, . . . man is not dependent on God," and Arminian preaching could only obstruct the work of the Calvinist ministry in bringing sinners to Christ.[40]

39. Edwards, "Personal Narrative," 134, 61.
40. Edwards to John Erskine, Aug. 3, 1757 in Dwight, *Life of President Edwards,* 560; Jonathan Edwards, *Freedom of the Will,* ed. Paul Ramsey (New Haven: Yale University Press, 1957), 469.

Arminianism, or the belief in the ability of unregenerate human beings to obey the law of God, was no abstract threat to Edwards in the 1750s but a nearly victorious force, not only in Christendom at large but over his own life and circumstances as well. He kept current with English tract wars and knew the arguments of Thomas Chubb, Daniel Whitby, Isaac Watts, and others in favor of human freedom. Almost yearly, while he was pastor in Northampton, Edwards visited Boston and heard some ministers there preach as if redemption could be earned. He participated in bitter fratricidal strife among the ministers in Hampshire County, joining especially in 1734 in Thomas Clap's ill-considered attack on Robert Breck's orthodoxy and qualifications to be minister at Springfield. This and other indications of heresy on the loose in his vicinity helped stimulate Edwards to preach the sermons on human inability that began the awakening in the Connecticut Valley in 1734. But by the early 1750s Edwards had given up the offensive. The awakening was past, thanks in part perhaps to the opposition and liberal preaching of Breck, who, having survived Edwards's 1734 attack, helped harry Edwards out of the Northampton pulpit and into virtual exile at Stockbridge. Deprived of the opportunity to preach in even so minor a center as Northampton, Edwards had clearly been bested by Arminian foes, but he loosed what arrows he could in the form of doctrinal tracts.

The extent to which Edwards's arguments in *Freedom of Will* depended on his idealist metaphysics has not been well understood. It is commonly known that the principal device by which he refuted the notion of human self-determination was the infinite regression: "If there be an act of the will in determining all its own free acts, then one free act of the will is determined by another; and so we have the absurdity of every free act, even the very first, determined by a foregoing free act."[41] But this and a great many of the other reductions to the absurd in *Freedom of Will* are simply extended elaborations of the principle of cause and effect, supported by Edwards's insistence that people can have no idea of nothing. That is, a person can always form an idea or image of one event, an "effect," and then an image of a previous event, a "cause." But to

41. *Freedom of the Will*, 176.

achieve ideal apprehension of the notion that an effect can be un-caused, a person would have to imagine an idea of an event pre-ceded by an idea of nothing, and Edwards believed that the mind cannot possess an idea of nothing. Hence he stated in "The Mind" that the notion that every event has a cause is an "innate principle" of human thought and in *Freedom of Will* called it a "grand prin-ciple of common sense."[42] Anyone who believed he or she had an idea of an uncaused or undetermined will had simply mistaken a speculative notion for an ideal apprehension.

The distinction between ideal apprehension and speculative knowledge also underlay Edwards's insistence that the Arminian notion of action "is something of which there is no idea." Armin-ians claimed to know from experience that they possessed free will, but they were actually relying on speculation. Their belief that the will determined itself implied an act of will before the first act of the will, an implication comparable to the claim of a "learned phi-losopher" that he had seen a beast that "when he moved, he always took a step before the first step; that he went with his head first, and yet always went tail foremost." Even if the philosopher called the beast "by a certain name"—just as the Arminians spoke of "free will"—he obviously had no ideal apprehension of the beast. The philosopher's opinion was not an idea but a speculation, so "it would be no impudence at all, to tell such a traveler, though a learned man, that he himself had no notion or idea of such an ani-mal as he gave an account of, and never had, nor ever would have."[43]

Believing that willful actions were determined not by prior actions but by the moral or spiritual quality of the soul, Edwards defended "that great and important truth, that *a bad will, or an evil disposition of heart, itself, is wickedness*."[44] Edwards believed there was such a thing as freedom of will—the title of his book, after all—but it was *natural* freedom, not *moral* freedom. Human beings are *naturally* free so long as they are physically unrestrained and able to act according to their will or desire. But they are not *morally* free to will to have different desires than they do. A per-

42. Edwards, "The Mind," 370; *idem, Freedom of the Will*, 182.
43. Edwards, *Freedom of the Will*, 345–346.
44. Ibid., 467.

son's willing or desiring, according to Edwards, is the result of an innate disposition that is not changeable except through divine grace. Edwards believed that though the human disposition determined human willing, human willing was not humanly determined—a notion understandably confusing to opponents who did not know that in his view the human disposition was not constituted of spriritual substance but of ideas upheld immediately in the mind of God.[45]

Edwards's frequent use of terms like "disposition," "inclination," "frame," "habit," and "propensity" indicate his skepticism about the power of reason to control behavior. In scholastic psychology the will was the rational appetite, charged with controlling irrational passions and affections. But Edwards sided with William Ames's rebellion against the scholastic interpretation of the will as rational appetite and thus with the long-term trend of piety to base moral life on the affections and passions. Like Charles Morton, Edwards was saying that human consciousness alone does not determine the human spirit. But Edwards's metaphysical idealism permitted him to avoid Morton's tendency toward natural religion. Where Morton had located the nonconscious determinant of human willing in the body, Edwards's metaphysics put it the mind of God and called the divinely determined pattern and order in human behavior by the name of "disposition."

Supporting the pietist devaluation of reason, Edwards attacked Locke's distinction between will and desire. Locke's psychology had remained deeply influenced by the faculty model, according to which willing was a rational power of choosing to act (or not to act) so as to obtain an object of desire. Locke (and hundreds of speculative psychologists after him) therefore held that psychological conflict showed will and desire to be two different things. A man with gout in his feet desires that the pain be eased, but apprehending

45. Many have suggested that Edwards missed the point that not only a motive or greatest apparent good but also a responding moral quality in the actor must determine action. See Lyman Beecher, *Autobiography,* ed. Barbara Cross (Cambridge: Harvard University Press, 1961), II, 117; Ramsey, "Introduction" to *Freedom of the Will,* 19; Horace Bushnell, *Nature and the Supernatural* (Hartford, 1858), 48–49. But Edwards actually said quite clearly that "the particular temper" of an individual mind "contributes to the agreeableness or disagreeableness" of an object (*Freedom of the Will,* 146).

"that the removal of the pain may translate the humour to a more vital part, his will is never determined to any one Action, that may serve to remove this pain. Whence it is evident . . . that the *Will* . . . is much more distinct from *Desire*." Edwards disagreed. The gout sufferer's conflict was with regard to two different objects— removal of present pain and prevention of worse in the future— "and in each, taken by themselves, the will and desire agree." To show that willing and desiring are two different things, they would have to be shown to differ "with respect to the very same object," which Locke had not done. Willing was not a rational choosing to act (or not to act) so as to obtain a desired object. Willing, according to Edwards, was simply a desiring to act. A drunkard with liquor before him does not act by the light of reason but merely does what he desires to do, does what seems "most agreeable."[46] Since in Edwards's view willing and desiring were two names for the same thing, the soul had no rational appetite capable of standing back from its desires and perceiving, with certainty, their moral quality. Edwards's metaphysical idealism thus permitted him, even while accepting the perceptual model of thought in the consciousness concept, to get back to something like the sixteenth- and seventeenth-century notion of conscience as a judgment or interpretation after the fact rather than immediate apprehension of the moral quality of an idea.

Metaphysical idealism also underlay, obscurely, Edwards's defense of original sin by enabling him to posit a common moral identity among all people. In the privacy of his notes on "The Mind" Edwards had rejected Locke's view that personal identity rests on continuity of ideas. For God might annihilate a person and subsequently create a new person with the same ideas as the former person, who yet would "be in no way concerned in it, having no reason to fear what that being shall suffer, or to hope for what he shall enjoy." Edwards therefore asserted in *Original Sin* what must have seemed a mere *ex cathedra* statement to friend and foe alike but in fact rested on his metaphysics: "there is no such thing as any identity or oneness . . . but what depends on *God's sovereign constitution*." The individual or personal identity of a human being

46. Locke, *Essay*, 250; Edwards, *Freedom of the Will*, 140, 143.

was therefore not necessarily the same as his or her moral identity: "There are various kinds of identity."[47] That is, God treats his creatures separately for some purposes but not for others. Since the world is constituted in the consciousness of God, separate things become one thing whenever God determines them to be so. And God determines that Adam's sinfulness is everyone's. The question of justice does not apply to relations between God and human beings any more than to relations between an individual human being and that person's thoughts and dreams.

Edwards's obscurity as to the way in which his published logic of determinism depended on his unpublished metaphysics may have been due in part to the fact that too much clarity in hemming in human action led straight back to God as the author of sin. Edwards tried unsuccessfully to wriggle out of the consequences of his absolute determinism with a privative theory of sin, that is, that God's only act in the chain of events leading inevitably to the Fall was to deprive Adam of the principle of virtue so that Adam, not God, took the positive action whereby sin came into the world. Even so, God initiated this series of events while foreseeing it would result in human iniquity. Liberals would therefore respond by asking if Edwards's doctrine did not contain the monstrously "plain consequence" that "God stands chargeable with doing wickedly?"[48]

This unattractive slipperiness in Edwards's defense of orthodox doctrines may indicate how great an opposition he thought he was up against in the middle of the eighteenth century. The contradiction of human moral freedom by the doctrine of divine sovereignty was not a result of his metaphysics but had existed as long as the doctrine itself had. What was new was a growing insistence on human freedom and autonomy. This new emphasis on human autonomy was supported by a whole range of sources including republican political theory, Whig belief in conspiracies against the liberties of Englishmen, and the consciousness concept in most of its mani-

47. Edwards, "The Mind," 386; Jonathan Edwards, *Original Sin*, ed. Clyde Holbrook (New Haven: Yale University Press, 1970), 404.
48. Edwards, *Original Sin*, 381–84; James Dana, *The "Examination of the Late Rev'd Edwards' Enquiry on Freedom of Will" Continued* (Boston, 1770), 50.

festations. In the face of all this, a privative explanation of original sin had no chance of success.

Yet Edwards would have better succeeded in his objective of defending not only Calvinist doctrine but also religious conversion by publishing his metaphysics, even at the expense of originating sin at God's door. Instead, he failed—evangelically if not theoretically—to reconcile conversion with the perceptualism in the consciousness concept. This failure was not as inevitable as it may seem in retrospect. Traditional religion lives on, but for the most part at odds with rather than subverting, as in Edwards's metaphysics, modern notions of thought and self.

Unpublished till 1830, Edwards's metaphysics became the road not taken in American speculation on thought and self. Edwards's actual historical importance, though not small, has been overestimated by twentieth-century thinkers impressed by his philosophical achievements. His theology, not his philosophy, most influenced his successors and with disastrous results for Calvinist orthodoxy and religious conversion. Although his metaphysics might unpopularly have implied that God was the author of sin, his theological heirs and disciples adopted the worse tactic of trying to get God off the hook by originating sin in the vagaries of the human self. This implied a conclusion far worse than that God was the author of sin; it implied that God had nothing to do with human behavior.

With little or no understanding of how Edwards had constituted human selfhood of God's ideas, his disciples would constitute the self, as Descartes had done, of an occult spiritual substance and would attempt on that basis to reconcile the doctrines of divine sovereignty and human responsibility. Even the most limited human ability to rise above the love of sin implied, as it always had, a divided mind. Edwards's successors would therefore attempt to continue the long tradition he had disrupted, the tradition of adapting the faculty model to descriptions of a religiously divided self.

Yet the perceptualism in the consciousness concept increasingly dominated speculative psychology and theology in the United States, thanks in no small part to Edwards's brilliant polemical use of the idealist vocabulary. Edwards's compromise with the way of ideas was not well understood. He had offered a system whereby holiness could be perceived but not with certainty. The perception required interpretation. After Edwards, however, aspiring believers such as Catharine Beecher tended to make desire for holiness an undoubtable inward perception. Certainty that the soul desired holiness subverted the humility that fueled the interpretive process of conversion.

Those of Edwards's successors who hoped to emulate him by reconciling secular learning and evangelical religion were perforce driven toward some new division of the mind. Since they believed that the mind was made of a substance, they did not need to believe, as had both Edwards and Locke from their different perspectives, that personal identity was coterminous with consciousness. Perhaps grounds for religious humility might still be found by supposing that some of the substance that constitutes the mind is unconscious.

CHAPTER FOUR

The Self Sign: From Hopkins to Finney

The Evangelical Roots of Unconscious Selfhood

"Consciousness" was "a magic word in the early Republic."[1] The consciousness concept helped make early nineteenth-century Americans into ardent proponents of free will, or, in their phrase, free moral agency. Human beings, it was generally agreed, possessed both natural and moral freedom. Jonathan Edwards had insisted in the eighteenth century that people do not have moral freedom, do not have the capacity to determine their own wills. Natural freedom, or liberty from external constraint, was the only possible freedom, according to Edwards. In the absence of external constraint, people were naturally free to act as they willed but not morally free to determine their wills. Most nineteenth-century thinkers disagreed with Edwards and defined freedom as moral freedom—the capacity to determine one's own will. Moreover, they asserted that everyone was morally free; everyone determined his or her own will. This confidence in human moral capacity undoubtedly had many sources: an expanding economy, self-congratulation born of prosperity, boundless territories promising still greater opportunities for the strong willed, and the triumph in the American Revolution and still more in Jacksonian America of egalitarianism over deference. But the theoretical clincher for free will was the consciousness concept, the notion that the self enjoys immediate knowledge of its own operations. The seemingly undeniable corollary of the consciousness concept was that subjective feeling was not

1. Perry Miller, *The Life of the Mind in America from the Revolution to the Civil War* (New York: Harcourt, Brace, 1965), 25.

to be denied. If human beings felt free, they were free, morally as well as naturally.

Congregationalist theologians led the way toward affirmation of free will by dint of the consciousness concept. Speculative psychology, like much of the rest of intellectual life in early nineteenth-century New England, was dominated by the clergy and their theological orientation. The clergy had helped import the consciousness concept in the eighteenth century, and in the nineteenth they had to deal with its effects. Moral freedom is so direct a repudiation of the doctrine of human inability that one would expect to find putative heirs of Edwards in opposition. But so overwhelming was the weight of the consciousness concept that many Congregational clergy were powerless to resist it and even became ardent advocates of free will because of it. "Let a man look into his own breast," said the Yale theologian Nathaniel William Taylor, "and he cannot but perceive inward freedom. . . . And liberty in the mind implies self-determination." Leading moral philosophy textbooks of the era were often informed by the theologians' adherence to the consciousness concept. When Professor Thomas Upham of Bowdoin College penned his *Elements of Moral Philosophy,* he was led by theologians to support moral freedom. Like the theologians, Upham believed that free will was an incontrovertible empirical fact established by "the evidence . . . of our consciousness."[2]

The science of the mind, not theology, became the path followed by illustrious clergy to their careers' typically crowning achievement—the presidency of a college or seminary. Young men

2. Nathaniel William Taylor, quoted in William McLoughlin, *Revivals, Awakenings, and Reform: An Essay on Religion and Social Change* (Chicago: University of Chicago Press, 1978), 119; Thomas Upham, *Elements of Moral Philosophy* (Boston, 1831), I, 43; cf. Upham, *A Philosophical and Practical Treatise on the Will* (Portland, Maine, 1832) 234–35; Catharine Beecher, "An Essay on Cause and Effect," *American Biblical Repository* (Oct. 1839): 393; Leonard Woods, *Works* (Andover, 1850), II, 59; and for a similar statement by a non–New Englander, Henry Philip Tappan, *The Doctrine of the Will, Determined by an Appeal to Consciousness* (New York, 1840), passim. These are a small sample of many dozens of such arguments that appeared in print. Additional sources on consciousness and free will are discussed in Bruce Kuklick, *Churchmen and Philosophers: From Jonathan Edwards to John Dewey* (New Haven: Yale University Press, 1985), 129n. For the theological influence on Upham, see Jay Wharton Fay, *American Psychology before William James* (New Brunswick, N.J.: Rutgers University Press, 1939), 93.

interested in mental philosophy were discouraged from taking up its study because they lacked appropriate social accoutrements to pursue their favorite discipline. A professorship in mental or moral philosophy was usually held by the college president and therefore required not only intellectual acumen but also "dignity and reputation."[3] The seemingly empirical and irrefutable evidence of consciousness became inextricably associated with both philosophy of mind and with the most powerful and prestigious positions in both church and academy.

Yet some of the same clergy who so ostentatiously embraced the consciousness concept were also its principal opponents. Forced by its seeming irrefutability to accept the consciousness concept and to involve it in the highest councils of their educational and religious institutions, some clergy nevertheless struggled quietly and even unwittingly against it because they hoped to salvage the doctrines of divine sovereignty and human inability. Even though they believed that consciousness proved human moral freedom, they also understood the evangelical importance of human helplessness and divine determinism. Human helplessness was basic to the humility on which conversion swung.[4] By the 1830s public opinion would not support punishment of the morally unable, as is suggested by changing views of criminal law.[5] If it was becoming debatable whether courts could justly punish people conscious of doing wrong but compelled to do so by mental derangement, God surely could not justly punish violations of his law if he created people morally disabled. For Calvinists striving to maintain a popular following, the only possible response to this situation was acceptance of the notion of human moral freedom, with whatever gymnastics and legerdemain were needed to maintain that they were also defenders of the Calvinist doctrines of divine sovereignty and human

3. Lucian Boynton, "Journal of Lucian Boynton," quoted in Donald M. Scott, *From Office to Profession: The New England Ministry, 1750–1850* (Philadelphia: University of Pennsylvania Press, 1978), 68.

4. On the continuing importance in this period of the doctrine of human inability in conversion, see Scott, *From Office to Profession*, 41.

5. Isaac Ray, *A Treatise on the Medical Jurisprudence of Insanity* (Boston, 1838), passim; Janet Ann Tighe, "A Question of Responsibility: The Development of American Forensic Psychiatry, 1838–1930" (Ph.D. diss., University of Pennsylvania, 1983), chap. 2.

inability. Attempting to preserve a determinist interpretation of at least part of the self and believing that consciousness supported freedom, they had to argue that part of the self was not conscious. Many early nineteenth-century clergy therefore rejected the belief of both Edwards and Locke that personal identity was constituted of consciousness alone. Only unconscious selfhood could preserve a saving remnant of dependence on God.

Samuel Hopkins, Nathanael Emmons, Asa Burton, Timothy Dwight, Nathaniel William Taylor, Lyman Beecher, and Charles Grandison Finney, with whom this chapter mainly deals, had little or no understanding of how Edwards's metaphysics had dispensed with substance and constituted the universe of ideas upheld in the consciousness of God. For the most part, they accepted the notion of spiritual substance as the basis of human identity. A substantial soul, constituted of something more than consciousness, might contain an unconscious element that was subject to divine determinism. Whatever one may think of the reasonableness of their defense of both human moral freedom and divine determinism, the combination had an interesting result in their notion that the battle for salvation is waged between conscious and unconscious parts of a sinner's soul.

Calvinist theology in New England in the century after Jonathan Edwards has been little studied.[6] The general impression has been that tedious theological disputation between and within the opposing camps of moderate "Old Calvinism" and Edwardsean "Consistent Calvinism" alienated many erstwhile Christians and weakened the congregations. The Consistent Calvinists were derided by enemies in their own day and by scholars subsequently as "logic choppers" who lost sight of the popular appeal of Edwards's heart religion as they worked out closely reasoned defenses of divine sovereignty and at least some measure of moral determinism. Tedious and prosaic they were, but out of concern, not unconcern,

---

6. Prior to Bruce Kuklick, *Churchmen and Philosophers* (1985), the most recent book-length studies are Joseph Haroutunian, *Piety versus Moralism: The Passing of the New England Theology* (New York: Henry Holt, 1932) and Frank Hugh Foster, *A Genetic History of the New England Theology* (Chicago: University of Chicago Press, 1907).

for popular feeling. Edwards, far more than his Congregational heirs, espoused unpleasant doctrines like infant damnation, infinite hell torments, and the moral inability of human beings. In a revolutionary, republican era that favored freedom and virtue, Edwards's successors chopped logic in an attempt to prove that divine sovereignty was consistent with human liberty. There now appears to be under way a revisionist turn in favor of the New England theologians, especially the Consistent Calvinists, who may not have been such unpopular preachers as has been thought.[7]

Regardless of how Edwards's near successors were perceived in their own time, by 1851 Horace Bushnell surely spoke the mind of many, in as well as out of the churches, when he listed as "indisputably mournful" the "theologic wars of only the century past,—the Supralapsarians, and Sublapsarians; the Arminianizers, and the true Calvinists; the Pelagians, and Augustinians; the Tasters, and the Exercisers; Exercisers by Divine Efficiency, and by human Self-Efficiency; the love-to-being-in-general virtue, the willing-to-be-damned virtue, and the love-to-one's-greatest happiness virtue; no ability, all ability, and moral and natural ability distinguished; disciples by the new-creating act of Omnipotence, and by change of the governing purpose; atonement by punishment, and by expression; limited, and general; by imputation, and without imputation; trinitarians of a threefold distinction, of three psychologic persons, or of three sets of attributes; under a unity of oneness, or of necessary agreement, or of society and deliberative council."[8] If ever there were men whose labors obstructed rather than helped create the future, they would seem to have been these theologians who sought with scholastic technicalities to defend Calvinism against modern thought. Yet out of these seemingly sterile and cer-

---

7. Joseph A. Conforti, *Samuel Hopkins and the New Divinity Movement: Calvinism, the Congregational Ministry, and Reform in New England Between the Great Awakenings* (Grand Rapids, Mich.: Christian University Press, 1981), 185. Mary P. Ryan reports considerable popular interest in upstate New York in "arid theological matters—searches through scripture for references to baptism, the source of grace, and the moral nature of infants," in *Cradle of the Middle Class: The Family in Oneida County, New York, 1790-1865* (Cambridge: Cambridge University Press, 1981), 66–67.

8. Horace Bushnell, *Christ in Theology* (Hartford, 1851), v–vi.

tainly intricate controversies came the first American statement of the modern view of human identity, the view that the self is not fully conscious.

The word "unconscious" must be read scrupulously in early nineteenth-century texts. The word may be found in the writings of nearly all the major figures treated in this chapter but never to suggest its most common twentieth-century connotation—subconscious mentality in human beings. Early nineteenth-century writers did not refer to unwitting mentality but to no mentality at all when they used the word "unconscious." To them a stove or toe or any other physical object was unconscious but never a thought. The argument of this chapter is not that they developed a conception of unconscious mentality but only that they, and especially Taylor, developed the idea of unconscious selfhood, that is, that the human self is not conscious of all of which it is composed.

The abandonment of the notion that the self has complete and empirical knowledge of itself was made all the more difficult by the vogue of "Baconian empiricism" among American Protestants in the early nineteenth century. "If I understand my own mode of philosophizing," declared Lyman Beecher, "it is the Baconian. Facts and the Bible are the extent of my philosophy."[9] Beecher and many other New England theologians were initially confident that the way to make natural philosophy support revealed religion was to avoid hypotheses and keep the physical sciences narrowly empirical. Their initial assurance on this point was based at least in part on the dominant philosophical movement of their time, Scottish realism, with its assertion that the mind perceives the world directly rather than through the mediation of Cartesian or Lockean ideas. Empirical study of a divinely created world could scarcely lead the mind away from divine truth if, as Thomas Reid and Dugald Stewart said, the mind perceives things in themselves, as they really are.

The Scots' substitution of immediate experience for representative ideas may have put the external natural sciences on a safely

9. Lyman Beecher, *Autobiography*, ed. Barbara Cross (Cambridge: Harvard University Press, 1961), II, 131; cf. Theodore Dwight Bozeman, *Protestants in an Age of Science: The Baconian Ideal and Ante-Bellum American Religious Thought* (Chapel Hill: University of North Carolina Press, 1977), passim.

empirical basis, but rather than resolving the threat posed by the consciousness concept to religious humility, Scottish empiricism lent all the more weight to the evidence of consciousness for moral freedom. Edwards had built his argument for moral determinism not on introspection but on logical inference from the way of ideas. His argument had been that it was logically impossible for the soul to perceive contradictory ideas such as a *first* act of will determined by a *prior* act of will. If, as the Scots said, the mind perceived things themselves rather than representative ideas, there seemed to be no basis for the startling ratiocination by which Edwards had argued against moral freedom. In rejecting Locke's epistemology of ideas, Edwards's successors, ironically, cleared the way for acceptance of Locke's introspective proof of free will. By dispensing with ideas, some of Edwards's Congregationalist successors were forced to dispense with his inferential logic and to accept what seemed to them the incontrovertible evidence of consciousness for moral freedom. Human will was not mere desire but the choice, as Locke had said, to satisfy or deny a desire. The New England theologians helped launch "the Victorian orgy with intellectualized will" in America.[10]

The Scots' empiricism thus threatened religious humility at least as much as the way of ideas, and the New England theologians therefore launched a quiet, almost unwitting revision of Scottish realism. That the theologians set their own philosophical agenda rather than being driven to it by imported movements is indicated by the fact that they did not swallow Scottish realism whole but rejected those aspects of it uncongenial to evangelical religion. The Scots were as certain as Locke that the mind completely and directly perceived its own operations. This Scottish perceptualism spilled over into early nineteenth-century New England textbooks in moral philosophy and speculative psychology. In addition to the principles of common sense inevitably intuited by the mind, said Thomas Upham in *Mental Philosophy Abridged*, there was a second source of "internal" knowledge, called "consciousness," and "nothing can ever prevent the convictions resulting from this

---

10. Norman Fiering, *Moral Philosophy at Seventeenth-Century Harvard: A Discipline in Transition* (Chapel Hill: University of North Carolina Press, 1981), 303.

source, and nothing can divest us of them."[11] Even Scottish realism thus failed to address and indeed exacerbated the basic problem faced by evangelical theologians. The self's direct perception of its own operations still threatened to make certain to the unregenerate soul that when it seemed to desire holiness it genuinely did so. Addressing the pressing evangelical need to preserve sufficient spiritual humility to convince the soul of its own helplessness, the New England theologians quietly subverted the Baconian empiricism they ostensibly espoused. Baconian empiricism left no room for doubt of the quality of inward experiences. But doubt of the genuineness of the feeling of striving for grace was crucial to conversion. In order to maintain that human beings are worse than they feel themselves to be, some of the New England theologians were forced to practice a science of the soul more hypothetical and less empirical than they supported in theory. Only by abandoning the belief that psychological science ought to rest on the mind's direct, experiential knowledge of itself did it become possible to posit within the unregenerate soul unconscious moral principles for which there was no empirical evidence of consciousness.

The Limiting of Empiricism and Consciousness

What had been a latent contradiction in Edwards's writings—the question whether God determines people's moral actions by immediately creating ideas in their minds or only mediately through second causes within the soul—became a clear problem in the conversion theory of his principal successor, Samuel Hopkins (1721–1803). An early abolitionist, Hopkins was a gentle man of good causes whose career was divided between long stints in two extremely different pastorates—first a tiny village in western Massachusetts and then the First Church in worldly Newport. That he fared better in the latter situation and there even befriended the moderate Calvinist Ezra Stiles, pastor of the Second Church, suggests that he was more human than the fierce character of legend.

11. Thomas Upham, *Abridgment of Mental Philosophy* (New York, 1835), 136, 138.

And in fact Hopkins intended to mitigate Edwards's harsh rigor, though the intention was obscured in his own time and since by the notoriety accorded his assertion that a person ought to be willing to be damned for the glory of God. The equally charming corollary that it is more damnable for a sinner to use than to spurn the means of grace earned Hopkins's system the sobriquet New Divinity.

Yet Hopkins did not mean that a sinner ought to wait passively for regeneration. Rather, he tried to encourage willful activity by distinguishing between "regeneration" and "conversion." He meant this distinction to give linguistic precision to Edwards's insistence that people may not conclude by inspiration that they possess a regenerate spirit but only by careful examination of their individual thoughts and deeds. "Regeneration," said Hopkins, was the silent transformation that the Holy Spirit effects in the underlying disposition of the soul. "Conversion," on the other hand, was the regenerate soul's continuous effort to grow in grace and become aware of its own holiness.[12] Any one may be regenerate without being conscious of it, and one therefore ought to make a willful effort at conversion. This was a clever and, among the theologians treated here, the last attempt to encourage human activity, while also trying to maintain the position that human beings cannot help themselves. But Hopkins's position was tenable only if the soul can exist in a state of which it is not conscious, which in turn requires that the soul be composed of something more than consciousness, be composed of some substance.

Hopkins was therefore nonplussed in 1770 by "the *new* notion of no spiritual substance."[13] His concern was due to the fact that he, Joseph Bellamy, and other New Divinity men had mainly continued the side of Edwards's thought that deemphasized God's arbitrariness in favor of God's just governorship. Edwards's privative explanation of the origin of sin, or, as his successors called it, the doctrine of the permission of sin, held that God bore responsibility for sin only in that he permitted rather than prevented it. But in that case human beings must act out of some constitutional bias or

12. Samuel Hopkins, *Works* (Boston, 1852), III, 545–46; cf. III, 555–57.
13. Ibid., I, 200.

disposition in the soul apart from God's immediate agency. That is, a person's moral identity must rest in a spiritual substance to which, in regeneration, God gives a new bias or disposition. But Hopkins accepted Edwards's belief that the Holy Spirit's regenerative act was not itself perceivable. So it was logically impossible for Hopkins to attempt to offer empirical support for the concept of a substantial bias toward evil in the sinful soul and toward holiness in the regenerate. In his and Edwards's view the only experiences a saint has of holiness—such as new affections of the heart upon reading scripture—are a consequence of regeneration rather than the thing itself. The saint might just as reasonably attribute these new "exercises," as they were called in Hopkins's time, to an immediate operation of the Spirit as to a change in a hypothetical soul substance.

The fact that Hopkins's system implied the existence of a spiritual substance for which he could offer no empirical evidence would eventually result in the once famous, now largely forgotten, controversy between the "exercisers" and the "tasters." The tasters would use the doctrine of the substantiality of the soul to attempt to create a human identity distinct from the immediate agency of God and thus relieve the almighty of immediate responsibility for sin. Human behavior, they would assert, is based on a substantial bias, "disposition," or "taste of the heart" existing in the soul prior to even its first actions in infancy. Regeneration is then the acquisition of a holy taste resulting from a substantial, or, as they often unphilosophically put it, a "physical" change in the soul. The exercisers, on the other hand, would hold that God's immediate agency is responsible for every human action, including sin. This was a strong view of the Creator, but it was consistent with New England's Calvinist heritage and with the lack of any empirical knowledge of a soul substance.

The controversy was only incipient in Hopkins's time, and he attempted to straddle the fence. Basing human activity on a "taste," he also verged on Edwards's occasionalism by saying that "taste" might possibly "be resolved into divine [i.e., immediate rather than substantial] constitution." Properly fearful lest "the *few* Edwardeans should get into divisions among themselves," Hopkins insisted that the question of the soul's substantiality had no practical implication for the saint's experience in regeneration.[14] Nevertheless, the Edwardseans eventually became divided between tasters who affirmed that regeneration was a substantial change of the soul and exercisers who denied it.

Foremost among the exercisers was the long-lived Nathanael Emmons (1745–1840), a country parson at Franklin, Massachusetts, renowned for his close reasoning, ministerial dedication, and conscientious unworldliness; he once refused the moment's effort required to repair a fallen fence bar lest it start him in the path of excessive care for his worldly estate. Born in Connecticut and educated at Yale, Emmons nearly became an Arminian at college and attributed his narrow escape to a timely reading of Edwards's *Freedom of Will*. Subsequently he studied theology with John Smalley, a well-known New Divinity man, and Hopkins himself participated in Emmons's ordination. This pedigree suggests that Emmons should have been a strenuous Calvinist, and he did orthodoxly uphold such doctrines as infant damnation and God's arbitrary sovereignty. His view of divine agency also was consistent with Edwards's occasionalism; God's "particular providence" is the immediate cause "of all that lives, and moves, and exists."[15] Yet as with Hopkins, Emmons's harshness was overstressed in his own time and since. He objected to the doctrine that regeneration required a substantial change in the soul both because it discouraged human effort and because it was unjust: "there could be no more propriety in God's requiring sinners to change their heart, than in requiring them to add another cubit to their stature." But in Emmons's exercise scheme, since the soul undergoes no substantial or physical change prior to regeneration, "it is just as easy . . . to love God, as to continue to hate him."[16]

Among the few scholars now interested in Emmons it is customary to assert that his metaphysics resembled Edwards's, but the statement cannot stand. Except for vaguely supported statements of occasionalism, Emmons's *Works* contains almost no metaphys-

14. Ibid.

15. Nathanael Emmons, *Works,* ed. Jacob Ide (Boston, 1860), II, 479.

16. Emmons, quoted in Edwards A. Park, *Memoir of Nathanael Emmons* (Boston, 1860), 379, 383.

ics. So little did he have to say on the constitution of the universe that there was something of a controversy down to the middle of the nineteenth century as to whether he accepted the concept of substance.[17] Emmons never offered any speculative system, substantial or ideal, remotely comparable in scope to Edwards's view that the universe is ideal and is constituted in the consciousness of God.

At least in part because of his lack of interest in metaphysics, Emmons disagreed with Edwards on both imputed depravity and personal identity. It was best for Calvinists, Emmons said, to abandon the "absurd idea of imputed or derived depravity" according to which a person would be justified in blaming Adam or God for his or her sinfulness. Innocent of any metaphysical speculation that might have weakened his confidence that a human being's thoughts are his alone, Emmons, unlike Edwards, believed that personal identity was not a difficult problem. The answer, as Locke had said, lay in consciousness which offers everyone empirical evidence that the actions of his soul pertain only to himself: "every man's corrupt heart is his own, and consists in . . . exercises."[18]

Believing that people possess an undeniable "consciousness of moral freedom,"[19] Emmons attempted to defend the doctrine of divine determinism by tempering his empiricism. The question of "how God upholds us every moment" was, he said, an ontological mystery which "we are utterly unable to explain." And we are similarly ignorant of the constitution of the soul. Although consciousness tells us that the soul can perceive, reason, remember, and desire, "we can form no conception of the soul as distinct from these properties or as the foundation of them."[20] Therefore consciousness of moral freedom could not rule out divine determinism. Emmons felt justified in trying to reconcile moral necessity and moral freedom through a kind of mental dualism. The two doctrines are

17. The controversy over Emmons's position on substance is well described in Kuklick, *Churchmen and Philosophers*, 59. In a review of Kuklick (*American Quarterly* [Spring 1986]: 142) I mistakenly stated that in Kuklick's view Emmons believed in substance.

18. Emmons, *Works,* I, 412; III, 123.

19. Emmons, quoted in Park, *Memoir,* 365.

20. Emmons, *Works,* II, 411; cf. Park, *Memoir,* 418.

demonstrated by "distinct faculties of the mind." One faculty—
"reason"—teaches us, as Edwards had done with powerful ratiocination in his *Freedom of Will*, of the moral necessity under which
our every thought and motion occurs. But the faculty of "common
sense" or consciousness intuits our moral freedom. By consulting
these two different faculties we "discover the consistency between
activity and dependence."[21] Unconvincing philosophy though this
is, there is also in it the attitude characteristic of modern psychoanalysis that empirical evidence of consciousness must be aided by
reason in order to form a just view of the mind or self.

The tasters, too, attempted to make human moral freedom pal-
atable to the orthodox by moderating their empiricism and tenden-
tiously adjusting faculty psychology according to the need of theology. Wanting to support moral freedom while preserving a morsel
of determinism, the tasters added to their model of mind a faculty
whose existence was not supported by empirical evidence of consciousness. Until this point, and contrary to textbook descriptions,
there had been no necessary opposition between faculty psychology
and empirical psychology. John Locke, despite his empirical psychology, accepted the centuries-old model of the mind as containing two major and distinct faculties of willing and understanding.
The empirical evidence of consciousness attested to Locke that it is
one thing to understand and another to will.[22] But the tasters could
not base their psychology on the mind's consciousness of two different powers of willing and understanding. They saw the logical
impossibility of Emmons's attempt to reconcile human moral freedom with a universe where everything is determined by God's immediate agency. The tasters therefore repudiated the exercisers'
idea that God immediately determines human willing. The tasters
held instead that while the faculties of understanding and willing
give an unregenerate human being moral freedom, that person is
simultaneously and inevitably depraved owing to the domination
of the will by evil desires originating in a third faculty of "taste."
Known not only as "taste" but also as "propension," "disposi-

21. Emmons, *Works*, II, 413, 415.
22. Fiering, *Moral Philosophy*, 106–7.

tion," or "heart," this third faculty was propounded most assiduously by a Vermont preacher named Asa Burton (1752–1836). Born to an impoverished rural Connecticut family, Burton lived the backwoods life typical of so many New Divinity men. Nearly disabled by hard farm labor as a youth, he deemed himself less fit for the plough than for college and cut his intellectual teeth on Locke and Edwards at Dartmouth. Subsequently he studied for the ministry with Levi Hart, a prominent Hopkinsian. During the next half century Burton preached to a tiny rural congregation, endured plagues and pestilence, survived Indian attacks, supported the Federalist party, and helped found the University of Vermont. Disenchanted with the clashing opinions he encountered in books of theology and moral philosophy, he early forswore reading and instead, with true frontier self-reliance, reasoned out his own system, taught it to the numerous disciples he prepared for the ministry, and as an old man launched it for posterity in a book. *Essays on Some of the First Principles of Metaphysicks, Ethicks, and Theology* (1824), now forgotten by all save a handful of scholars, was considered by many nineteenth-century divines to be "one of the great influential philosophical books of the world."[23] The grandeur of Burton's system lay, as he succinctly stated in his autobiography, in the empirical observation that the "first principles" known to consciousness are pleasure and pain, from which he concluded that there "is a feeling faculty in the mind, and we can trace actions back no further."[24]

Why were such ordinary thoughts heralded by some New England divines as a marvelous discovery answering their theological needs? After all, the pleasurable and painful sensations of Burton's "feeling faculty" were nothing more than the affections and passions, reflexive knowledge of which surely antedates Christianity itself. And in New England literature one can find earlier adumbrations of a heart faculty. For instance, Edwards himself had often used the terms "heart," "taste," "disposition," and "propensity."

23. Foster, *Genetic History*, 243.

24. Asa Burton, *The Life of Asa Burton Written by Himself*, ed. Charles Latham, Jr. (Thetford, Vt.: First Congregational Church of Thetford, 1973), 63; cf. Asa Burton, *Essays on Some of the First Principles of Metaphysicks, Ethicks, and Theology* (Portland, Maine, 1824), 53–61.

But Edwards represented the culmination of the long-term trend that Fiering has called "Augustinian voluntarism." Thinkers in this tradition, though according great significance to the faculty of will-ing, gradually deprived it of any intellectual significance until, as with Edwards, it was synonymous with desire. The opposing "scho-lastic voluntarism" was the position that the soul's ability to will was to some degree independent from the passions and affections. In one sense, then, the New England tasters of the early nineteenth century had been pushed back behind Edwards toward a centuries-old scholasticism, toward an insistence that the soul's faculty of willing differed from its affections and desires. A crucial point, however, separated Burton from the schoolmen and must have been the secret of his doctrine's appeal. The schoolmen had held that the will should check the passions. Burton insisted that it was the other way around, that the heart or taste "determines the will." By rooting willing in a still deeper aspect of human nature, the heart, Burton, more explicitly than any New Englander before him, offered a way to avoid the exercisers' implication that sinful volitions result from "the immediate agency of God."[25]

But Burton failed to offer, indeed could not offer, empirical evi-dence of consciousness to prove the existence of this third faculty. His many tedious pages arguing that heart and will are separate faculties boil down to an assertion that in the case of a thirsty man who has a drink within reach, "If desire and volition were the same thing, . . . his desire for the drink would bring it to his mouth," yet it does not do so in many cases. A reformed drunkard, for in-stance, though he may desire a drink before him, does not bring it to his lips—certain evidence, Burton thought, that a person's heart or passion is one thing and his will another.[26] But Jonathan Ed-wards the younger had already shown the inadequacy of such an argument in the context of any model of thought as perception. A person may desire something "with some degree of reluctance occa-

25. Burton, *Essays*, 89, 215; cf. Nancy Cott, *The Bonds of Womanhood: "Wom-an's Sphere" in New England, 1780–1835* (New Haven: Yale University Press, 1977), 163–64.

26. Burton, *Essays*, 88. Burton's confusion is indicated by the fact that this exam-ple implies that the soul's faculty of willing controls its faculty of heart (desire or taste) rather than, as he thought, vice versa.

sioned by some other bias or motive."[27] A person does not choose every apparent good but only, in the words of Edwards senior, the greatest apparent good. The reformed drunkard knows of no other reason for his choice than that sobriety appears more desirable to him than drink. Therefore the reformed drunkard lacks empirical data—evidence of consciousness—for the conclusion that tasting or desiring is different from willing.

Of all the New England theologians, the bumptious Burton best revealed the desperation into which Calvinists were pushed by the demands of doctrine on the one hand and consciousness on the other. Free will was attested by consciousness and determinism by orthodoxy. Unlike pietists of several centuries past, Burton and other New England theologians were not in favor of conflation but separation of will and desire in a desperate attempt to overcome the religious dangers of psychological empiricism. Rationalization triumphed over empiricism as Burton addressed the question why the will exists at all if it has nothing to do except the "executive" function of prompting the body's motion according to the heart's desire? Why cannot the heart directly prompt the body instead of acting through the will? "Answer, why men were not made differently, does not belong to us to determine. God knew what was necessary."[28]

Unconscious Selfhood

Some tasters, among them Timothy Dwight (1758–1817), knew that they had to deal better than had Burton with the limitation of consciousness as a source of empirical data on the mind. Grandson of Edwards, president of Yale, theologian, poet, preacher, revivalist, Federalist, fighter of French infidelity, and author of the justly celebrated *Travels in New-England and New-York*, Dwight would continue Emmons's and Burton's attempt to justify God's punishment of human sin by modifying Edwards's dim view of human moral capacity. Dwight had studied for a time with his acute uncle,

27. Jonathan Edwards, *A Dissertation on Liberty and Necessity* in *Works* (Andover, 1842), 301.
28. Burton, *Essays*, 108–9.

Jonathan Edwards the younger, who stated as succinctly as anyone that a consciousness composed of nothing but Lockean ideas can prove neither that willing is morally free of, nor that it is determined by, factors outside the mind. Locke believed that ideas were positive—that is, things existing rather than not existing in the mind. It is therefore "impossible for us to be conscious of a negative," impossible to be conscious "that our volitions are not the effect of an extrinsic cause."[29] Consciousness as defined by Locke proves that people feel free when they act according to their wishes but not that they are free to wish differently—Edwards's distinction between natural freedom and moral necessity. Since Dwight wanted to prove moral freedom in order to justify God's punishment of sin, Locke's "way of ideas" was not for him, and he gladly embraced the Scottish philosophy.

Thanks to the Scottish philosophers' insistence that the mind perceives objects rather than ideas, Dwight felt able to depart from Burton by locating the origin of sin in the understanding rather than in a substantial bias or taste of the heart. If sin originates in a divinely created heart bias, God has rigged the game from the start and human beings labor "under a physical impossibility" of doing what he has commanded. Refusing to accept a "consequence so monstrous," Dwight viewed conversion not as a physical change but as "a voluntary conformity to truth." So he invoked the authority of the Scots to assert that human failure to perceive divine truth does not result from any substantial bias in the soul. God has so constituted affairs that objects "uniformly present to the mind their real state and nature." Sin is humanity's fault, not God's, for people's failure to see the truth is an intellectual rather than sensory error. It is one thing accurately to perceive a proposition and another to reason correctly about it. Everyone accurately perceives the proposition that "he that believeth shall be saved," but not everyone gives a reasoned assent to it. This "speculative" assent requires a subsequent emotional or "cordial consent" to be saving. Nevertheless, the speculative aspect of the faith required for regeneration can be achieved by anyone regardless of the condition of his or her

29. Edwards, *Dissertation on Liberty and Necessity*, 423.

heart. Since speculative faith is arrived at freely and is "absolutely required" as a basis of saving faith, Dwight concluded that even saving faith "is an act of the mind, which is in such a sense voluntary, as to be the proper object of a command."[30]

Yet Dwight qualified his acceptance of the Scots' perceptualism in order to remain in the tasters' camp. It might be undeniable that a religious proposition present in consciousness was so present. But once a voluntary, speculative assent to the proposition was achieved, only a subsequent consent of the emotions or heart was saving, and Dwight located its origins offstage from consciousness. Where the lack of empirical knowledge of the heart faculty had been the weakness of Burton's system, Dwight made it the strength of his. The empirical limitation of consciousness enabled him to leave open the possibility that people form their own hearts while refusing as a scrupulous "Calvinist" to affirm that they do. A "new heart" is only a name for an unknown cause of the habit of virtue, and Dwight was happy to be empirically "ignorant" of the "metaphysical nature of this cause." Who is to say that the Holy Spirit does not regenerate the heart through second causes, including perhaps even—contrary to Samuel Hopkins—the sinner's self-interested efforts? Moreover, it may once have worked the other way round, with Adam's originally holy heart degenerating by second causes within the soul. In Adam's case, his "holy heart" was an unknown cause of hitherto virtuous volitions, with no guarantee that it would be equal to every future temptation, no matter how strong. Unequal to the apple, Adam fell from grace of his own accord, not God's, and launched himself on a course of action that ruined his heart.[31] What Dwight had not done, however, was to relieve God of responsibility for giving Adam a "heart" insufficiently holy to resist all temptation.

Heir to this difficult problem was Nathaniel W. Taylor (1756–1858), born to a prominent Connecticut family and raised in the Old Calvinist tradition disdainful of revivalism, New Divinity, and

---

30. Timothy Dwight, *Theology; Explained and Defended in a Series of Sermons* (Middletown, Conn., 1818), II, 531–42.

31. Ibid., II, 543; III, 63; I, 546–47.

Edwardsean rigor. But Taylor entered Yale in 1800 just as Dwight
was fostering the college revival sometimes credited with beginning, in New England at least, the Second Great Awakening.
Moved in his junior year by Dwight's affecting quotation in a
chapel prayer of the passage "A bruised reed shall he not break,"
Taylor achieved hope in the mercy of God and went over to the
evangelists.[32] According to those who knew him, the arrogant tone
of Taylor's prose was present, too, in his personal bearing. But he
was also intellectually gifted and uncommonly handsome. He
could afford to wait for a congregation till the right opportunity
came along, so even though illness had delayed his Yale graduation
till 1807, he stayed on for four years of postgraduate study. Two
years he lived in the president's home in order to serve as amanuen-
sis to the weak-sighted Dwight. Then in 1812, at twenty-six, he was
called to New Haven's First, or "Center," Church, easily the most
prestigious pulpit in Connecticut. Taylor's was as fast a track as anything one might witness in the modern academic or corporate
worlds, but still greater things lay ahead. When the Connecticut
clergy determined in 1822 that orthodoxy required an intellectual
defense more adapted to modern thought than the Andover Theological Seminary was providing, they created a professorship of divinity at Yale and named Taylor to the post.

Some of the orthodox got more than they had bargained for and
were soon appalled at how perilously close Taylor came to removing
all supernatural causes from transformations of human personality.
Taylor's sympathetic biographer, Sidney Mead, agreed with one of
Taylor's contemporaries that "Taylorism meant the forsaking of
[Calvinism]" and in particular the doctrine of divine determinism.
Taylor rejected Edwards's distinction between natural freedom and
moral necessity, telling his Yale students that "Edwards' mind was
all confusion on the subject."[33] Edwards had held that people are
powerless to will differently than they do. Taylor responded in his
legalistic prose that people have "power to choose otherwise than
this present choice with the same antecedent." He tried to reconcile

---

32. Sidney Earl Mead, *Nathaniel William Taylor, 1786-1858: A Connecticut Liberal* (Chicago: University of Chicago Press, 1942), 28.
   33. Ibid., 191, 112.

divine determinism with human moral freedom in his famous formulation that human action is characterized by "certainty, with
power to the contrary." When orthodox Calvinists like Bennett
Tyler objected sensibly enough that God could not possibly possess
certain foreknowledge if people have genuine power to the contrary, Taylor humbly relied on the empirical limitation of consciousness as regards God's operations: "what if we cannot see *how* . . . ?
Does this *prove* that he cannot do it?"[34]

Taylor's system implied an answer to the question that had baf-
fled Dwight—why had God not given Adam a heart sufficiently
holy to resist all temptation? God *had* given Adam a heart that
could have avoided sin, for like the rest of humanity Adam had
power to the contrary. Taylor's departure from Edwards is usually
seen to lie in this assertion of a liberty of indifference, a liberty to
will either way (to choose or not to choose) in any situation. But in
terms of the New England theology's psychological tradition, the
crucial departure from Edwards was Taylor's insistence, at least as
regards depravity, that people form their own hearts. Even
Dwight's view that heart is a changeable habit but that it is impossible to know what changes it stopped short of Taylor's position.

"Taylorism" was a middle path between the exercise and taste
schemes, a way to relieve God of the onus of being either the immediate cause of sin or the vicious creator of a sinful human nature.
Taylor agreed with the exercisers that human depravity does not
originate "in any essential property or attribute of the soul." And
he agreed with the tasters that sinful people possess a sinful disposition. But that sinful disposition, in Taylor's view, is created by people, not God: "does God . . . damn them for the very nature he
creates. Believe this, who can." Believing instead that morality is a
quality pertaining only to acts of free choice, Taylor held that human nature was not originally sinful. Sin has a sinless source: "that
which is the cause of *all* sin is not itself sin." Sin's sinless source is
"self-love," which is the innate disposition of all souls. Being innate, self-love is not the result of a free choice, and Taylor therefore
attached no moral quality to it. To the question of how a person's

34. Nathaniel Taylor, *A Further Reply to Dr. Tyler, on the Doctrine of Decrees*
(n.p., n.d.), 18–19.

moral character is first formed, Taylor empirically announced that the "answer which human consciousness gives, is, that . . . [humanity, because of self-love] desires to be happy" and chooses as the supreme object of its affections what it mistakenly believes will prove most pleasing—mammon rather than God.[35]

Taylor did not wish to imply that, human souls initially choosing sin, God must poorly dispose the original principle of self-love itself. He therefore argued circularly that while the disposition usually determines willful actions, a willful action creates the evil disposition. The soul's original, amoral principle of self-love "prompts to the choice (not determines it)."[36] That is, self-love moves the soul to action, but the soul then willfully chooses sin without reference to any heart bias. Being indeterminate and free, this willful choice possesses a moral character: "We mean by depravity, a sinful volition itself, or rather, a sinful elective preference which becomes predominant in the soul."[37] By this first choice people create in their hearts a new "selfish principle," the somewhat confusing name for a sinful disposition that Taylor borrowed from the Scots. The new "selfish," or sinful, principle of the heart then dominates the neutral principle of "self-love." Selfishness determines the will's subsequent moral choices, always sinful unless the selfish principle somehow loses control of the soul. Of this there is hope, for just as the soul initially chose an evil disposition, it may subsequently opt for "a *change* of this preference."[38]

Like the other theologians in this chapter, Taylor was struggling and flailing against the tendency to make desire for holiness a perception rather than an interpretation. He insisted that the formation of a holy disposition, no less than the initial adoption of a sinful one, is as much an action as a perception. A soul in the process of regeneration must choose between God and mammon as potential sources of happiness. As to how the sinner with an evil, selfish disposition may truly consider God as a possible source of

35. Nathaniel Taylor, *Concio ad Clerum* (New Haven, 1828), 5, 7; *idem*, "On the Means of Regeneration," *Quarterly Christian Spectator* 1 (1829): 21.

36. Taylor, "On the Means of Regeneration," 22.

37. Nathaniel Taylor, *Essays, Lectures, Etc. upon Select Topics in Revealed Theology* (New York, 1859), 204.

38. Taylor, "On the Means of Regeneration," 21.

happiness, Taylor again resorted to self-love, or the heart's original desire for happiness. A candle that will secretly "thrill in the soul of the worst sinner," self-love may flame up and suspend the selfish principle. Initially Taylor spoke carelessly of a "suspension of the entire influence" of the selfish principle, but this brought up the same problem that, in his discussion of a person's first act of sin, had forced him to reason circularly. Self-love is a "tendency which, if wholly *uncounteracted* would flow out in holy love to God." So when the selfish principle is totally suspended (or, to begin with, nonexistent), holiness should be the inevitable result. Yet in discussing regeneration, as opposed to the adoption of a sinful disposition, it is not desirable to minimize God's responsibility. Taylor scarcely wished to conclude that there is no need of gracious assistance from the Holy Ghost. Backing off from a total suspension of the selfish principle, he subsequently held that the suspension is total only intermittently and perhaps not even total at any time since "the mind is capable of opposite *tendencies* at the same time."[39]

Here, in the possibility of two conflicting tendencies or dispositions existing simultaneously in the soul, was the advantage of a soul constituted of spiritual substance rather than mere consciousness. A soul consisting of nothing but consciousness could not possess two tendencies or dispositions, for the conscious activity of the selfish (sinful) principle would preclude the existence of self-love and vice versa. But a soul constituted substantially could contain a struggle between conscious and unconscious principles since their existence does not depend on consciousness. Responsibility for sin then rested with human beings who freely create their selfish dispositions and whose free choice of holiness is necessary before the Holy Ghost will ensure its triumph in their souls.

By using the idea that the self may be composed of elements of which it is not conscious to defend Trinitarianism, Taylor became a pioneer theorist of multiple personality. To the charge of the Unitarians' leading theologian, William Ellery Channing, that viewing the deity as three persons or consciousnesses implied polytheism, Taylor replied by distinguishing between a unified being and a con-

39. Ibid., 227, 34, 231, 227.

scious person. God was *"one being in three persons."* The unity of a deity with several consciousnesses, no less than the identity of a human being with conscious and unconscious tendencies, rested in substance rather than consciousness. Taylor admitted, as had Dwight, that the "common" conception of substance was "phenomenal," but he refused to reason commonly, refused to conclude that the three different phenomena or persons of God are three distinct substances and therefore three different Gods. Instead, he brought the empirical limitation of consciousness into play. The Unitarians, he said, presumptuously assert that human consciousness is the measure of all things, that because people ordinarily think of a substance as having one phenomenal nature it cannot have more than one. The same argument, that people are conscious of nothing but phenomena, had led Edwards to reject the concept of substance and to assert that humanity is constituted of nothing but phenomena or ideas. Taylor moved in exactly the opposite direction by insisting that since phenomena were no indication of substance, what was phenomenally impossible might be substantial reality: "who shall undertake to say on *a priori* ground, whether anything more can or cannot be true of a substance?"[40]

Taylor helped create the modern view of human personality as merely a group of phenomenal or behavioral traits which do not necessarily characterize the entire being. It was perfectly reasonable, he said, to conceive of "one man, as consisting of one substance and of three human natures," or personalities. Only traditional word usage, Taylor pointed out, made multiple personality seem unreasonable, either in human beings or in Trinitarian doctrine. In a question suggestive of later nineteenth-century psychological speculation in general and Robert Louis Stevenson in particular, Taylor asked what linguistic practice would be followed if a divine revelation made clear that one person's body may contain three personalities. Ordinary human economy in language is such that people would still call this creature a *man* when there was no reason to recognize his "tri-personality."[41] Only when people

40. William Ellery Channing, *A Sermon Delivered at the Ordination of the Reverend Jared Sparks* (Boston, 1819), 13; Taylor, *Essays, Lectures, Etc.*, 10, 27, 36.
41. Taylor, *Essays, Lectures, Etc.*, 20.

wanted to differentiate between the personalities would they find the word *man* inadequate and be obliged to coin different names, say Jekyll and Hyde, for the different personalities.

Yet it is important not to overestimate the modernity of Taylor or underestimate the distance that separated his view from modern mental science. Except for the analogies he drew between the Trinity and human personality, there is no suggestion in his writings of the possibility of unconscious mental events. In Taylor's view, unconscious tendencies or dispositions were only bases for mental action rather than actions themselves. He never really imagined the possibility of unconscious *thought*. His was a much more preliminary step—the insistence merely that the human self is not entirely conscious of all that composes it.

The Unconscious Self Interpreted Evangelically

The great evangelists Lyman Beecher and Charles Finney well illustrate the impact on the work of the ministry of the drift of New England theology from Hopkins to Taylor. Beecher, a close friend of Taylor, was a practical worker, a harvester of souls in the fields of the Lord, and his infrequent attempts at critical thought reveal a narrow, poorly trained mind. Missing, for example, the whole point of the revolt by Edwards, Locke, and others against treating psychological faculties as more or less independent entities, he argued that "if language has any meaning, a free will is a will which is free."[42] Incapable of genuinely participating in speculative psychology and theology, Beecher nevertheless kept superficially abreast of them and was in the mainstream of New England "Calvinism" when he repudiated Edwards's teachings, not only on free will but also on original sin and the moral accountability of infants. A man of action rather than a speculative thinker, Beecher worked off his enormous excess of energy by shoveling a pile of sand from one side of his basement to the other. He also conducted from 1826 to 1832 the largest revival in Boston since the Great Awakening.

Beecher's strategy as a revivalist was to emphasize conscious ability. Enjoining sinners to make salvation their first object in life, he

42. Lyman Beecher, *Autobiography*, I, 285.

preached, "You can do *that*. Are you not conscious that you can?" Because of his own religiously troubled youth, "high Calvinism" and humility were anathema to him: "For cases like mine, Brainerd's Life is a most undesirable thing. It gave me a tinge for years. So Edwards on the Affections—a most overwhelming thing, and to common minds the most entangling. The impressions left by such books were not spiritual, but a state of permanent hypochondria—the horrors of a mind without guidance, motive, or ability to do any thing. They are a bad generation of books on the whole." Practicing a "clinical theology" based on the evidence of consciousness for a mild degree of moral ability in the sinner, Beecher guarded against pushing troubled souls into total abjection. Like his seventeenth-century predecessors, he cautioned against taking the soul at its worst. For the unduly distressed he prescribed, according to his daughter Harriet Beecher Stowe, a week or two "of almost entire cessation from all religious offices, with a course of gentle muscular exercise and diversion."[43]

Yet humility had a place in Beecher's scheme, for the consciousness concept could not be allowed to usurp understanding of the spiritual life. Consciousness could be invoked as evidence of the sinner's capacity to try, but the sinner must not be allowed to conclude that, conscious of having tried, he or she was entitled to leave the rest to God. Beecher chastised his unregenerate daughter Catharine for her "presumptuous reliance upon her own consciousness." When she replied that a consciousness devoid of any willful aversion to God must eventually conclude that the almighty unjustly denied grace, Beecher sprang on her the trap prepared by Taylor: "It is a common thing for men to be actuated [activated] by motives . . . of whose existence they are unconscious."[44]

In addition to Catharine, Lyman Beecher had another daughter who, of all his verbose and scribbling children, wrote the greatest book. *Uncle Tom's Cabin* touched the nerve of a once pious and still putatively Christian nation because Harriet Beecher Stowe more firmly than her father refused to allow confidence in consciousness to subdue conscience of sin. Lyman's faith in the evi-

43. Ibid., II, 86; I, 29–30, 48–49.
44. Ibid., I, 382.

dence of consciousness for moral freedom became, for Catharine, an absolute. But Harriet implicitly denied the consciousness concept by drawing on the tradition of New England piety that Lyman unsuccessfully attempted to reconcile with the consciousness concept. Jacksonian Americans, accepting the evidence of consciousness, had conceived of human willing as self-conscious and self-controlled. They had therefore seen not moral danger but moral rectitude in an economy based on self-interest. Harriet Beecher Stowe brought to the bar of justice not only slavery but also the ethos of American avarice when she wrote that "the *interest* of the master" was not "a sufficient safeguard for the slave" against "the fury of man's mad will."[45] Ironically, Lyman Beecher could not employ the self-denying language of piety as emphatically as did his novelist daughter precisely because he was an evangelist. He urged potential converts to make self-interested efforts to save their own souls.

The impossible feat of balancing assertions of human capacity with traditional piety defeated not only Beecher but also the age's other great revivalist. Charles Grandison Finney (1792–1875), though born in New England, spent most of his life representing the region's evolving religious culture in the great valley of the West where he preached, more plainly even than Beecher, "that the divine agency was that of teaching and persuasion, that the influence was a moral, and not a physical one." But his meaning was no different from that of his Eastern brethren when he asserted that "we must cultivate an habitual sense of our dependence," for it is not to "be presumed, that we should learn our dependence, by the results of our experience." For "experience" was "a matter of consciousness," and consciousness attested to freedom.[46] So did the supposedly fluid society and boundless opportunity of Jacksonian America, suppositions that humiliated individuals by the relative poverty of their accomplishments. Revivals and conversions in the

45. Harriet Beecher Stowe, *Uncle Tom's Cabin*, ed. Kenneth S. Lynn (Cambridge: Harvard University Press, 1962), 420.

46. Charles Grandison Finney, *Memoirs* (New York, 1876), 317; *idem*, "Report of the Suffolk South Association," *The Spirit of the Pilgrims* 6 (1833): 199; *idem*, quoted in Miller, *Life of the Mind in America*, 30.

1820s and 1830s could concentrate into days and even hours the religious humiliation that once would have taken months or years because they subjected a worldly but anxious people to a social and searing moral scrutiny.[47] What had once been left to God and sinner to accomplish slowly and even tediously was pressed hastily forward by the weight of the community. In such circumstances, dependence was certain to be remembered but not necessarily the qualification, dependent *on God*. Pressed by the consciousness concept to avow more autonomy in spiritual life than human beings found in their material and social circumstances, the revivalists of the era cast desperately about for spiritual limitations: "We are not to expect to feel our minds in direct physical contact with God. If such a thing can be, we know of no way in which it can be made sensible."[48] Despite all the changes since the seventeenth century, piety still required that some things be learned through interpretation of signs rather than immediate, conscious perceptions.

But the clerical compromise—conscious and unconscious elements within a substantial self—was only superficially less damaging to piety than was the unadulterated consciousness concept. Because the religious quests of Catharine Beecher and Charles Finney had opposing outcomes, it is easy to overestimate the difference between them. Catharine, conscious of no willful aversion to God, refused to be humbled. Finney, on the other hand, was humbled by sin, but his shame originated in his conviction that he had sinned freely, voluntarily. In early Boston, Jane Holmes had been humiliated by the sense of her inability to avoid sin. Two centuries later, for Finney, it was the very avoidableness of sin that made it a cause for humiliation. The crucial moment in Finney's conversion came when, praying for salvation in the woods, he thought he heard someone approaching and interrupted his prayer to see if it were so: "An overwhelming sense of my wickedness in being ashamed to have a human being see me on my knees before God, took such powerful possession of me, that I cried at the top of my voice and exclaimed that I would not leave that place. . . . The sin

47. Scott, *From Office to Profession*, 80–84.
48. Charles Grandison Finney, *Lectures on Revivals of Religion*, ed. William G. McLoughlin (Cambridge: Harvard University Press, 1960), 95.

appeared awful, infinite. It broke me down before the Lord." Just then his mind was flooded with the light of a scripture passage: "Then shall ye go and pray unto me, and I will hearken unto you." Finney "seized hold of this with my heart. I had intellectually believed the Bible before; but never had the truth been in my mind that faith was a voluntary trust instead of an intellectual state."[49] Finney and Catharine Beecher, despite the different outcomes of their religious quests, accepted a degree of moral freedom alien to seventeenth-century pietists like Jane Holmes.

Not only the nature of conversion but also postconversion piety was threatened by the belief that reconciliation of human freedom and divine determinism depended on viewing the mind as a substance divisible into conscious and unconscious elements. The division contributed to a model of postconversion spirituality that did not sufficiently allow for backsliding and renewed humiliation. If the substance of the soul was changed, it was changed, and its new disposition should be permanent. There was a profound irony in the coming into use during this period of the phrase "religious experience." For it showed that the evangelists had not escaped, as they had tried so hard to do, the irreligious effect of the consciousness concept. They conceived of regeneration as an inner "experience" as undeniable as any other thought to the knowing self. The soul, once it had undergone a conscious "religious experience," had no reason to expect, and indeed good reason to avoid, the humiliation and guilt that had driven seventeenth-century saints to redouble, after conversion, the intensity of their spiritual search. For humiliation and guilt, rather than being interpreted as holy scrupulousness, could only be indications that the earlier "experience" was not genuine.

Finney's case is again instructive. Once he had achieved faith, "I was as conscious as I was of my existence, of trusting at that moment in God's veracity." Alone one evening in the law office he would soon abandon for the ministry, Finney, as it seemed to him, "met the Lord Jesus Christ face to face," an event he could recount because, as it occurred to him afterward, it "was wholly a mental state" but still, of course, an experience within the self. Wave after

49. Finney, *Memoirs*, 16.

wave of holiness coursed intolerably through him. A great and substantial change had occurred in his soul, and some of its effect was conscious: "My sense of guilt was gone; my sins were gone; and I do not think I felt any more sense of guilt than if I never had sinned. . . . I felt myself justified by faith; and so far as I could see, I was in a state in which I did not sin."[50] Finney marked a new mood of certainty—impious certainty—in American Protestantism, a mood in which the devout would be less given than formerly to humbling reinterpretation of their spiritual lives.

Doubtless there had been such cocksure believers in every previous generation, but then prevailing theory would have cautioned their fellows to be skeptical of those who could find no doubt or wrong in themselves. Now, thanks to the prevalent faith in the sureness and immediacy of self-knowledge encouraged by the consciousness concept, a man like Finney, who looked within and saw no guilt, could be admiringly launched on a career as a great revivalist. Endowing evangelicalism with the confident countenance of a good lawyer with a strong case and a well-heeled client, Finney helped make it likely that future explorations of the inner life would come from beyond the fold.

The voluntarism and, in effect, Christian perfectionism of early nineteenth-century revivalists and theological revisionists, it has been pointed out, surpassed and even subverted the conservative political goals of many of them, if not of the abolitionist Finney. The reforms for which many, such as Beecher and Taylor, worked were "moral rather than social."[51] Prohibitionism and Sabbatarianism marked the limits of their reform impulse. Yet Beecher and Taylor probably eventually understood that their defense of free will helped raise the question, by what right one human being deprived another of the free moral agency that even God did not enslave. But giving impetus to abolitionism was not the only way Beecher and Taylor subverted their conservatism, nor does one have to move from the moral sphere to the social to find irony in their story. Even within the moral sphere, Beecher and Taylor proved to be

50. Ibid., 16, 19, 23.

51. John L. Thomas, "Romantic Reform in America, 1815–1865," *American Quarterly* (Winter 1965): 679.

their own worst enemies. For if part of the self is not known to consciousness, the evidence of consciousness can scarcely prove the moral freedom on which Beecher and Taylor rested their case for human effort in revivals of religion. If part of the self is not known to consciousness, the self may feel free and yet be determined by something out of consciousness. The next generation of thinkers, in addressing the question of selfhood, would realize the deterministic possibilities of unconscious selfhood but would locate the determining power in material nature rather than a sovereign God.

Late eighteenth- and early nineteenth-century New England theology offered fertile soil for growth of theories about the inner life, especially the notion that personal identity rests in an emotionally divided and partly unseen self within which human beings must reestablish harmony if they are to be happy. Before such new subconscious elements could be hypothesized within the self, mental philosophy had to be liberated from the crudely empirical attitude that knowledge of the self depended entirely on consciousness or introspection. In the history of Anglo-American philosophy, this liberation is often attributed to John Stuart Mill's *Examination of Sir William Hamilton's Philosophy* (1865). But decades earlier New England Calvinists, even while relying on the Scottish realists' rejection of the way of ideas, had begun to move away from empiricism and toward the position characteristic of modern psychology that introspection alone is not a sufficient basis for study of the mind. Liberation from unaided introspection was never totally achieved in the context of the New England theology, for proponents of that tradition continued to cite the empirical "evidence of consciousness" whenever it suited them. But they bred a new generation, a few of whom would finally abandon hope of saving Calvinism while nevertheless working out to its logical conclusion their predecessors' belief in a self composed partly of something unconscious. A mind constituted of something other than consciousness might perceive without perceiving that it perceives, might think without thinking that it thinks. It might think unconsciously.

CHAPTER FIVE

The Self Sign: Bushnell, Holmes, Hall

The Unsuccessful Compromise between Consciousness and Determinism

So successful were the New Divinity men and the Taylorites in moving doctrinal emphasis toward the moral capacity of human beings that by the mid-nineteenth century scientifically minded critics charged the New England theology with not being deterministic enough. Early nineteenth-century theologians, moved partly by republican condemnation of monarchical absolutism, had defended God's justice in punishing sin by minimizing divine determinism and expanding on human freedom. It was not tyrannical of God to punish people for sin if they had the ability to choose virtue. Shortly, however, the physical sciences replaced republican celebration of human capacity for self-government as the principal challenge to the theologians. In this context of increasing attention to causal relationships in the natural world, deterministic interpretation of human behavior again became intellectually respectable. Religious thinkers who had been convinced of human freedom by the evidence of consciousness began to have second thoughts. Political and scientific discourse, however, were only partial determinants of the development of the self sign.

The concept of consciousness continued to complicate self-understanding. A distinctly mental substance capable of perceiving its own actions supposedly attested to free will. Conversely, the subjective feeling of free will attested to the mentality of the self, to its distinctness from material nature. This interdependency of the notions of self and conscious will has now largely disappeared, for most twentieth-century psychologists believe that even conscious thought is at least partly determined or unwilled. Before mental philosophers could take that view, however, they had to get rid of the notion that the evidence of consciousness supported free will. But to get rid of free will was to dispense with what had come to be considered the basic evidence for the mentality and spirituality of the self. Clinging desperately to free will, some nineteenth-century mental philosophers unsuccessfully attempted a compromise with the new determinism.

The attempt to compromise between freedom and determinism led to frank acknowledgment of the possibility of unconscious thought. New England theologians had hoped to preserve traditional religiosity by blending conscious freedom and an unconscious element within the self. Their heirs admitted the law of cause and effect into that unconscious part of the self. Needing free will as evidence of the self's consciousness or mentality, they suggested that any determinant of human willing must affect the unconscious part of the self. But the unconscious part of the self is presumably as immaterial as the conscious part of the self. The unconscious part of the self can therefore only be determined, not by material force, but by a thought. But before the unconscious part of the self can be determined by a thought, it must know the thought. And being unconscious, it must know the thought without knowing that it knows the thought. The hypothesis of unconscious thought thus made its way among the New England establishment as a device for preserving the freedom and mentality of the self.

But the compromise failed. Unconscious mentality proved unsuccessful as a way of preserving belief in the self's spirituality and moral freedom. It was eventually seen that if unconscious thought is capable of determining human willing, the hitherto vaunted evidence of consciousness did not prove free will. For determined, unconscious thoughts might determine conscious thoughts, which were thus not necessarily as free as they felt. The only way to have preserved the evidence of consciousness for free will would have been to assert that unconscious, determined thought occurs outside the self. But the thinkers treated in this chapter sought to preserve the self's traditional role as the creator and container of all thought, so they reached another conclusion. It may be that the evidence of consciousness does not conclude for free will nor indeed for immediate self-knowledge of any kind. But that does not necessarily mean that the self is not in charge. It may mean only that consciousness is a delusion or at best an insignificant phenomenon and that the self is an organic body rather than a soulful mind.

Three men in whom this logic progressed were Horace Bushnell (1802–76), Oliver Wendell Holmes, Senior (1809–94), and G. Stanley Hall (1844–1924). They are disparate. The plain but controversial Bushnell painfully accommodated the New England theology to the needs of his middle-class Hartford congregation. Holmes, the famous physician and Harvard professor, litterateur and urbane wit, mocked the scholastic intricacies of Calvinism. Hall, somewhat frustrated and jealous, lifted himself by enormous energy and ability out of rural poverty to take the first doctorate in psychology ever granted by an American university. Yet Holmes, through his father, who was raised in Connecticut and trained in orthodoxy at Yale, had contact with many of the intellectual forces that shaped Bushnell's thought. And Hall was a Calvinist divine before he was a psychologist. Although Holmes and, eventually, Hall worked in secular genres, their writings betray an impulse both religious and theological and were meant, like Bushnell's, to bring New England's inherited culture to terms with modern thought. That task was much more difficult for Bushnell than Holmes and Hall, who had abandoned the technical intricacies of their parents' faith. Yet the psychologies articulated by these three thinkers represented a developmental process. By tracing that process, this chapter will show the large degree to which spiritual questions continued to dominate psychology as it became a secular and even a physical science.

Toward Unconscious Thought

Bushnell was born and raised in a reasonably prosperous Connecticut farm family, who were not concerned about the fine points of New England theology or prone to strenuous piety. Slow in his religious development, only at age nineteen did he become a church member. Late in his education as well, he graduated from Yale at twenty-six and then spent several years in New Haven preparing for possible careers in teaching, journalism, or law before entering the Yale Divinity School at twenty-nine. Graduating two years later, he

went to the North Church in Hartford where he tried unsuccessfully to raise revivals. Slowly, he abandoned dramatic conversion
experiences in favor of a gradual, imperceptible growth in Christ
more suitable to the taste of an urban, middle-class congregation.
His relations with his parishioners, not always comfortable early in
his ministry, were eventually successful. When he embroiled himself in controversy by questioning the literalness of the doctrine of
the Trinity, his church loyally protected him against a heresy trial by
withdrawing from its local consociation. Yet Bushnell was restless in
the ministry and tried unsuccessfully for a university professorship.
Illness required ("permitted" would possibly be more accurate)
travel to Europe, Cuba, and California before a generous settle-
ment from his church enabled him to retire at fifty-seven.

In his earliest major publications Bushnell could scarcely have
been more conventional in his belief that consciousness implies a
unified self. Although he had studied with Taylor at Yale, Bushnell
differed with his mentor on many points. Taylor had defended the
Trinity by a theory of multiple personality that Bushnell abhorred:
"a Living Person having in Himself, first, the attributes of a person,
and secondly, three more persons" would be a "monster." But it
would be equally horrible to suppose that the three divine persons
are not also one person, for then God would not be a unified spiritual being. This unnavigable Scylla and Charybdis was the result,
Bushnell said, of a mistaken attempt to analyze what, to the finite
human mind, must always be an unanalyzable mystery—the internal character of God. The human mind needs the Trinity, and especially the person of Christ, as a symbol of an incomprehensible reality. But the limited knowledge attained through Christ is
insufficient to comprehend divinity in its entirety. The mystery,
however, pertains to the Trinity and not to the personal unity of
God as "one mind, will, consciousness."[1] If we do not understand
the nature of God, we at least know something of ourselves, and it
is impossible, Bushnell thought, "*for us* to admit such a threeness
of person, and retain any real belief in the divine unity at all."[2]

Bushnell nevertheless recognized that the consciousness and

1. Horace Bushnell, *God in Christ* (Hartford, 1849), 132, 136.
2. Horace Bushnell, *Christ in Theology* (Hartford, 1851), 143.

conversion concepts were irreconcilable in their traditional purity, and he attempted a reconciliation by modifying them both. The notion of conversion as a "technical experience" was harmful to children who were in effect told that until they were blessed with a miraculous and undeniable perception of holiness they should expect no good of themselves: "Christian families . . . take their own children to be aliens . . . and even tell them that they can do nothing right or acceptable to God till *after* their hearts are changed. . . . They are thus discouraged, and even *taught* to grow up in sin." Why not raise children, then, to lie and steal? Bushnell did not understand the degree to which Puritan conversion had been a dynamic, interpretive process, but he certainly understood how the prevalence in his time of the consciousness concept and the implication that the soul possesses certain knowledge of its own moral quality blocked spiritual change and development. His desire to aid spiritual growth would eventually lead him, not to reject the consciousness concept in favor of an older psychology, but to modify the concept by allowing for unconscious thought. Conversion could then be regarded not as a perception but as a process of growth: "the child is to grow up a Christian . . . not remembering the time when he went through a technical experience, but seeming rather to have loved what is good from his earliest years."[3]

Bushnell's much remarked adjustment of theology to middle-class domesticity was basically an elaboration of Taylor's idea that the struggle for regeneration is a contest between two principles in the soul. Taylor had thought that the regenerate made two choices—first, the choosing of sin soon after birth and, much later, holiness. Bushnell thought one choice would suffice for regeneration, provided only that the choosing process stretched from infancy to adulthood. If Taylor was right that good as well as evil tendencies are present from the beginning, Bushnell reasoned in *Christian Nurture* (1847), then sanctification need not depend on a dramatic conversion in adulthood. Certainly there is evil in the soul of even the best child, as any reasonably objective observer must admit. But sanctified adults also live a mixed, flawed life. Just as Taylor had thought that the adult sinner might actively will a new

3. Horace Bushnell, *Christian Nurture* (Hartford, 1847), 166, 6.

heart despite his or her dependence on an omnipotent God, Bushnell thought that a child might submit to adult authority for a better reason than the parent's superior strength. Middle-class parents were understandably receptive to Bushnell's notion that their children might obey "lovingly" and because it is "right and good."[4]

Bushnell believed that consciousness attested to free will, yet he was also well aware of increasing respect for determinism, which seemed to be sanctioned by explanatory science. He paid his respect to both voluntarism and determinism by dividing the entire universe into two realms of nature and supernature. Most of the soul was natural. But the will, as part of God's supernatural order, was the one point in the human soul where the natural law of cause and effect does not apply. Against "naturalists" (those who believed that there was nothing supernatural about the universe), Bushnell cited the evidence of consciousness for the existence of a spiritual, supernatural realm: "we find another kind of existence in ourselves, which consciously does not fall within the terms of nature." Like Taylor, Bushnell attacked Edwards's and earlier pietists' conflation of desire and will. The evidence of consciousness shows conclusively, Bushnell thought, that willful choice and emotional desire are two different things: "we even shudder it may be in the choice, at the sense of our own perversity—that we are . . . casting away the gold and grasping after the dirt."[5]

Having paid obeisance to free will, Bushnell gently tipped the New England theology back toward determinism, which he believed most consistent not only with explanatory science but also with middle-class domesticity. Parents, like the almighty, wanted not only voluntary love from their children but also absolute sovereignty over them. On the basis of scientific determinism and an organicism acquired from German sources, Bushnell assured parents that physical separation between mother and child at birth does not mean "that no organic relation remains." Because a person is responsible for no sins except his or her own, "it does not therefore follow that there are no moral connections between individuals

---

4. Ibid., 16.
5. Horace Bushnell, *Nature and the Supernatural* (Hartford, 1858), 86, 49.

by which one becomes a corrupter of others." Rejecting absolute individualism, Bushnell held that moral "character may be, to a great extent, only the free development of exercises previously wrought in us . . . when other wills had us within their sphere." The infant's will is partly exercised by the parent, whose smile or frown will often produce a similar phenomenon in the child. There is thus no reason that a sanctified parent should not attempt to exercise the child's will in the direction of holiness. Even at the disturbing point where the child begins to have the voluntary power to mold his own character, "he is still under the authority of the parent, and has only a partial control of himself."[6]

Organic, scientific determinism enabled Bushnell to proclaim the truth of Calvinism, or at least its symbolic truth, far more aggressively than Taylor. Although Bushnell rejected the literal meaning of the doctrine of imputation—that God imputes the sins of parents to their children—he still offered a familial explanation for the continuance of sin in the world. If parents may hope to exercise their child's soul in a holy manner, they surely also often do so in a sinful manner. The "taint derived . . . under the law of family infection" bears resemblance to the doctrines of original sin and federal headship which, though literally erroneous, nevertheless contain, symbolically, "a great and momentous truth . . . that in Adam all die, that by one man's disobedience many were made sinners." Parents exert not an "influence" but a "force" in the shaping of a child's character. Even adults, despite the evidence of consciousness, are determined: "we are never at any age, so completely individual as to be clear of organic connections that affect our character."[7]

If, despite the evidence of consciousness, adults are determined, they must be determined by something unconscious. Bushnell elaborated more fully than had Taylor the notion that religious conversions of the dramatic sort are based on an unconscious element in the soul. Following upon a Christian's willful choice of God, "What was before unconscious, flames out into consciousness."[8]

---

6. Bushnell, *Christian Nurture*, 19, 192, 20, 196.
7. Ibid., 187–93.
8. Bushnell, *Christian Nurture* (New York, 1861), 247–48.

The dramatic conversions of adults in revivals might amount to no more than the conscious recognition of a right disposedness that had long existed unconsciously in the soul. This was scarcely revolutionary. No unconscious thought was implied in the unconscious existence of a religious disposition. One could be unconscious of a holy disposition in a substantially constituted soul in the same way that one is often unconscious of the existence of a part of one's body.

Because Bushnell had given up on dramatic conversion "experiences," he could also give up the attempt of Taylor and other post-Edwardsians to reconcile the perceptualism in the concept of consciousness with Christian humility. Bushnell's views justified the unrepentance of aspiring converts like Catharine Beecher who believed that since they perceived a desire for holiness in themselves, they could do no more than they already had, and the rest was up to God. Catharine eventually gave up on achieving conversion, and according to Bushnell's theory it would have been better if she had never tried. He wanted to bring the child's conscious free willing into accord with its unconscious holy disposition so early that there would be no need for humiliating self-examination and dramatic conversions in adulthood. Christian faith would be more natural and steady, and the soul, less often at war with itself, would be more at home in this world: "if it were understood that Christian education, or training in the families, is to be itself a process of domestic conversion, . . . The homes would be Christian homes, and life itself a stream of genial piety."[9]

Despite his attempts to defend religious growth, Bushnell greatly limited the possibility of literal belief in humanity's potential for living in the spirit. Bushnell has been rightly read as a pioneer American symbolist, but it has not been equally well understood that his symbolic theory of language limited humanity's acquaintance with the world of spirit just as much as the empiricism he opposed.[10] The principal influence on Bushnell's theory of

9. Bushnell, *Christian Nurture* (1847), 247.
10. Philip F. Gura, *The Wisdom of Words: Language, Theology and Literature in the New England Renaissance* (Middletown, Conn.: Wesleyan University Press, 1981), 51–71; Charles Feidelson, *Symbolism and American Literature* (Chicago: University of Chicago Press, 1953), 142–61.

language was his Yale professor, Josiah Willard Gibbs, who in turn
had been influenced by German philology and the new nineteenth-century textual criticism showing the Bible to have been
amended and corrupted so often that it could scarcely be thought
to have been dictated directly by God.[11] Influenced by Gibbs and
also by Schleiermacher and Coleridge, Bushnell decided that Scripture was divinely inspired but not divinely spoken. In communicating with human beings, God had expressed himself through finite
human language. Human words for spiritual or mental phenomena, Bushnell had learned from Gibbs, were metaphors derived
from physical nature. For instance, the word "spirit" originally
meant "breath." Since the Bible's language was human rather than
divine, its spiritual import could be best understood by forfeiting
faith in its literalness and reading it for symbolic meaning.
Bushnell enthused rapturously that whoever "will offer himself to
the many-sided forms of the scripture with a perfectly ingenuous
and receptive spirit . . . shall find his nature flooded with sense
. . . such as it is even greatness to feel." But such "sense" was only
poetic rather than, as he confusedly put it, "an immediate, experimental knowledge of God." Bushnell himself had some pages earlier cautioned logic-chopping theologians against assuming a monistic "identity" between spirit and nature when the relation was
only "analogical."[12] Poetry might offer the possibility of greater
emotionality than logic, but that emotionality was nevertheless
symbolic representation of God rather than "immediate" experience of him.

The limitation of consciousness sanctioned Bushnell's romantic
attack on self-examination as a means for determining the state of
the soul: "in simply noting things as they pass in us, which is all we
mean by consciousness, we scarcely do more than to just have a look
on the huddle of their transition." He therefore lamented
Edwards's *Religious Affections*—"one of the most mistaken books
that a good and saintly man was ever allowed to write"—for its
encouragement of belief in a new spiritual sense.[13] Grace, Bushnell

---

11. Jerry Wayne Brown, *The Rise of Biblical Criticism in America, 1800–1870*
(Middletown, Conn.: Wesleyan University Press, 1969), 170–79.
12. Bushnell, *God in Christ*, 25, 69, 93, 38.
13. Horace Bushnell, *Sermons on Living Subjects* (New York, 1858), 229, 239.

believed, is not a particular feeling but a general feeling so that "over and above the little, tiny consciousness [the soul] has of itself, it may have a grand, all-inclusive consciousness of God."[14] Bushnell's "consciousness of God" is a good example of his tendency to turn the language of the New England theology inside out in order to give it a symbolic meaning entirely opposed to literal orthodoxy. By "consciousness of God" he did not mean the positive idea of holiness that Edwards and the Puritans, in different ways, had attempted to describe. Bushnell was describing, in Edwards's terminology, mere "speculative understanding" rather than an "ideal apprehension" of holiness. To Bushnell, "consciousness of God" was only a negative phenomenon. Holiness was not a thought perceived in the self but merely an escape from self-consciousness: "Such a disciple grows less conscious and not more conscious in his habit, and there is such plain, forward-going simplicity in him, that he visibly bears the stamp of God's approving, not of his own self-approving."[15] For the regenerate Christian, Bushnell wanted personal harmony rather than the spiritual travail that Puritans had expected not only to precede but also to follow conversion. The saint's assurance of righteousness, in Bushnell's view, was based not on the continuance of a severe conscience but on its absence.

Yet an absolutely quiet conscience was morally and theologically abhorrent, an obstacle Bushnell overcame by implying, for the first time among New England theologians, the possibility not merely that part of the human soul is unconscious but that it thinks unconsciously. The quieting of the sinner's conscience, the falling away of self-accusation and the emergence of personal harmony, raised the traditional Lockean question of how far it was possible "to change the consciousness of a soul, without any breach of its identity."[16] To Bushnell it seemed clear, as regards personal identity, that the redeemed Christian is in some basic sense the same person as formerly. Grace is miraculous precisely in its restoring the old, corrupt soul to its proper state rather than in any literal sense making a

---

14. Horace Bushnell, *Christ and His Salvation* (New York, 1864), 301–2; cf. *idem, Sermons on Living Subjects,* 236.

15. Bushnell, *Sermons on Living Subjects,* 241.

16. Bushnell, *Christ and His Salvation,* 298.

"new man" or "new woman." But if the saint is metaphysically the same person as before, ought not the saint's conscience continue to be disturbed by past sins? Here is what seems to be a "metaphysical impossibility," for either the accusing conscience must have been "extirpated, which decomposes the man," or else the conscience lies, which means that the saint is no saint after all. Bushnell answered: "The conscience of sin—it may be that he has it in a sense; for, being an eternal fact, he must eternally know it; but the Christ-consciousness in him ranges so high above the self-consciousness, that he lives in a summit of exaltation, which the infinitesimal disturbances of his human wrong and shame can not reach."[17] If the renewed soul unself-consciously perceives its sinfulness, it must perceive its sin without perceiving that it perceives it. Bushnell found it not only possible but necessary to imagine within a human being the phenomenon he had rejected in Taylor's doctrine of the Trinity—one living person who includes more than one consciousness, or, more precisely, conscious and unconscious thought.

Unconscious Thought

This study must depart for a time from theology and permanently from the line promulgated by Bushnell, whose otherwise loyal disciples did not share his loyalty, however ambivalent, to the individual self. His theological successors such as Theodore Munger and Newman Smyth tended to deindividualize the soul. By counseling against excessive reliance on the conscious self, they helped develop the modern theology of "self-realization." Proclaiming a "theology of experience," they helped shape the thought of the young John Dewey[18] and thus played back into the sacrifice of self to thought that is discussed in chapters 6 and 7 of this book.

The concern here is with those who reluctantly sacrificed thought, or at least the consciousness of some thoughts, to preserve a basically unified self. Bushnell's most visible, immediate successor in this line was not a theologian but a physician, Oliver Wendell

17. Ibid., 307.
18. Bruce Kuklick, *Churchmen and Philosophers: From Jonathan Edwards to John Dewey* (New Haven: Yale University Press, 1985), chaps. 15–17.

Holmes. Only seven years younger than Bushnell, Holmes was longer lived and had two careers, medicine and literature. His literary career, beginning as Bushnell's was ending, opened in a more liberal time and place. The possibility of unconscious mental events, which Bushnell had only implied, was insisted on by the more liberated Holmes.

Born into the mercantile and clerical aristocracy, Holmes eventually supplied it with a famous name—the "Brahmin caste of New England"[19]—whose elitism rested, in his original conception, not only on social standing but on scholarship. Raised in Cambridge and educated at Harvard, he vacillated like Bushnell among many possible careers, including law and literature. After a brief, popular success as a poet in his early twenties, he studied medicine in Paris, practiced it in Boston, and eventually taught it at Harvard. His research on "The Contagiousness of Puerperal Fever" (1843) saved the lives of many new mothers. Only in middle age did he seriously take up his pen, beginning with his 1857 *Atlantic Monthly* series, "The Autocrat of the Breakfast Table," which was followed by numerous and popular essays, poems, and novels. Holmes was also in demand on the Lyceum circuit as well as being a pioneer microscopist, amateur photographer, and by some accounts, the inventor of the stereoscope. His facility at all he attempted, combined with his fluid, Latinate prose, may account for his present reputation as a glib and superficial thinker. And as regards mental philosophy, Holmes was a distinct amateur as compared to clergymen like Bushnell and Taylor, who devoted years to pondering psychological issues where they impinged on theology. Yet Holmes enjoyed a profitable relationship to theological tradition, simultaneously knowledgeable and disdainful of it, a relationship which enabled him to innovate somewhat in mental philosophy.

Holmes's father, Abiel, is known mainly through his austere history, *American Annals* (1805), and through the memories of his son who later painted a dour picture of his father's house and Puritanical ministry. Abiel's Cambridge parishioners, however, considered him "liberal—for a Connecticut man," and though they ultimately dismissed him, they complained of neither his preaching

19. Oliver Wendell Holmes, *Elsie Venner* (Boston, 1861), 41.

nor doctrines but only of his refusal to exchange pulpits with liberals.[20] Associated with the Beecher-Taylor wing of Congregationalism, Abiel was hardly the seventeenth-century throwback his son later made him out to be. This failure of discernment informed the son's novels, which would disdain liberal theologians almost equally with conservatives. But though Doctor Holmes mostly abandoned the Reverend Holmes's theology, he would address, in the secular form of the novel, the same moral questions that troubled his father's generation and would arrive at conclusions that advanced somewhat on Bushnell's.

A principal character in Holmes's first novel inquires whether "there may be predispositions, inherited or ingrafted, but at any rate constitutional, which shall take out certain apparently voluntary determinations from the control of the will, and leave them as free from moral responsibility as the instincts of the lower animals."[21] The question pertains to the title character of *Elsie Venner* (1861), who is literally full of venom. Her mother had been bitten by a rattlesnake and had survived only long enough to give birth to a beautiful dark daughter possessed of small, entrancing eyes and the habit of coiling whatever was at hand. Incapable of love or even normal human warmth, the child could be roused to murderous passion and was then likely to employ a vial of poison that she hid beneath the floorboards of her bedroom. It was no wonder that Holmes's preface disclaimed the "scientific doctrine" that a daughter might imbibe, through her mother's poisoned blood, the character of a snake. The appeal of this preposterous theory lay not in any scientific evidence for it but rather, as Holmes admitted, in its offering him an opportunity to explore the old questions of imputed sin and human responsibility.[22]

Like Bushnell, Holmes placed a greater emphasis on determinism than did the Beecher-Taylor wing of Congregationalist theology, but unlike Bushnell, Holmes repudiated the Calvinist notion of human responsibility for predetermined sin. Bushnell's organic interpretation of the moral relation between generations was

---

20. Eleanor Tilton, *Amiable Autocrat: A Biography of Doctor Oliver Wendell Holmes* (New York: H. Schuman, 1947), 43–49.
21. Holmes, *Elsie Venner,* 220.
22. Ibid., vii–ix.

meant to show that Christian parents could raise a sanctified child without benefit of a dramatic conversion experience. The corollary, charming to Calvinists, was that sinful parents determined sinful children. Holmes's point in *Elsie Venner,* however, was that a determined soul could not be sinful. People should no more be held responsible for an illness of the soul than of the body, asserts one of Holmes's characters who is, just as Holmes was, a professor in a medical school. Elsie has committed crimes but not sins. She dies in the end, but the snake in her dies first, allowing a brief glimpse of her mild, "true character." She has "lived a double being," her human moral state overborne but unblemished by "the blight which fell upon her in the dim period before consciousness."[23]

Holmes's avowed antisectarianism did not so much escape as continue and advance the tradition of New England's religious culture which, with a mixture of horror and fascination, had long struggled with the temptations of the consciousness concept. For instance, Holmes's next novel, *The Guardian Angel* (1867), could scarcely have been harsher toward the Calvinist ministry, depicting a vain, cruel, lascivious preacher of hellfire named Joseph Bellamy Stoker. Near victim of the seductive Stoker is an erratic young woman, Myrtle Hazard, who suffers from the inherited temperament of her part-Indian grandmother, Virginia Wild. Elaborating the themes of *Elsie Venner,* Holmes wrote that "it is by no means certain that our individual personality is the single inhabitant of these our corporeal frames." Myrtle's true, gentler self has been so obscured by her ancestral, aboriginal spirit that her hypocritically pious maiden aunt, Silence Withers, despairs of Myrtle's soul and any chance of her regeneration. But in Myrtle's discovery of love "a transfusion of . . . spiritual being might well seem to manifest itself."[24] Although Holmes mocked belief in dramatic transformations of the soul, his novelistic description of multiple personalities, with unconscious personalities leaping into consciousness, resembled such transformations as they had come to be understood in the era of Beecher and Finney. By helping to develop the notion of unconscious mentality, Holmes did not become an advocate of

23. Ibid., 226, 445–46.
24. Oliver Wendell Holmes, *The Guardian Angel* (Boston, 1867), 22, 410.

traditional piety. But he stood on the battlement of unconscious selfhood that the evangelists had erected in their failed attempt to preserve piety. Their dalliance with the consciousness concept had ironically subverted the piety that they had hoped to preserve. Holmes's more open questioning of the concept would help return human beings, if not to piety, at least toward the notion that the self is not immediately known in consciousness but requires interpretation.

Although Holmes would not hold humanity morally accountable for involuntary actions, he at least agreed with Bushnell that a good deal of human life was involuntary. Only in extreme cases was Holmes ready to suggest that the failure of the will to dominate the other faculties constituted an illness. Complete failure of will, Holmes lectured his readers, was a "morbid condition . . . which in ignorant ages and communities is attributed to the influence of evil spirits, but for the better-instructed is the malady which they call hysteria." To Holmes, hysteria was a moral illness, a failure of will that left a person "drifting without any self-directing power."[25] The difference, however, between hysteria and moral health was a narrow one since Holmes believed that will power is quite limited in even the most healthy people. "Do you want an image of the human will?" Holmes had asked in a famous passage of *The Autocrat:* "A drop of water, imprisoned in a crystal."[26]

Yet belief in freedom, not determinism, was the heritage of the mid nineteenth-century religious establishment, and Holmes's espousal of freedom, despite his belief that science supported determinism, was the strongest evidence for the influence of the inherited religious culture on his thinking. On the basis of the traditional evidence—consciousness—Holmes attributed a limited freedom to the will. The drop of water imprisoned in a crystal possesses freedom of movement within its limited sphere, and so do human beings within their physical and biological constraints. The Brahmin Holmes believed that the constraints were greatly underestimated because the consciousnesses cited as evidence of freedom

25. Ibid., 131, 137; cf. Holmes, *Elsie Venner,* 322.
26. Oliver Wendell Holmes, *The Autocrat of the Breakfast Table* (Boston, 1858), 86; cf. Bushnell, *Nature and the Supernatural,* 234–40.

"belong to the thinking class of the highest races, and they are conscious of a great deal of liberty of will. . . . [But] they talk as if they knew from their own will all about that of a Digger Indian!"[27] Even the "thinking classes," who enjoy more moral freedom than other people, are not entirely free. Yet arguments against freedom "leave a certain undischarged balance in most minds"—evidence of consciousness. When Holmes succinctly drew together the psychological speculation of his novels into an 1870 Phi Beta Kappa address on "Mechanism in Thought and Morals," he rejected "the mechanical doctrine which makes me the slave of outside influences."[28]

The significance for this study of Holmes's address on "Mechanism in Thought and Morals" is the clarity with which it shows how the nineteenth-century proof of free will by the evidence of consciousness led to the view that determined mental actions must be unconscious. Physician that he was, Holmes compared thinking to breathing—a basically involuntary activity over which the self nevertheless has some control. People are free to a degree to choose the subject of their thoughts by making a conscious effort, just as they can choose briefly to hold their breath. But they can no more choose to stop thinking than breathing. Even though the self does not willfully control all or even most thought, thought is nevertheless perception by the self or mind. With such premises, it was only a short leap to the conclusion that the self thinks unconsciously: "it is a great source of error to believe that there is no perception in the mind but those of which it is conscious."[29]

Common everyday experiences, Holmes pointed out, implied the existence of unconscious thought—the action of walking, for instance, while paying no attention to what one is doing. Or again, a name sometimes leaps into consciousness hours after a person has tried unsuccessfully to remember it. Apparently the mind has found through an unconscious search what it could not find consciously. Moreover, unconscious thought offered a solution to the traditional conundrum of associationism: "What happens when

27. Holmes, *Elsie Venner,* 323.
28. Oliver Wendell Holmes, "Mechanism in Thought and Morals," *Pages from an Old Volume of Life* (Boston, 1899), 302, 303.
29. Ibid., 261, 276.

one idea brings up another?"[30] It seemed as evident to Holmes as it had to Hume that one atomistic idea could not be associated with another except by a thinking self. If the self does not consciously associate the two ideas, it must unconsciously associate them. Such possibilities, long noted as indications of unconscious perception by philosophers like Leibniz and Hartley, received increasing attention in the middle of the nineteenth century as the concept of consciousness began to lose its dominance of Western self-understanding.

Holmes strained to avoid the more or less obvious conclusion that if the self was not constituted consciously in the mind, it might be constituted unconsciously in the body. Thought, he admitted, was probably a "mechanical" bodily action like the involuntary breathing to which he compared it. But that had no significance for the spiritual quality of moral decisions: "The moral universe includes nothing but the exercise of choice: all else is machinery." The same amount of molecular action in two different brains may represent "a certain equivalent of food, but by no means an equivalent of intellectual product." Religious thinkers should not fear materialism, even if materialists succeeded in showing that mental phenomena have a material basis. In fact that would confirm, albeit in an unexpected way, the original determinism of New England Calvinism. Slyly, Holmes compared the unconscious mind to the actions of "a divine visitor who chooses our brain as his dwelling-place." Determinism was tolerable so long as conscious, willed thought remained supernatural, remained above natural laws of cause and effect. Holmes pointed out that whereas experience caused people to associate understanding with the brain and emotions with the heart, willing had no apparent organic seat. The will "is the least like an instrument of any of our faculties; the farthest removed from our conceptions of mechanism and matter."[31] He hoped to preserve the self as conscious and morally free, but he was whistling in the dark.

Holmes's system implied that "consciousness" was only a sub-

30. Ibid., 285.
31. Ibid., 261, 293, 301, 284–85, 271.

category of a more comprehensive operation called "thought," a devastating implication for his spiritually constituted self which was supposed to be capable of free will. Only so long as "consciousness" and "thought" were considered synonymous could consciousness be assumed to attest to the spirituality of the self, to its independence from material nature. Holmes missed the contradiction between his two assertions: first, that conscious thoughts were freely willed and, second, that unconscious thoughts "make their influence felt among the perceptible mental currents."[32] Since those unconscious thoughts were determined, their exerting an influence on conscious thought suggested that even conscious thought was not freely willed. And if conscious thought could be determined, the evidence of consciousness for freedom was an illusion. Evidently, the self was not so independent from physical nature, not so "spiritual" as it seemed. Unwilling to abandon the notion of thought as perception by and within a self, Holmes drove himself into a corner. But because of contradictions like his, many thinkers eventually lost all confidence in the "evidence of consciousness" on which so many New Englanders had rested their case for a morally free and spiritually constituted self.

Unconsciousness as a Normative Ideal

Although G. Stanley Hall was a member of a new generation, his background, early development, and psychological theories bore a far closer resemblance to those of Holmes, Bushnell, and even Taylor than to such contemporaries as C. S. Peirce and William James. Raised on a farm in western Massachusetts' ambience of backwoods Calvinism, Hall was the first member of his family to attend college, and he traversed a greater intellectual distance than any other figure in this book. James, Peirce, and James Jackson Putnam reached farther points but began much nearer to the end of their journeys than did Hall, whose adolescent search for vocation dragged on into his mid-thirties from divinity to philosophy to psychology.

As a freshman at Williams College, Hall was converted in an

32. Ibid., 282.

undergraduate revival, and his conversion superficially followed the standard model laid out in Brainerd's *Diary*. The only difference was that Hall accomplished in a day what had taken Brainerd more than a year. An "infant in spiritual knowledge," as his parents called him, Hall listened one winter Sunday in Williamstown to a sermon on "The Ark of Safety." Convicted of sin and terrified of doom, he tried for the rest of the day to give himself away to Christ but got no light till the next morning when he felt a burden "gradually" lift from his mind. By Monday afternoon he was counseling awakened sinners. And by his sophomore year he was done forever with personal religion, noting that the least intelligent students were the most pious.

No doubt it is correct to attribute Hall's college conversion, as Dorothy Ross does, to freshman insecurity, but it would be a mistake to think that he did not possess a potentially religious temperament. Formidably impersonal and austere to all but his most intimate friends, he finally became the unlucky first president of Clark University, where his secretiveness and craving for control were partly responsible for the loss of many brilliant faculty. His repressed passions periodically surfaced, both scandalously and admirably, as for instance in his explicit treatment of adolescent sexuality. Hall came far closer than Bushnell or Holmes to possessing the character and temperament of a Puritan. Had he lived in an earlier time, he might have grown in grace through a turbulent struggle with a sinful heart, and then triumphant interpretation of it. As it was, he lived out his life in secular institutions and sought a new form of self-understanding by helping to create the secular science of psychology.

After Williams, Hall reluctantly prepared for the ministry at Union Theological Seminary, where Professor Henry Boynton Smith stimulated his interest in philosophy more than theology. Another potent influence was Henry Ward Beecher, whose Brooklyn congregation Hall joined and whose questioning of many orthodox doctrines did not so much stimulate doubt in Hall as authorize him to express doubts he already had. Beecher arranged the loan that permitted Hall to interrupt his theological training for a year of philosophical study in Germany. There he acquired interests in mental philosophy and especially empirical psychology; in biology, especially physiology; and in developmental theory, especially Hegelianism. The continuous development and revision of these three interests were the main threads of Hall's career as a psychologist, upon which he finally entered after completing his divinity degree, teaching languages for four years at Antioch College, and enrolling for graduate study in philosophy at Harvard. There, in 1878, he was awarded the first American doctorate in psychology for his thesis "The Muscular Perception of Space," which had been directed by William James.

Hall's graduate study with James was an opportune intersection of both men's careers, when their originally different interests converged in physiological psychology before diverging again. James, a medical doctor, was about this time embarking on the intellectual odyssey that would have its first significant achievement in *The Principles of Psychology* (1890), a book with the avowed purpose of limiting psychology to conclusions based on conscious experience and physiological experimentation, but which in fact slipped time and again into philosophical and epistemological conjectures. James would more frankly abandon physiological psychology for philosophy in the 1890s, and he eventually arrived at a bold phenomenalism. Hall's movement from theology through philosophy to physiological psychology and then finally developmental, genetic psychology was exactly the opposite of James's intellectual direction. Yet Hall was never to be free of philosophical and theological emphases, even though he repudiated as a useless distraction the problem of knowledge that had put the consciousness concept at the center of Western philosophy for the previous two centuries. He often drew grand speculative conclusions on the basis of limited scientific data, and Dorothy Ross has aptly characterized his psychology as prophecy.[33]

At the time Hall studied with James, the first American psychological laboratory was still some years away, but to a small group of Americans familiar with European medicine and physiology the possibility of liberating psychology from the thralldom of speculative philosophers and delivering it into the hands of scientists al-

33. Dorothy Ross, *G. Stanley Hall: The Psychologist as Prophet* (Chicago: University of Chicago Press, 1973), 16.

ready seemed an exciting possibility. By 1868 it was becoming difficult to maintain, as did Nathaniel Taylor's son-in-law, Noah Porter of Yale, that psychology, as the "science of the soul," is "distinguished from physiology," which "studies man as a material organism."[34] The demolition of that view had already begun eighteen years earlier, in Germany, when Ferdinand Ludwig von Helmholtz constructed an ingenious myographion and measured the speed of the nervous impulse in frogs. Conventional physiologists had thought that this feat would never be accomplished because of the short distance traversed by the impulse at a speed believed to equal or even exceed that of light, but Helmholtz measured it at ninety feet per second. Helmholtz was also the originator of the law of conservation of energy that led Gustav Fechner to infer in the early 1860s that the subjective intensity of neural sensation must bear a constant relation to the objective stimulus—an idea that became widely accepted in the late nineteenth century under the ugly rubric of "psycho-physical law." Meanwhile, neurologists, encouraged especially by new understanding of aphasia, believed that it might become possible actually to accomplish what phrenologists had long and spuriously claimed to be able to do, to locate mental functions in precise regions of the brain. These rapid advances into once impenetrable and unmeasurable regions resulted in Wilhelm Wundt's greatly influential lectures on physiological psychology (published in 1863), his authorship of the first textbook on physiological psychology (1874), and his founding of the world's first psychological laboratory at Leipzig (1879).

Laboratory psychology was not initially a rejection of the concept of consciousness but rather an attempt to study consciousness objectively. Although sensations could not be measured objectively, stimuli could. If Fechner was right that the relation between stimulus and intensity of sensation was constant, one could reason inductively about subjective sensation on the basis of objectively measured stimuli. The way seemed open to apply the methods of physical science to questions hitherto reserved for moral philosophers. To its German pioneers, then, this new physiological psychology did not initially imply the conclusion subsequently drawn

34. Noah Porter, *The Human Intellect* (New York, 1868), 6.

by behaviorists that psychology could get along quite well without the concept of consciousness. Fechner was a panpsychist and viewed the entire universe as conscious and spiritual. Wundt was committed to psycho-physical parallelism and held that all increase or expenditure of nerve force was registered in consciousness. It was not accidental that the two earliest American proponents of psychology as a laboratory science—Hall and James—abandoned the laboratory before they abandoned the consciousness concept. The laboratory, at first, was not a spur but an obstacle to any revolutionary change in mental philosophy.

But Hall eventually realized, perhaps more quickly than any other of the early psychologists, that the new physiological approach to consciousness would force a choice between either a bodily self or the notion of thought as a spiritual process. Whereas James would eventually attempt to abandon the substantial self, Hall opted for it. His Harvard doctoral thesis was mainly theoretical and argued that the origin of spatial perception was the subjective sensation of muscular motion rather than, as Hegel had said, the self-objectification of pure thought. Thought was not perception by a spirit or soul but literally a self-experience, an immediately apprehended bodily feeling. Hall went over to the view of Adolf Trendelenburg, with whom he had studied at Berlin, that not thought but rather bodily motion was the "prius" and "medium" of all experience. Trendelenburg had rejected Hegelian idealism because it was subjective and offered no plausible explanation for, in Hall's words, "the most important of all logical transitions, viz., from the subjective-intensive to the objective-extensive." But if, as Wundt had suggested, "pure sensations may be described as an immediate knowledge of physical states," muscular sensations of exertion and innervation, being subjective in the first place, must be the most native experiences. But they were also objective bodily motions. Subject and object were thus intimately related from the beginning, and "mind and matter may even be proven identical to the understanding."[35] It is as clear in Hall's early writings as anywhere how those with sentimental attachments to the notion of an

---

35. G. Stanley Hall, "Notes on Hegel and His Critics," *Journal of Speculative Philosophy* (January 1878): 98–99, 94–95, 101.

experiencing self were forced by the new physiological sophistication toward the notion of the self as a sentient body, not a perceiving mind.

In Hall's view, the only genuine consciousness was unconscious, an indication of the bankruptcy of mental philosophy's traditional terminology. He pointed out that the "simplest elements of sensation that common consciousness recognizes" are "resolvable into yet more ultimate states." A visual image, for instance, is a "cosmos" of still simpler psychic states, each of them having as a counterpart in the nervous system some molecular or electrical change. If Wundt was correct that all nervous effort and innervation are immediately known, surely the cosmos of unconsciously felt states that constitute a visual image or any other conscious sensation "are not unconscious, but are the most innate forms of self-consciousness—the mother-tongues of sensation."[36] Unperceived feelings, in Hall's view, were properly described as "self-conscious" because they were felt in the bodily self. But they were not "self-conscious" in the traditional sense of the consciousness concept, according to which a spiritual self or mind not only knows but knows that it knows.

Hall was left with a difficult question to which he devoted much of the rest of his life—how to explain the phenomenon, as he had called it, of "common consciousness," the feeling of self-consciousness that, in the consciousness concept, was described as the self's knowledge that the self is a knower. The difficulty for Hall's predecessors had been to move beyond the traditional identification of "thought" with conscious knowledge to the possibility of unconscious thought, that is, thought by the self that was not known to the self. Hall's problem was the exact opposite. Since he believed that all thought was primarily an unconscious bodily process, "common consciousness" was a secondary phenomenon. The question was why this feeling of personal self-consciousness—"consciousness" in the "common" sense of the word—should ever have arisen?

Compounding Hall's difficulty was the fact that some psychological phenomena, such as hypnotism, were easier to discuss in

36. Ibid., 101.

terms of "common consciousness" or mental function than in terms of physiology. In 1882, when Hall was appointed to the philosophy department at Johns Hopkins, he began to study hypnotism and concluded that it was due to a concentration of attention. If so, Hall reasoned, reaction times ought to be shortened under hypnosis, and he attempted to prove this with laboratory experiments. But despite the fact that he used experimentation to support his theory, the theory itself was functional. He had not offered a physiological explanation of hypnotism but had only suggested that hypnotism was a result of the self's attentive function. Explanation by way of "function" was the same method that had created the ancient psychology of "faculties." But given the limited neurological knowledge available, Hall decided that it was foolish to ignore psychological functions. The difficulty of using physiology as psychological explanation and possibly also the influence of his Hopkins colleague, Charles Sanders Peirce, led Hall to conclude that it was better not to hypothesize the identity of thought and brain processes but to study them as if they were concomitant series.[37] But this was only a grudging admission that physiology had so far proved inadequate to the investigation of some phenomena, not an acceptance of consciousness as independent, or even the equal, of bodily sensation.

In the 1890s, after assuming the presidency of Clark, Hall continued to find it difficult if not impossible to study consciousness through physiology. Moved partly by a deteriorating financial situation, he tried to prove the University a useful asset to Worcester and environs by launching a child study program. The growing corps of professional, well-educated teachers was eager for scientific guidance on methods and curriculum. But Hall was also drawn to child study by his prophetic temperament and by clerical tradition, which had always emphasized the importance of moral and religious education of the young. And as the child study movement developed under Hall's guidance it rested not only on one of the newest methods in behavioral science—the questionnaire—but also on the oldest method of New England religiosity—self-interpretation. Hall sent questionnaires to hundreds of adult correspon-

37. Ross, G. Stanley Hall, 151.

dents, mainly teachers, on lies, fears, anger, play, and so on. His correspondents either questioned children in their charge or else answered the questions themselves on the basis of their childhood memories. The method was of course criticized as a departure or regression from the objective laboratory work that was supposed to make psychology into a science. For that reason and also because of distrust and dislike of Hall by Dewey, James Mark Baldwin, and others interested in developmental psychology, Hall's movement gained little support from psychologists outside his circle of colleagues and students at Clark. Desperately, Hall employed what objective methods he could, building a physiological argument for the early development of the sense of self not only on questionnaires but also on observation of infantile development of physical self-consciousness as evidenced in the child's first noticing of his or her own mouth, hands, and feet.[38]

Hall found the solution to his intellectual difficulties in Darwinism. By discrediting the scriptural account of the creation of the human body, Darwinism made it equally doubtful that "common consciousness" arose through the tacking on of a soul. Darwinism seemed to imply what laboratory psychology had proved unable to establish—the self was physiological. If thought was a biological phenomenon, ontogeny might recapitulate phylogeny not only in physical but also in mental development, a possibility which justified, Hall said, the genetic psychologist's use of "introspection in the old way."[39] Prior to the 1890s Hall had shown little interest in evolution, at least partly because he had come to psychology through philosophy and physiology. But like others among the new university psychologists, Hall began in the early 1890s to take evolutionary considerations into account. For Hall and perhaps for many other late nineteenth-century thinkers as well, Darwinism did not significantly challenge the traditional conception of human spirituality, for the traditional conception had long since begun to break down. Rather, Darwinism appealed to Hall by its offering the possibility of an evolutionary answer to the question that had

---

38. G. Stanley Hall, "Some Aspects of the Early Sense of Self," *American Journal of Psychology* (April 1898), 352–60.

39. G. Stanley Hall, *Adolescence* (New York: D. Appleton, 1904), II, 67.

interested him almost from the beginning—the origin of self-consciousness.

Consciousness, wrote Hall in his two-volume study, *Adolescence* (1904), is a "wart raised by the sting of sin, a product of alienation or a remedial process."[40] He believed that self-consciousness had had an important corrective role in the evolutionary process and suggested that older species may once have possessed it but, developing instinctual responses to most of the situations they encountered, had outgrown the need for consciousness. As humanity matured, it, too, should allow self-consciousness to atrophy. Even without self-consciousness the bodily self would unconsciously feel and act like a self. Indeed human selfhood would be enhanced in the absence of self-consciousness. Holmes, out of Brahmin superiority, had questioned the representativeness of the consciousness of the "thinking classes," but Hall expressed inferiority when he blasted the "sedentary and mentally pampered thinker" who assumed that his own consciousness offered an accurate picture of the inner life of all people. Little acquainted with "willing and far less with the floods of feeling that have irrigated the life of man in the past, the 'experience' of the adult consciousness he so persistently analyzes is at best but a provincial oracle of the soul, which is incalculably older, vaster, or more organized than it."[41]

Hall's interest in adolescence was due to his belief that it was the deepest and most vital phase of modern life, a period when consciousness exerted little control over the bodily self. The awakening of intense sexual appetite gave the adolescent experiences in willing and feeling denied to modern adults and thus made adolescents the best subjects through which to study human emotion. After a period of life in which consciousness held easy sway over the passions and instincts, the adolescent was suddenly "reduced back to a state of nature." The ethical life of the adolescent was immensely enriched by new possibilities for sin, while the "knowledge of self is less adequate" than it had been in childhood. Just as infancy recapitulated primordial life, so in adolescence "the voices of . . . our

40. Ibid., II, 67.
41. Ibid., I, vi.

later and more human ancestry, are heard in the soul."[42] Heredity, said Hall, was the adolescent's teacher, putting him or her in touch with forces in the soul unknown to consciousness.

There was personal and even religious satisfaction for Hall in this notion of unconscious soul qualities in human life, but it was nevertheless a biological view of the soul: "Mind is almost, possibly quite, coextensive with life, at least animal life." The difference between people and animals was only a difference of degree. He deplored Christians' refusal to ask what the soul was made of and also their belief that every soul was newly made at birth. The truth was that an infant's soul as much as his body was a result of the parents' procreation. The biological basis of the soul meant that the larger self "is beneath and not above us, immanent and not transcendent, and if only rightly interpreted it is veridical in a sense and degree our voluble ratiocination knows not of."[43]

Pascal's aphorism that the heart has reasons the reason knows not of was confirmed, Hall believed, by religious conversion wherein "perhaps more than anywhere else, consciousness is a very poor witness to what takes place in the abysses of soul-life." Like Holmes, Hall was an ostensibly secular thinker. But like Bushnell, Hall gave more weight to the concept of conversion than of consciousness. By collecting and comparing narratives of individual conversions, Hall hoped to find grounds for inductive conclusions about unconscious mental life. He had queried Dwight Moody and numerous other revivalists for their observations about conversion. Their reports, together with more systematic data from religious organizations and the statistics gathered by Hall's fellow psychologist, E. D. Starbuck, showed that conversion happened most often in adolescence, a fact known to casual observers for centuries. But Hall offered a biological explanation for the synchronicity of religious conversion and sexual awakening. Love was the new voice in the soul that exhorted: "find the joy of sacrifice, get only to give, live for others. . . . Henceforth the race, not the self, must become supreme."[44]

42. Ibid., II, 71.
43. Ibid., 63, 342.
44. Ibid., 341, 303.

Hall's enthusiasm for geneticism was due partly to what he saw as its potential for integrating his commitment to the secular profession of academic psychology with his religious upbringing and education. Genetic psychology promised a "union and identity [between religion and science] so complete that we shall . . . realize that science must be taught in our theological schools . . . while religion . . . will pervade the laboratory and observatory." Hall believed that his psychology was in the tradition of "ultra and especially American Protestantism," which had entered the soul "at pubescence" and attempted "to prescribe and normalize its states and changes."[45] But he meant to improve on that tradition by bringing scientific psychology to the aid of the self in its traditional, pietist quest for union with an Other. He cautioned against judging spiritual testimony by normative standards, for those standards bring in an element of self-consciousness that gets in the way of feeling, the avenue to the unconscious on which he believed conversion depended.

Hall thus rejected, like Bushnell, the tendency of Finney to collapse conversion into a blazing moment of "religious experience," a momentarily conscious perception. This view had informed the religious culture of Hall's youth. His adult skepticism that conversion was a moment's or even a day's work may have been due partly to what had happened to him as a freshman at Williams. But neither did the mature Hall view conversion after the Puritan fashion as a work of self-interpretation. Even though he had abandoned the notion that conscious thought was immediate experience within a self, he continued to assume that *un*conscious thought was immediate experience within a *bodily* self. Conversion was therefore a process of biological growth that could not be hurried.

Hall's biologism seemed to suggest that other orthodox doctrines also contained an at least symbolic truth. Like Bushnell, Hall became a believer in original sin. In view of the the fact that the unconscious elements in the human soul are derived from our biological heritage, Hall concluded that "we suffer for the sins of our forebears" back not merely to Adam but to the amoebae.[46]

45. Ibid., 330, 280.
46. Ibid., 309.

This untraditional support for traditional doctrine scarcely comforted the orthodox. Hall was a bit circumspect about drawing his system's obvious conclusion for hope of survival of individual consciousness in the hereafter, but it was clear to careful readers that he believed that the death of the brain meant the death of the individual soul or "self" as that word was understood in the traditional consciousness concept. He attributed, for instance, the opposition of his fellow psychologists to genetic psychology to their fear of its implications for the doctrine of an afterlife.[47] Hopes for eternity must depend on progeny, for the only life there was was biological: "bodies, brains, automatisms, and instincts."[48]

The irony in Hall's defense of the self was that he had sacrificed the conscious mentality that had once been considered the essence of the soul. He had preserved the self and, in his view, its spirituality as well. But while biological geneticism established the kinship of all life, it rendered conscious thought insignificant and meaningless. The whole logic of the proponents of the self sign had pointed in this direction from the time of the New Divinity men. As it had gradually dawned on them that the consciousness concept with its description of thought as total and immediately available self-knowledge posed a threat to piety, they had attempted to preserve piety by retreating to something like the Puritans' description of the self as not totally self-conscious. Conscious thought thus eventually became a superfluous rather than essential activity of the self. Yet Hall was correct that the substantial self could be preserved only by sacrificing "consciousness" in the "common" sense of the word. For as the next two chapters show, those who viewed conscious thought as the essence of spirituality were eventually forced to abandon the substantial soul or self.

47. Ibid., 41.
48. Ibid., 342.

CHAPTER SIX

The Thought Sign
from Gay to Brownson

The Expansion of Thought

G. Stanley Hall rightly feared for the self, for the seventeenth-century consciousness concept not only had related the self sign and the thought sign but had located the latter in the former. As the consciousness concept gradually broke down, defenders of the self in the line from Hopkins to Hall watched with dismay the rise of an argument—a minority argument to be sure—for the superiority of thought.

Just as the New England theologians were pushed more or less against their will to divide the self into conscious and unconscious elements in order to defend evangelical religion from unorthodox implications of the consciousness concept, so too the defenders of rational religion, with great misgivings, were pushed by their acceptance of the consciousness concept to elevate thought at the expense of the perceiving self. The early liberals and Unitarians never intended to deny that the self was the locus and ought to be the controller of thought. But there was a self-denying tendency in their respect for the authority of thought.

Accordingly, proponents of the consciousness concept could be influenced by James Marsh's attempt to revivify traditional piety by invoking Kant against Locke. Marsh's most radical successors, including Emerson and Thoreau, used transcendentalism to extend the principle of self-denial even though they were prophets of the self. To them the enhancement of the self was not an end but a means, a strategy for achieving so complete a union with the One that the self would ultimately lose its individual human consciousness and identity. Sharing with the Puritans an ideal of selflessness, Emerson and Thoreau felt forced by the consciousness concept to substitute for their forebears' belief in human inability, an over-bearing confidence in the power of human thought to draw on divine power. If thought was contained within a self, the only way to annihilate the human self was to join the divine self by thinking its thoughts.

Transcendentalists like George Ripley and Theodore Parker, whose backgrounds and proclivities were more Calvinistic, less Unitarian, than Emerson's or Thoreau's, did not wince so much at human self-consciousness, but they nevertheless believed transcendental reason was available to humanity. Transcendental reason appealed to some religiously enthusiastic but non-Calvinist New Englanders because it was a thoughtful equivalent to "taste" in New Divinity schemes, a faculty disposing the soul prior to perception and thus liberating people from the tyranny of fact. Believing in consciousness, they could not locate the basis of human freedom and autonomy in an unconscious element of the self. In spite of themselves, they had to locate the basis of freedom in thought. If thought were to be a basis for self-transcendence, it had to be larger than the self. And if transcendental reason was available to the human self, it was not exclusively God's.

Drawing back in horror from such antinomianism, Orestes Brownson attempted to contain thought within the self while nevertheless making it possible for thought to give people contact with the external authority of God. Asserting that every thought was an indissoluble relation between subject and object, Brownson attacked the notion that the mind could meaningfully distinguish between those thoughts that seem clearly to originate in the self and those that, bursting unexpectedly into consciousness, seem to originate outside the self. Since every thought contained both objective and subjective elements, no thought offered entirely objective knowledge of absolute truth as the transcendentalists had mistakenly believed. Still, Brownson was saying that every thought contained an element of objective truth. He therefore attempted to guard against excessive confidence in the mind's ability to grasp that truth by attacking the notion that philosophy could be based on any supposedly empirical evidence of consciousness. Asserting that any single thought was too fleeting to be grasped, he argued that whatever knowledge the mind possessed of its own operations was indirect rather than empirical. Yet he also believed that analysis of this indirect knowledge of the mind's operations could provide inferential knowledge of divine Reason. He thereby failed in his goal of reconciling the subjectivity of thought with the objectivity of religious truth. Even if thought could only be interpreted indirectly through signs rather than known empirically in ideas, a human thought that contained divine truth was evidently larger than the mortal self.

The Diminution of Self

The wisdom of Jonathan Edwards in attacking Lockean empiricism was confirmed within a year of his death when Ebenezer Gay, the liberal pastor at Hingham, delivered Harvard's 1759 Dudleian lecture on the topic of natural religion. Describing conscience in conventional language as "his [God's] voice, telling them [humanity] their duty," Gay unconventionally added that conscience was not innate but was acquired through experience: "In the due exercise of their natural faculties, men are capable of attaining some knowledge of God's will, and their duty . . . *as if* it were written in legible characters on the tables of their hearts" [italics added].[1] Gay's "*as if*" was a proffered sop to evangelical tradition, but the implications were nevertheless revolutionary. The traditional role of innate conscience was both to encourage unregenerate effort at righteousness and then, by the feebleness of that effort, to condemn and humiliate the sinner so that he or she would turn despairingly to an Other. But if conscience, rather than being innate, is acquired by exercising the natural faculties, the awakened sinner is not helpless. Rather than surrendering to an Other, the sinner should continue to exercise his or her faculties in the pursuit of more conscience. Although it is "only by grace that sinful men can be saved," nevertheless, "by good use of their rational powers," the unregenerate "may be in a better preparation of mind to comply

1. Ebenezer Gay, *Natural Religion, as Distinguish'd from Revealed* (Boston, 1759), 11. For more forthright statements of Lockean empiricism by liberals, see Gad Hitchcock, *Natural Religion* (Boston, 1779), 19 and Jonathan Mayhew, *Christian Sobriety* (Boston, 1763), 72.

with the offers and operations of divine grace."[2] Gay did not quite say that grace was resistible and would have balked had it come to that. His lecture was less of a threat to the doctrine of an omnipotent God than to the morphology of conversion. Listeners were encouraged to comply with God's law because of their perception of its reasonableness rather than out of a helplessness born of humiliation.

Gay's sermon was merely the exposed tip of what was, by the middle of the eighteenth century, an iceberg of Arminianism afloat in orthodox waters.[3] It had drifted in slowly and, for the most part, unobtrusively. Ministers of liberal opinion did not nail theses to church doors but, as an orthodox critic later noted, quietly dropped the doctrines of election and original sin and, instead, delivered sermons on practical conduct.[4] Although there were liberals in outlying regions, the center of Arminian tendencies was Boston and its environs, as Gilbert Tennent understood when he charged that the "greatest part" of the clergy there held "damnable Arminian principles."[5] Tennent's observation was confirmed by the later memories of John Adams, whose boyhood pastor in Braintree was Lemuel Briant, an early Unitarian and author of a well-known tract, *The Absurdity and Blasphemy of Depretiating Moral Virtue* (1749). In old age Adams recalled a number of other clergy whom he believed to have been Unitarians "65 years ago" and added, "Among the laity, how many could I name, lawyers, physicians, tradesmen, farmers! I could fill a sheet."[6]

The consciousness concept provided one of the intellectual bases for the early eighteenth-century Arminianism that subsequently flowered into Unitarianism. A leading historian of the beginnings

---

2. Gay, *Natural Religion*, 21.

3. Robert J. Wilson, *Benevolent Deity: Ebenezer Gay and the Rise of Rational Religion in New England, 1696–1787* (Philadelphia: University of Pennsylvania Press, 1984), 63–64, lists an impressive number of Arminian pastors in New England by the 1730s. Cf. Stephen A. Marini, *Radical Sects of Revolutionary New England* (Cambridge: Harvard University Press, 1982), chap. 3.

4. Samuel C. Thacher, *Review of American Unitarianism* (Boston, 1815), 1–2.

5. Gilbert Tennent, quoted in Charles Chauncy, *Seasonable Thoughts on the State of Religion in New England* (Boston, 1743), 147.

6. John Adams to Jedidiah Morse, May 15, 1815, Microfilm copy, Massachusetts Historical Society. Original Copy, Library of Congress.

of Unitarianism in America agreed with the proposition that not the Trinity but original sin was the Calvinist doctrine "most eagerly struck at."[7] The New England argument against original sin depended heavily on Locke's argument that consciousness was the basis of personal identity. The English theologian John Taylor had argued that Adam's descendants, not being conscious of his sins, could not share Adam's identity and consequently had no personal guilt for his sins.[8] This was the argument that Edwards's idealism had brilliantly answered by making human identity dependent on divine rather than human consciousness. But among Edwards's contemporaries and near successors, neither his disciples nor his opponents knew of the metaphysical basis of his argument. The liberals believed that contemporary mental philosophy was all on their side: Adam's descendants, conscious of their individuality, could not possibly perceive any just imputation of guilt for his sins.

The argument for personal identity on the basis of consciousness thus became well established as a result of Arminian discussions of original sin and only subsequently became the basis of anti-Trinitarianism as well. When Jonathan Mayhew boldly challenged the Athanasian creed in 1755, he merely ridiculed inconsistencies in the doctrine, for "with the metaphysical abstract nature, or essence of the Deity, I am not bold enough to meddle." But no such restraint hampered William Ellery Channing in 1819 when, in preaching the most famous American sermon of the nineteenth century, he objected "to the doctrine of the Trinity, that it subverts the unity of God" by its suggestion that "each of these three [divine] persons . . . has his own particular consciousness." Moses Stuart of Andover replied for the Calvinists that they used the word "*person* . . . not to describe independent, conscious beings" but "merely to designate our belief of a real distinction in the Godhead."[9] Stuart rested this interpretation of "person" on philologi-

---

7. Samuel Niles, quoted in Conrad Wright, *The Beginnings of Unitarianism in America* (Boston: Starr King, 1955), 60.

8. John Taylor, *The Scripture-Doctrine of Original Sin* (London, 1740), 384–85.

9. Jonathan Mayhew, *Sermons* (Boston, 1755), 269n; William Ellery Channing, *Sermon at the Ordination of the Reverend Jared Sparks* (Boston, 1819), 13; Moses Stuart, *Letters to the Reverend William Ellery Channing* (Andover, 1819), 34.

cal scholarship surpassing anything the liberals could muster, but scholarship was beside the point. Not historical philology but the concept of consciousness controlled early nineteenth-century understanding of personality, be it human, divine, or both. In his sermon at the ordination of Jared Sparks, Channing had pointed out that Christ incarnate did not share divine omniscience, but as an equal partner in the Godhead he must have shared it: "The doctrine, that one and the same person should have two consciousnesses, . . . this we think an enormous tax on human credulity."[10]

Because the liberals so readily subscribed to consciousness as the basis of personal identity, they realized more quickly than the evangelicals the danger of the representational quality of ideas and therefore asserted the directness of at least some perceptions. It is customary in histories of American philosophy to assume that the same skeptical conclusion about cause and effect that made Hume's extension of the way of ideas unpalatable on the other side of the water did so on this. According to the conventional account, because God's word was written in the book of nature as well as in the Bible, religious thinkers could not tolerate a philosophy that rendered suspect the conclusions of natural science. New Englanders too numerous to name did eventually so argue, but there was another, earlier, and more basic reason for liberals to question the way of ideas, which had been used by Calvinists not to challenge the principle of cause and effect but to confirm it. Edwards had used the mind's inability to possess an idea of an uncaused effect as the basis of his argument that all human willing is determined, is caused. By 1784 Charles Chauncy had had many years to ponder Edwards's distinction in *Freedom of Will* (1754) between natural freedom and moral necessity, between physical liberty and psychological determinism. Chauncy evidently had Edwards's argument much in mind: "It is not true, that our perceptions go no further than to assure us, that we can do as we have willed, and are pleased to do so. Besides this, and far beyond it, they certify it to us, that we are at liberty to will or not to will, to chuse or not to chuse, the doing of these and those actions. We feel in ourselves a power over

---

10. Channing, *Sermon at the Ordination*, 19–20; cf. Henry Ware, *Letters Addressed to Trinitarians and Calvinists* (Cambridge, 1820), 69.

our volitions, and such an one as enables us to direct, suspend, and overrule, or put an intire stop to them." Only direct perception of this liberty of willing would constitute empirical evidence of consciousness and thus assure us that "we be agents" rather than merely "conscious machines."[11]

The most basic objection to representational ideas was that ideas were a threat to the self. Liberals and Unitarians wanted unmediated and therefore undeniable perception so that the self could not be supposed to be, as in Hume, a mere construct of thought, a mere bundle of ideas. Liberals and Unitarians did not so much reject Locke as attempt to improve upon him by maintaining the distinction between mind and thought, which the way of ideas had originally been meant to explain, not subvert. Unitarians proudly claimed that Locke had been a Unitarian,[12] and their title pages sometimes epigrammatically quoted him.[13] Unitarian assertions of unmediated perception contradicted the way of ideas but not the notion of a spiritual, soulful self as the subject of thought. Liberal insistence on direct perception or intuition of human identity and free will was not only a rejection of the way of ideas but also a result of the confidence in self-perception that had been inspired by the consciousness concept.

The way of ideas was a contributor to the increasing respectability of self-assertion and confidence in human moral ability. So was the new belief that consciousness was perception so direct that it was unmediated even by ideas. Of course economic, social, and political developments also contributed. But it was consciousness to which Jonathan Mayhew referred when he said that human individuality or the fact "that we exist is what we have an immediate and intuitive certainty of."[14] It was a "needless and fruitless in-

11. Charles Chauncy, *The Benevolence of the Deity* (Boston, 1784), 132–34. Cf. Charles Chauncy, *The Mystery Hid from Ages and Generations* (London, 1784), 2; Gay, *Natural Religion*, 11–13; and Channing, *Sermon at the Ordination*, 34.

12. William Ellery Channing, *Objections to Unitarian Christianity Considered* (n.p., n.d.), 14.

13. Luther Hamilton, *Reasons for the Unitarian Belief* (Boston, 1830), and Jared Sparks, *An Inquiry into the Comparative Moral Tendencies of Trinitarian and Unitarian Doctrines* (Boston, 1823).

14. Jonathan Mayhew, *Seven Sermons* (Boston, 1759), 27.

quiry, what determines our will. . . . [for] in all those respects, wherein we are actually free, . . . nothing determines us. . . . We are arbiters here, chusing for, and determining ourselves." The very feeling of being "free to act one way or another," said Ebenezer Gay, was the best proof that human beings were spiritual creatures rather than "lumpish matter."[15] Channing complacently accepted the logical acuity of Edwards's argument for moral determinism, for what was logical was not necessarily empirical: "Happily it is a demonstration which no man believes, which the whole consciousness contradicts."[16]

Even though liberals insisted on direct perception of the actions of the human self, they could not tolerate similarly direct perception of divine actions, and they therefore clung to at least some representational ideas. When arguing against Calvinists and in favor of free will, liberals might claim to follow the Scottish common sense thinkers in their attack on the way of ideas. But as soon as the liberals turned to theology, they returned to representationalism and for good reason. A very large part of liberal criticism of revivalism, from Chauncy to Channing, was directed against evangelicals' claim that the convert had a new and direct knowledge of holiness thanks to a new faculty, a new sense produced by a "physical" change in the soul. While fighting against the arrogance and fanaticism of antinomian claims of direct communication with the Almighty, liberals scarcely wished to deny that human beings could attain some knowledge of God. The safe middle ground was to allow indirect, representational knowledge of God through ideas. Therefore, Chauncy held that the same process in natural knowledge whereby "ideas . . . serve as a light to our understanding-faculty" was characteristic of spiritual perception as well. Channing maintained that moral sentiment was "the very image of God in the human soul," or in short, an idea.[17]

15. Ibid., 292–93; Gay, *Natural Religion*, 12.
16. William Ellery Channing, *Works* (Boston, 1845), I, xiii; cf. I, 254 and Levi Hedge, "Essay Concerning Free Agency," *North American Review* (October 1821): 392.
17. Charles Chauncy, *Twelve Sermons* (Boston, 1765), 282–83; Channing, *Objections*, 7; cf. Ezra Stiles Gannett, *A Comparison of the Good and Evil of Revivals* (Boston, 1831), 10.

Pietists from Ames to Edwards had attempted to guard against dreaded conclusions about human conscience, which now rushed in through the Unitarians' explicit perceptualism and implicit representationalism. Ames had insisted on an element of will in conscience and Edwards on innateness lest regeneration come to be thought of as an enlightening of the understanding through natural perception. But eighteenth-century liberals like Chauncy were inspired by Locke to make conscience or moral knowledge solely a matter of perception, not something engraved on the heart. The tendency to make conscience a result of perception devalued it from a uniquely human faculty to one possessed by all creatures capable of perception. God creates "a balance of pleasure," Chauncy said, in the lives not only of people but of all creatures "endowed with a perceptive power." Ebenezer Gay, like Charles Morton, distinguished people from animals, not on the basis of conscience, but rather on humanity's being *"a Creature capable of Religion."*[18]

Human conscience, thanks to the vaunted evidence of consciousness for moral freedom, did not bear witness as the Puritans had thought to the soul's inability to avoid sin but rather confirmed Arminian self-determination: "Now if there be one plain principle of morality," said Channing, "it is this, that we are accountable beings only because we have conscience, a power" not only "of knowing" but also "of performing our duty." It was unthinkable to liberals that regeneration could be a renovation of the willing faculty, for that faculty "cannot be immediately touched without destroying moral action. The appetites and passions cannot [be immediately touched], without destroying temptation. . . . There remain, then, only the understanding and the moral sense. And these are the very powers which need not miraculous interference."[19]

God of course possessed the power directly to influence the operation of the understanding as well as any other part of the mind,

18. Chauncy, *Benevolence of the Deity*, 145, 157; Gay, *Natural Religion*, 16.
19. Channing, *Sermon at the Ordination*, 28; George W. Burnap, *Lectures on the Doctrines of Christianity* (Boston, 1848), 270–71; cf. Daniel Walker Howe, *The Unitarian Conscience: Harvard Moral Philosoph, 1805–1861* (Cambridge: Harvard University Press, 1970), 54.

but he restrained himself from using it. As Henry Ware, Junior, observed, there was no reason for God to employ so tyrannical a power when through second causes "analogous" to those he used in the external natural world he might accomplish all he desired in the internal spiritual realm as well. And even if God did exert "immediate and direct influence upon the mind," human beings all perceived through the same faculties of sensation and reflection so that God must still make himself known to human beings, as John Toland had said, in "common notions" or not at all. Edwards's metaphysical idealism had aimed at showing the possibility of a new spiritual sense reserved to saints. But Ware knew nothing of Edwards's metaphysics and sided with Toland: "It will not, I presume, be pretended, that the direct influence of the spirit of God upon the mind is of such a nature, that men can be conscious of it at the time."[20]

Common, not holy, ideas were the object of Unitarian religion, which was not immediate, miraculous perception and love of God but only natural, "clear perception . . . and veneration of his moral perfections" as represented in divine laws. In God's ordinances, Channing said, "his character is fully displayed." The test of people's religion is, "do they love God's commands . . . and give up to these their habits and passions. Without this, ecstasy is a mockery." Channing did not wish to exclude "warmth and even transport" from religion, but his ardor differed in kind from that of evangelical Christians.[21] Religious ardor, to Channing, was love of representative ideas that were distinguished from all other ideas only in the thing they represented—God.

Since in the liberal view religion was attainable through common perception rather than an interpretation of the self as joined with an Other, there was no more point for them than for Bushnell in the ritual humiliation of self that led unregenerate Calvinists to turn helplessly to God. The difficulty of assurance had been the engine of Puritan humility, but Charles Chauncy lamented the difficulty: "assurance . . . 'tis the attainment of but few; and the experience of the greatest part of true Christians is a sad proof of

---

20. Ware, *Letters to Trinitarians and Calvinists*, 76–77.
21. Channing, *Sermon at the Ordination*, 36–37.

this." Channing, believing that evangelical abjection was fruitless, redefined "humility" as high respect for all the Creator's works, including human nature. Shame, Henry Ware said, should properly arise not from helplessness but from ability: "Humility and self-condemnation should spring only from the consciousness of a course of life not answering to the powers . . . of our nature. What God has made us, we should think of with unmingled satisfaction; what we have made ourselves, we cannot think of with too deep regret."[22]

The Unitarians' respect for the human self was partly a result of their admiration for the self's power in thinking and perceiving as described in the consciousness concept. Charles Chauncy had tried to find a middle ground between traditional piety and the consciousness concept by defining humility as not an abject emotional state but rather low esteem for the idea of the self. But once the self was understood to have immediate perception of and control over all its own thoughts and actions, it was difficult to hold the self in low esteem. Instead of being an incubus of sin, the self became a resevoir of virtue. The anonymous author of "One's Self," a meditation published in an early Unitarian magazine, admired the self in proportion to its thoughtfulness and especially its reflexive self-consciousness: "There is no reflection, which confers such perfect dignity on ourselves . . . as that of our own individuality; the consciousness of a separate being. . . . How vapid and empty is life, if we have not in reserve. . . , certain dignities and consolations of thought, which belong only to our own nature, and which constitute the sovereignty of one's self."[23]

Even though the Unitarians subscribed to the consciousness concept and its rooting of thought in the self, they had a foreboding that thought might turn on the self and overrun it. Their admiration for human prowess in perceiving and thinking was therefore also a principal source of their moral anxiety. The writings of Unitarian moralists are replete with injunctions to deny appetites and

---

22. Charles Chauncy, *The New Creature* (Boston, 1741), 31; William Ellery Channing, *Memoir of William Ellery Channing, with Extracts from His Correspondence* (Boston, 1848), I, 366–74; Ware, *Letters to Trinitarians and Calvinists*, 37.

23. Chauncy, *Seasonable Thoughts*, 113; "One's Self," *Monthly Anthology* 4 (October 1807): 543–44.

control impulses. It has been rightly emphasized that Unitarian moral optimism was highly qualified and that "in the realm of moral action, the Unitarian expression of faith in self and the Puritan expression of self-distrust generated remarkably similar results."[24] But in the realm of psychological action there was an immense difference. When Channing attacked the romantic notion that "genius" was "a kind of fever, madness [or] intoxication," he offered in its place an ideal that sounded conventional—"self-mastery"—but that would have seemed strange to Puritans.[25] For in Channing's view the self was not so much to be mastered as it was to do the mastering. Puritans contradictorily urged the self to annihilate the self sign, but Unitarians reasonably urged it to subdue the thought sign.

Unitarian nervousness that thought might run amok and trample down the self was due to a large contradiction between the Unitarians' theory and practice in mental philosophy. In theory, thought originated in the self, but in practice and especially polemics, the Unitarians based certainty of selfhood on thought. The evidence of consciousness was the avowed basis of many other Unitarian principles, including the principles of moral conduct, which were not inevitably "intuited," as the Scots had said, by all rational minds. Even knowledge of God was, to Unitarians, a matter of reasonableness rather than an affective state. Jared Sparks was stymied not by the Trinitarian belief in a "'mysterious threefold mode of existence' in the Deity" but rather by the fact that these words "convey no ideas whatever. . . . is it necessary to talk of the Supreme Being without ideas, and to describe his nature in combinations of words to which we can affix no meaning?" Conservatives objected that reason should judge the *meaning* of divine revelation rather than "what it *ought* to mean." But liberals placed a much less restrictive interpretation on the power of reason. Regarding the doctrines of free will and original sin, Henry Ware admitted that because of "the limitaton of our faculties" people cannot know

24. David Robinson, *Apostle of Culture: Emerson as Preacher and Lecturer* (Philadelphia: University of Pennsylvania Press, 1982), 27; cf. Howe, *Unitarian Conscience*, 61.

25. Channing, *Memoir*, II, 344.

"what the goodness or justice of God would require; [but] we *have* faculties capable of deciding with certainty, what they will *not admit.*"[26] Unitarian moral philosophy was a fundamentally unsuccessful attempt to enlarge upon the power and independence of thought without diminishing the self in which thought was supposed to originate.

Self-Conscious Selflessness

The transcendentalist movement that grew out of and rebelled against Unitarianism contained, less latently, the same contradiction between an expanding thought sign and the self in which thought was supposed to be contained. It is lopsided to consider Emerson's great spiritual ambition as "an avatar of the Self."[27] The transcendentalists did self-consciously attempt to expand the self by putting to their own purpose the insights of transcendental reason, but their purpose was to lose self-consciousness in a larger realm of thought. Even though transcendentalists hoped to achieve selflessness and union with an Other through a quite different spiritual strategy than had the Puritans, there was a self-denying tendency in their enlargement of human reason. It is understandable, then, that they could draw inspiration from a pietist like James Marsh.

Raised on a Vermont farm, Marsh (1794–1842) studied at Dartmouth, where he passed through a traditional religious experience—humiliation, conversion, and renewed doubt interpreted as a sign of grace—and then prepared for the ministry at Andover, admiring and learning from the philological scholarship of Moses Stuart. After stints as tutor at Dartmouth and Professor of Oriental Languages at Hampden-Sidney College in Virginia, Marsh became, at thirty-two, president of the University of Vermont. There he pursued a distinguished scholarly career in German literature that included a translation of Herder's *Spirit of Hebrew Poetry*

26. Sparks, *Inquiry into Comparative Moral Tendencies,* 143–44; Enoch Pond, *A Sermon on the Divinity of Christ* (Boston, 1829), 17; Ware, *Letters to Trinitarians and Calvinists,* 11.

27. Sacvan Bercovitch, *The American Jeremiad* (Madison: University of Wisconsin Press, 1978), 199.

(1833). Although this translation would help touch off the "miracles" controversy that led some to rebel against Unitarianism in favor of transcendentalism, Marsh believed that only English-language sources could offer an effective antidote to the Lockean and Scottish empiricism that deplorably failed to "keep alive the heart in the head."[28] Accordingly, he had published in 1829 his famous and influential edition of Coleridge's *Aids to Reflection.*

Marsh admired the way Coleridge put philosophy to the service of piety in such aphorisms as "Yea, blessed is the calamity that makes us humble."[29] Like Coleridge and Edwards, Marsh saw that the Lockean model of consciousness as perception was a threat to the traditional objective of pious humility—union with an Other. Edwards's metaphysical idealism, posthumously published in the same year as Marsh's edition of Coleridge's *Aids,* was unknown to Marsh, who nevertheless rightly believed that the conventional view that Edwards was a Lockean was a hindrance to piety.[30] Unaware of Edwards's theological idealism, Marsh opted for transcendental idealism. The self, said Marsh, is not passive in perception but, as Kant had said, "combines the manifold in the affections of sense" into the "subjective unity of a perception." Edwards believed that God's ideas formed the human self and Marsh that the human self formed ideas, but the object of both was to limit pride and belief in human moral ability. The appeal of Kantianism to Marsh was that the German philosopher's description of the formation of unitary perceptions out of the manifold of sensation meant that the process of perception was not "under the direction of the will."[31] As Coleridge put it, "Man was and is a *fallen* Creature . . . diseased in his Will."[32]

Marsh echoed the opinion of his age that consciousness made it undeniable that human beings possessed a "self-determining power" and then, pietist that he was, qualified that opinion by insisting that the unregenerate self was not all-determining. The

28. James Marsh, *Remains,* ed. J. Torrey (Boston, 1843), 43.

29. Samuel Taylor Coleridge, *Aids to Reflection,* ed. James Marsh (Burlington, 1829), 126.

30. Marsh, Introduction to ibid., xxix.

31. Marsh, *Remains,* 318–20.

32. Coleridge, *Aids to Reflection,* 90.

limitation of human willing in determining behavior was due, in Marsh's words, to the fact that "I am at no time distinctly conscious of all the knowledge which I possess, or of . . . all the powers of thought which are active at a given moment; and to become conscious of them, must employ a vigorous effort of attention." This implied unconscious thought in the modern sense, implied that people sometimes think without perceiving that they think. But Marsh did not develop that line, for he was a prophet of consciousness rather than the unconscious. Wanting to expand the power of regenerate human willing to determine behavior, he urged the faithful to bring unconscious actions under the dominion of consciousness by expanding their self-knowledge. An increase in reflective knowledge of the self was the end to which he had offered Coleridge's *Aids to Reflection.* Consciousness would be complete, Marsh said, only if there were no unconscious thought, only if it were possible for people "to possess simultaneous intuition of all the powers of living action which belong to us . . . so that our being and our knowing should be identical."[33]

Objective spiritual knowledge was not to be obtained through studying nature but rather through exploring the spiritual realm, which was the dwelling place of the soul, just as the external world was the dwelling place of the body. Just as the physical senses and powers had "correlative objects," so did the internal sense and the mental faculties have correlatives in the spiritual realm. Just as the natural philosopher pondered sensory data in order to arrive at scientific law, people properly reflected on their own mental operations in order to discern the "law of reason" that governed the spiritual world.[34] Through self-reflection human beings could attain spiritual knowledge, or "reason," rather than mere "understanding," or natural knowledge, which, as Marsh said, was shared to some extent by animals.[35] By reflection, people became "distinctly conscious of that in our immediate experiences, of which we were not before conscious." For instance, reflection upon conscience as a "fact of consciousness" established the principle "that the will is in

33. Marsh, *Remains,* 269, 279, 284.
34. Ibid., 142, 363.
35. Marsh, Introduction to Coleridge, *Aids to Reflection,* xlii.

itself, essentially supernatural, having its true correlatives" in God. Indeed, it suggested, as Coleridge said, that conscience "is the ground and antecedent of human (or *self-*) consciousness, and not any modification of the latter."[36] Cultivating conscience was the means to spiritual knowledge, Marsh believed, for "in proportion as the conscience is awakened, does it become impossible to doubt the existence of God." That such spiritual knowledge was often in doubt indicated the degree to which human spirituality was tainted by "the self-seeking principle of nature." Consequently, pietists were right that "the individual self-will in man must be slain."[37]

Transcendentalism proved inadequate to the task of renewing piety and humility. Marsh thought of himself as attempting the feat at which he believed Edwards had failed, the feat of philosophically defending piety. His editing of Coleridge and especially his addition to the *Aids* of passages from seventeenth-century writers like Henry More were meant to assure conservative readers that Kantian transcendentalism fell safely within the bounds of traditional religion.[38] But though Marsh asserted that transcendent reason was available only to the regenerate mind, he did not philosophically support the assertion. There was no basis in Marsh's system for believing that regeneration depended on God or that human beings were helpless to accomplish it. Regeneration was evidently nothing but self-conscious cultivation of conscience and the study of transcendent reason, a process possible for anyone who of his or her own free will adopted the Kantian method. The admirably objective Marsh seems to have understood his failure and sagely predicted to a friend that the "spiritual philosophy" would appeal to the proud, self-assertive "young men about Cambridge and Boston" determined to honor impulsive thought rather than reason.[39]

---

36. Marsh, *Remains*, 358, 384; Coleridge, *Aids to Reflection*, 76.
37. Marsh, *Remains*, 142, 383, 387.
38. Coleridge, *Aids to Reflection*, 316–20; cf. Ronald Vale Wells, *Three Christian Transcendentalists: James Marsh, Caleb Sprague Henry, and Frederic Henry Hedge* (New York: Columbia University Press, 1943), 22.
39. Marsh, *Remains*, 83, 124.

Yet even Marsh lacked the prescience needed to conjure up Jones Very, Harvard's twenty-five-year-old tutor in Greek. In September of 1838, possibly moved in part by having heard Ralph Waldo Emerson's address at the Divinity School two months earlier and by other contacts as well with the Concord seer, Very called on Professor Henry Ware, Junior. To the latter, who was planning to answer Emerson with a sermon on "The Personality of the Deity," Very must have seemed a providential manifestation of the danger of Emerson's neglect of the distinctness of God's individuality from that of human persons. For Very told Ware "that it was the father who was speaking thro' him." The next day Very announced to students that he was infallible and cried out in resounding tones, "Flee to the mountains, for the end of all things is at hand." Relieved of his teaching duties and returned to his family at Salem, he unexpectedly visited his friend Elizabeth Peabody, placed his hand on her head, baptized her "with the Holy Ghost and with fire," and added, "I am the Second Coming." Emerson, with whom Very had recently "staid a few days confounding us all with the question—whether he was insane," was now untroubled by reports of his follower's strange doings and pronounced him "profoundly sane." The Concord prophet had the advantage not only of conversation with Very—"Talk with him a few hours and you will think all insane but he"—but also of having read the brilliant essay on Shakespeare that Very had written during his "mono*Sania*."[40]

In the Shakespeare essay and in a lecture on "Epic Poetry" that Emerson had heard at the Concord Lyceum some months earlier, Very had articulated his radical views on the history and future of consciousness. Using Homer as evidence that the early Greeks had believed in the visibility of the gods and had looked "upon themselves in all reflex acts, whether external or internal, as patients rather than agents," Very argued that they had not thought of themselves as spiritual beings but had conceived of human existence in strictly physical terms.[41] With the rise of self-conscious-

40. Edwin Gittleman, *Jones Very: The Effective Years, 1833–1840* (New York: Columbia University Press, 1967), 189, 190, 216, 217, 250.

41. Jones Very, *Poems and Essays*, ed. James Freeman Clarke (Boston, 1886), 11; cf. James Marsh, "Ancient and Modern Poetry," *North American Review* (July 1822):

ness, which Very attributed to Christianity, the poet inevitably possessed "an introspective mind" and gave "an inwardness of meaning to his characters." Epic, Homerian poetry of war was therefore succeeded by the drama, for the latter reflected the modern awareness that "the mightiest conflicts are born within." The fact that the greatest dramatist, Shakespeare, was also the most mysterious of all modern poets, the most difficult to know personally through his works, indicates how little of his universality the rest of humanity possesses and how difficult it is to achieve his "unconscious" naturalness. Much of this drew conventionally on the romantic cult of genius, but Very went on to argue that "there is a higher action than that we witness in [Shakespeare]; where the will has not been borne down and drawn along by the mind's own original impulse; but, though capable of resistance, yields flexibly to all its natural movements, presenting that higher phenomenon which genius and revelation were meant to forward in all men,—conscious nature."[42]

These essays support Emerson's judgment as to Very's basic sanity by indicating that his strange actions were the result of deliberation and resolve rather than insane delusion. For it is evident that while Very probably possessed much of his mother's eccentric temperament that had made her a notorious crank in Salem, he also intentionally exploited his excited mind in order to achieve the "conscious nature" denied to Shakespeare. Very was trying to return to a primitive mental world similar to the early Greeks' where his own thoughts were to be received as divine utterances. But since he understood them to be thoughts in himself, his submission to them, unlike that of the Homeric heroes, could only be voluntary and conscious. These thoughts being acts of his own mind did not preclude their also being acts of God. All that was required was that he had not consciously originated them so that they could be interpreted as a "sensible will that was not my own."[43] He had to

104–8; for a recent, similar argument, see Julian Jaynes, *The Origin of Consciousness in the Breakdown of the Bicameral Mind* (Boston: Houghton Mifflin, 1976).

42. Very, *Poems and Essays*, 30, 11, 41–42.

43. Very, quoted in Gittleman, *Jones Very*, 187.

wait passively for impulses, then consciously obey them while trying not to "will" or initiate any thought of his own. Thus Very
never claimed to have lost self-consciousness and was willing to discuss with Channing, for instance, which of his actions were done of
his "own accord and which in obeisance to the Spirit."[44] This set of
beliefs about consciousness probably helped lead Very to bizarre
actions he might otherwise have avoided. Honoring impulses according to their degree of apparent foreignness seems likely to encourage extreme behavior. But it also mitigated the egotism of believing that the second coming was in him. For he also believed
that it could be in all other human beings if they would only consciously subject their will to the divine will as he had done; his
identification with Christ was not exclusive.

Inevitably, Very was only partly successful in his attempt to become conscious nature. To stipulate as a condition of unification
with the One a consciousness of the union's being a voluntary act is
to stipulate an incomplete union; an individual self totally identified with the Other could not be conscious of its separate actions.
In Very's system the self was supposed to accomplish the impossible
feat of retaining self-consciousness while not acting like a self.
When Very sent his Shakespeare essay to Emerson, he complained
that whereas most of it was written according to the Holy Spirit's
dictation, his own self had interfered somewhat.[45] Very became increasingly distrustful of his system. After a month's involuntary
confinement at McLean Hospital, where he wrote his great essay,
"Hamlet," he was released to his family. To them he made a promise and kept it to forsake the thinking of divine thoughts and "return to the ways of men in a year."[46] Meanwhile, lovely sonnets
flowed from his pen at an astonishing rate—one hundred in six
months. Some of these, together with his essays, have had a small
audience to the present day. Very, however, lapsed into a sad re-
cluse, soon lost touch with his transcendentalist friends, and lived
forty barren years with his sisters in Salem.

44. Clarke, Introduction to Very, *Poems and Essays,* xxv.
45. Gittleman, *Jones Very,* 193.
46. Ibid., 309.

Unconscious Selflessness

While Very's actions were the most extreme of any of the major
transcendentalists, his willingness to retain individual self-consciousness was a more moderate position than that of Emerson or
Thoreau, who longed for an eclipse of the human self in favor of
divine thought. Emerson found it consistent with his role as
prophet of self to urge the necessity of self-renunciation, and when
Thoreau planned "to go soon and live away by the pond," he
added, "It will be success if I shall have left myself behind." He
prayed, "Why, God, did you include me in your great scheme?
. . . Did it need there should be a conscious material?"[47] There was
no fundamental inconsistency between these deprecations of self-
consciousness and the transcendentalists' better-known method of
self-exaltation. Consciousness of individual selfhood was celebrated as a window on the Universal Self but simultaneously deplored as evidence that the transcendentalist had not achieved
complete union with the One. Only a limited self, detached from
absolute Self, could be self-consciously aware of the poverty of its
own attributes as opposed to the rest of creation. Distaste for any
intentional pursuit of limited selfhood led Thoreau to call the
church the ugliest building in every village because it was "the one
in which human nature stoops the lowest and is most disgraced."
Emerson subscribed to Channing's view of humility as high respect
for divinely created human nature and added that the most successful study of nature involves "self-recovery," for "man is the dwarf of
himself." It has been rightly said of the Unitarians but is still truer
of the transcendentalists that they had a common purpose with
their Puritan forebears—"a clear impression of God's all-embrac-
ing presence." The difference lay in the transcendentalist's strategy
of attempting "to raise *himself* to God, not languish in hope and
fear awaiting supernatural grace."[48]

47. Ralph Waldo Emerson, "Divinity School Address," *Works* (Boston, 1883), I,
122; Henry David Thoreau, *Journal* (Boston: Houghton Mifflin, 1949), I, 299, 327.
48. Henry David Thoreau, *Week* (Boston: Houghton Mifflin, 1906), 77; Emerson,
Nature in *Works*, I, 70, 74; Howe, *Unitarian Conscience*, 118.

On the level of spiritual strategy, however, self-exaltation does contradict self-disgust, which created a problem within the dynamics of transcendentalism the opposite of that in evangelical self-interpretation. When Emerson said that "humility is properly the exaltation of the Spirit,"[49] he spoke aloud what had been the not quite secret truth of Puritanism, the connection between abjectness of self and joyous recognition of the Other within. This awareness of the element of self in conversion, or rather, the making of conversion a process of self-interpretation, was the most native element in transcendentalism. Many of the more philosophically acute transcendentalists—thinkers like George Ripley, Theodore Parker, and Orestes Brownson—were raised in the ambiance of New England's backwoods Calvinism and in youth were converted or at least passed through spiritual anguish. They moved easily from Puritan self-abnegation to transcendental self-exaltation because in both cases the goal was a union of self and Other. The closer transcendental and Puritan interpretations moved toward their ideal types, the more similar they became, for the absence of any consciousness of Otherness precludes any consciousness of self and vice versa. But the danger for Puritans had lain in a humility so absolute that it denied the propriety of even the modicum of selfhood needed to recognize the Other. The spiritual danger for Emerson and Thoreau was exactly the reverse. Their prideful soul sickness was the refusal to accept any indication that the self was not all inclusive, the refusal to accept any self-conscious perception of Otherness.

In the absence of any institutional requirement of a profession of faith, the transcendentalists left no formal spiritual relations comparable to those of their Puritan ancestors, but their numerous books, journals, and letters reveal the process by which their pride was chastened. In the early volumes of Thoreau's *Journal* he tended self-consciously to analyze thought, attempting to wring out its utmost symbolic meanings. He was not insincere in those passages where he deplored self-consciousness. Rather, he hoped to make his self all conquering so that his self-consciousness would become all-consciousness. In an early entry, with "closed ears and eyes," he

49. Emerson, *Journals* (Cambridge, Mass.: Riverside Press, 1909), II, 300.

subjected "Consciousness" itself to this technique and found it a symbol of the soul's proper relation to the universe, dissolving "all lesser lights in my own intenser and steadier light." Under the heading "Self-Culture" he asked, "Who knows how incessant a surveillance a strong man may maintain over himself . . . ? By a strong effort may he not command even his brute body in unconscious moments?"[50] But as the years passed both the self-consciousness and symbolic analysis fell steadily off. By the late 1850s and early 1860s it took the excitement of the slavery controversy or of a John Brown to provoke him to self-conscious symbolizing. Most of the latter volumes of the *Journal* are much less self-referring, and the symbolic analysis is less strained. The later volumes do not indicate an abandonment of his early resolve to "live thus deliberately for the most part," but they do reveal a tempered spiritual strategy. By 1856 his willingness to wait somewhat on thought rather than subject it to the self is indicated in his conclusion that "both a conscious and an unconscious life are good. . . . The wisely conscious life springs out of an unconscious suggestion."[51]

The self could no more entirely conquer the Other for Emerson and Thoreau than it had been able, for the Puritans, to wait in entire passivity for transformation by the Other. Emerson believed that "the height, the deity of man is to be self-sustained, to need no gift, no foreign force," but he also felt "like other men my relation to that Fact which cannot be spoken."[52] Stephen Whicher's *Freedom and Fate* is unquestionably the finest statement of this tension in Emerson. Whicher found that Emerson "perforce splits into two distinct personalities: the believer, who sees through to the mystical perfection of things, and the detached observer, Mr. Emerson of Concord, who gives their due to the facts."[53] Emerson understood that a religious ecstasy based on self-exaltation was bound to be as episodic as the Puritans' experience of grace in humiliation. The generalized self, Whicher's "believer," had inevitably to accept the individuality of "Mr. Emerson of Concord." But

---

50. Thoreau, *Journal*, I, 54, 79.
51. Ibid., II, 421; IX, 37.
52. Emerson, "The Transcendentalist," *Works*, I, 316–17.
53. Stephen Whicher, *Freedom and Fate: An Inner Life of Ralph Waldo Emerson* (Philadelphia: University of Pennsylvania Press, 1953), 32.

what Whicher saw as an increasingly mature and somewhat resigned acceptance of "Beautiful Necessity" was also a strategy of
self-interpretation. What Whicher calls a split mentality was to
Emerson not only a "double consciousness" but also a "key . . . to
the old knots of fate, freedom, and foreknowledge." When the
universe is recalcitrant and refuses to be subsumed by the self,
"when a man is the victim of his fate, has sciatica in his loins and
cramp in his mind . . . he is to rally on his relation to the Universe,
which his ruin benefits. Leaving the daemon who suffers, he is to
take sides with the Deity who secures universal benefit by his
pain."[54] Since consciousness of individual selfhood was retained,
Emerson's scheme did indicate a chastened spiritual ambition, but
he still refused to let the ultimate if unattainable objective slip
from view. Thereby, Emerson's notions are reminiscent of Increase
Mather's and Thomas Shepard's device of making pride a ground
for humiliation. But in Emerson's case the process was reversed and
humiliation was a basis for pride.

Whether through forthright self-exaltation or the strategic indirection of humility, the tendency of transcendentalists was toward
increasing the independence of thought from self. Neither Emerson nor Thoreau explicitly doubted that thought was an activity of
the self. Their self-deprecation was due to the inability of their
selves to think the thoughts they desired to think. Their self-exaltation was aimed at identification with a larger Self that did think
such thoughts. Yet just because of their vagueness on the question
of where the human self ended and the divine self began, they
tended to see thought as coursing in and out of humanity. In contrast to the New Divinity men who had divided the self into conscious and unconscious elements, transcendentalists continued to
identify the self with consciousness. The formulations of the New
Divinity men allowed for the possibility that thoughts not originating consciously within the self originated in an unconscious part of
the self. But the transcendentalists assumed that any such thoughts
must have originated outside the self.

Because Calvinists had been pushed more or less unconsciously,
as it were, toward the idea of an unconscious element within the

54. Emerson, "Fate," *Works*, VI, 49–51.

self, they had not formulated the idea clearly enough for opponents to pounce on it, but the transcendentalists opposed the means, the humble pie of metaphysical ignorance, by which Taylor and other ostensible Calvinists had split the personality of the Godhead as well as the selves of individual human beings. Where the New Divinity men had gradually toned down their empirical reliance on consciousness in favor of reasoned inference about unobservable elements of the self, the transcendentalists retained confidence in the evidence of consciousness. Thoreau advised his sister Helen, a teacher, that knowledge of the mind was best acquired through introspection: "One of your young ladies wishes to study mental philosophy, hey? Well, tell her that she has the very best text-book that I know of in her possession already." Mental science, said Sampson Reed, was merely the mind's consciousness of the growth of its own powers. The limitation of consciousness had even less appeal to transcendentalists than to Unitarians. From Channing's insistence that "we cannot take a step in reasoning or action without a secret reliance on our own minds," it was only a step to Emerson's assertion that the idealist measures things by "the *rank* which things themselves take in his consciousness."[55] Unconscious selfhood could not be known in consciousness and therefore took no rank at all.

American transcendentalist writings of course teem with the word "unconscious," but the word seldom if ever refers to an unconscious element within the human self. At its most prosaic, the phrase "unconscious life" in Emerson's writings indicates not unwitting thought but a complete absence of thought—standard nineteenth-century usage. More specific to transcendentalism, however, was the view that to say a person is motivated by unconscious thought is to imply that the thought was not so much his as a higher being's: "There is less intention in history than we ascribe to it," wrote Emerson. "We impute deep-laid, far-sighted plans to Caesar and Napoleon; but the best of their power was in nature, not in them." The origin of thought is not in unconscious mental

55. Henry David Thoreau, *Writings* (Boston: Houghton Mifflin, 1906), VI, 25–26; Sampson Reed, *Observations on the Growth of the Mind* (Boston, 1826), 17; William Ellery Channing, "The Moral Argument against Calvinism," *Works*, I, 226; Emerson, "The Transcendentalist," I, 314–15.

processes within humanity but in the consciousness of the Over-Soul: "so is it with thoughts. When I watch that flowing river, which, out of regions I see not, pours for a season its streams into me, I see that I am a pensioner. . . . from some alien energy the visions come." This uninterrupted continuum of thought from God to humanity was the "impersonality" to which Emerson's opponents objected. Emerson's latter-day antinomianism was made clear in his belief that individual self-consciousness and strivings of will based on it vitiated the moral life, which ought to be spontaneous and unconscious in the sense of originating outside the human self: "Either God is there or he is not there."[56]

Thought above Self

The career of George Ripley (1802–80) reveals that even transcendentalists more willing than Emerson to accept some distinction between human and divine personalities nevertheless had difficulty containing thought within the self. By nature a religious enthusiast, Ripley had had an intense exposure to Unitarian coldness. In his fundamentalist youth he had hoped to attend Yale but was frustrated by his theologically liberal father, who sent him to Concord for tutelage by the boy's uncle, the local Unitarian pastor, Ezra Ripley, and then to Harvard. After fifteen years in the Unitarian ministry during which he became more and more disenchanted with the antienthusiastic position of liberal orthodoxy, Ripley resigned his Boston pulpit in 1841 to found the utopian community Brook Farm and then subsequently became literary editor of the *New York Tribune*. These later roles developed logically out of his years in the ministry, when he helped organize the Transcendentalist Club and the *Dial*.

As editor of the fifteen influential volumes translating *Specimens of Standard Foreign Literature* (1838–45), Ripley helped introduce American transcendentalists to their European counterparts. Ripley himself translated and wrote about the speculations on willing and selfhood of French Kantians and anti-Lockeans such

---

56. Emerson, "The American Scholar," *Works*, I, 97; *idem*, "Spiritual Laws," *Works*, II, 128; *idem*, "The Over-Soul," *Works*, II, 252; *idem*, "Spiritual Laws," 127.

as Victor Cousin, Maine de Biran, Royer-Collard, Theodore Jouffroy, and Benjamin Constant. Believing that personal identity was
both proved by and founded on consciousness, Ripley rhetorically
asked the Kantian question, "How is the unity of our personal being to be derived from the multiplicity of sensible phenomena?"
Lockeanism, or, as its French opponents often called it, "sensual-
ism," destroyed personality and liberty. For in the hands of French
Lockeans such as Condillac the willing faculty had been material-
ized and made passive. In response, the French Kantians maintained that human willing was causative and that the proof lay in
human consciousness of willing's resulting in muscular effort. And
since people were conscious that "it is We who make the effort,"
Ripley breathtakingly concluded that "the liberty of what we call
SELF is identical with its existence and immediately perceived by
consciousness."[57]

Holding that knowledge of the me—of free will, personal identity, and human spirituality—depended on reflection and self-consciousness, the New England transcendentalists also believed that
objective knowledge of the not-me—of reason—depended on
spontaneous thought. Here they parted company with Marsh.
Emerson was notoriously not a Kantian in any exact sense, but he
was scarcely alone in his refusal to accept the inability of the Kantian system to validate the objective truth of intuitions. Emerson
passed airily over the issue and identified transcendentalism as
merely a "tendency to respect the intuitions and to give them, at
least in our creed, all authority over our experience." But Ripley
criticized Emerson's view as impersonal and tending to produce the
religious coldness it was meant to avoid. More philosophically rigorous than Emerson, Ripley sought a more solid base than creedal
assertion and believed he found it in Victor Cousin. The French
philosopher protested Kant's ontological skepticism by researches
based on the empirical evidence of consciousness: "More faithful
than ever to the psychological method, instead of departing from
observation, I plunged into it more deeply . . . and at a depth to
which Kant did not penetrate . . . I detected and unfolded the

---

57. George Ripley, *Philosophical Miscellanies, Translated from the French of
Cousin, Jouffroy, and B. Constant* (Boston, 1838), I, 12, 24–25.

fact, instantaneous but real, of the spontaneous perception of truth." The laws of thought depend only on themselves and are therefore objective: "the spontaneous perception is so pure that it escapes our notice," and it is only upon reflection, "in relation to the free and voluntary me," that it becomes subjective.[58] Reason belongs to no individual nor even to humanity but rather humanity to it, a conclusion horrifying to Theodore Parker.

Parker feared that if the human self could be formed by thought, so might the divine self. Like Ripley, Parker unsuccessfully attempted to find a basis for distinguishing between mortal and divine personalities that would nevertheless allow natural human beings access to divine truth. Raised in rude circumstances at Lexington and largely self-educated despite his having once enrolled at Harvard on a noncredit basis, Parker resembled Ripley, his closest friend, in many ways—in reform zeal, in his strenuous philosophical interests, and in his refusal to believe that true religion depended on obliterating the distinction between the me and not-me within. Influenced even more strongly than Ripley by European, post-Kantian speculations about relations between the me and the not-me, Parker criticized Emerson for believing that his method of ecstasy, "in which the man loses his individual self-consciousness," revealed religious truth. Self-conscious awareness of the separation of the me from the not-me, rather than separating people from God, was the basis of religious life. "As soon as man has any personal self-consciousness, and feels 'I am a *me*,' he has also religious consciousness, and feels this consciousness of a power about him everywhere, within him at all times, and yet above him."[59]

Religious sentiment depended on self-consciousness because it depended even more fundamentally on the self's awareness of otherness, of not being all. "See how the baby comes to consciousness

<hr>

58. Emerson, "The Transcendentalist," I, 321; Cousin in Ripley, *Philosophical Miscellanies*, I, 128–29.

59. Theodore Parker, "Ralph Waldo Emerson," *Works* (Boston: American Unitarian Association, 1907), VIII, 83; Parker, "The Innermost Facts of Religious Consciousness," *Works*, VI, 233–34.

of its body, and learns to distinguish between the *me* of the body and the *not-me* of the body. So at a later date he . . . learns to distinguish between the me of the soul and the not-me of the soul, the me and something other. This is the first fact of religious experience." In an explanation that he owed to Schleiermacher and that resembled the explanation Freud would offer a century later for the origin of religious emotions, Parker held that religious sentiment "is indeed logically inseparable from [self-consciousness], for we cannot be conscious of ourselves except as *dependent* beings."[60] The difference between Parker and Freud lay in the former's belief that this "sense" had a real object—God. Nevertheless, Parker admitted that "no more than the eye or ear discovers the essence of light or sound" does this sense "itself disclose the character . . . of the object on which it depends."[61]

Unable to rest content with so vague a "sense," Parker held that the soul could fathom the nature of God by self-reflection, by analysis of the relations between the me and the not-me of the soul. Since the sense of dependence reflects the me's imperfection and weakness, human beings attribute perfection and omnipotence to the not-me. Similarly, the inability to believe that two plus two equals three indicates that the me is governed by a not-me who is Reason. From their affections people induce that God is Love; from their moral natures that he is Justice; from their spirits and their bodies that he transcends all substance. "Yea, with great groanings which cannot be uttered," concluded Parker in typically crude phrasing, "the ten hundred millions of mankind cry out, 'Show us the Father, and it sufficeth us! . . . [But] In our own consciousness lies the evidence."[62]

Parker unconvincingly asserted that locating the evidence for the nature of God within human consciousness did not subvert belief

---

60. Theodore Parker, "Innermost Facts of Religious Consciousness," 236; Sigmund Freud, *Civilization and Its Discontents*, trans. James Strachey (New York: Norton, 1961), 11–12; Parker, *A Discourse of Matters Pertaining to Religion*, in *Works*, I, 11.
61. Parker, *Matters Pertaining to Religion*, 7.
62. Parker, "God in the World of Man," *Works*, I, 282–84.

in his being an "object independent of us." But Parker himself at-tributed the divisiveness of sectarian opinion to failure to separate "the me of the spirit from the not-me. We give outness to much which is really only inward in us." Ghosts, devils, and visions, he said, are products of the me: "Martin Luther threw his inkstand at the visible devil, and it hit Martin's own whim." But Parker offered no evidence for his location of, on the one hand, ghosts and devils in the me and, on the other hand, the divine qualities of love and justice in the not-me of the mind. Even the not-me is ascertained "in my mental consciousness," and the me alone views it as an ex-ternal "cause and providence." Parker's writings showed that tran-scendentalism contained impious tendencies. As Orestes Brownson said much later of Parker, "his theology became simply anthropology."[63]

The most philosophically acute thinker in America in the period between Edwards and Peirce, Brownson (1803–76) was well situ-ated to explode the religious and transcendental fallacies of his day, for he had proved susceptible to the gamut. Raised as a Congrega-tionalist, he nearly became a Methodist and did go over to the Pres-byterian, Universalist, Unitarian, and Catholic Churches, in that order, with skeptical and transcendentalist phases mixed in. Politi-cal radical and social reformer, newspaper and periodical editor, Brownson had an outwardly varied career. But he was consistently dedicated to self-education. Placed at age six with an elderly Ver-mont couple because his widowed mother could not support her half-dozen children, Brownson was bereft, lonely, and longing for belonging. An eccentric man of fierce passions, he embarked on a spiritual journey, described in his aptly titled autobiography, *The Convert,* that was eminently understandable. Perhaps it is true, as he claimed, that the difference between him and most others who think for themselves is that they prudently keep most of their changes of mind to themselves. Few people have to conduct so much of their own education in public as did Brownson, by dint of his late start and his need to make a living as editor and writer.

63. Parker, *Matters Pertaining to Religion,* 9; Parker, "God in the World of Man," 270, 276; Orestes Brownson, *The Convert* (New York, 1857), 348.

What was to his credit in his lengthy and varied intellectual pilgrimage was that it genuinely resulted from his being unwilling "to purchase . . . consistency" at the expense of "virtue."[64]

He should have been more charitable, though, to those transcendentalists like Parker who eventually became his enemies, for his own early views contained the impiety he later condemned in others. Like Parker, the youthful Brownson had been influenced by Cousin's distinction between the subjective me and the subjective not-me. Since reflective thought indicates an awareness of *me,* and since the Bible seemed to Brownson to be spontaneous rather than reflective, its writers and prophets were genuinely inspired by the *not-me* of the spirit. Their inspiration was not exclusive, however, since all other people possess in their own consciousnesses the spontaneous thought of the *not-me.* Everyone has access to divine reason within: "Religion is natural to man," as is proved "by what we are conscious of in ourselves."[65] Even divine creation itself can be understood "by noting what passes in the bosom of your own consciousness. . . . The world is God's will or intention, existing in the bosom of his consciousness, as my will or intention exists in the bosom of mine." Although he condemned Parker's theology as mere anthropology, Brownson himself had written that since God created people in his image, "The study of man then is still more the study of Divinity."[66]

The potentially godless implications of attempting to base religion on the inward distinction between the *me* and the *not-me* became clear to Brownson in the autumn of 1841 as he sat in Boston's Masonic Temple and listened to Parker deliver the lectures later published as *A Discourse Pertaining to Matters of Religion.* In Parker's hands, the *not-me* was simply a part of the self not perceived as such. Therefore, all questions, even those pertaining to, say, the authority of Jesus, could be referred to the self. People know, Parker said, that Jesus spoke the truth because they recognize it as truth, just as they instantly recognize that they exist, that

64. Orestes Brownson, "Charles Elwood Reviewed," *Works* (Detroit: T. Nourse, 1882–1907), IV, 357–58.

65. Brownson, *New Views of Christianity, Society, and the Church,* in *Works,* IV, 3.

66. Brownson, *Charles Elwood,* in *Works,* IV, 280–82.

a half is less than a whole, or that it is impossible for a thing both to be and not to be. This meant that "man is himself the standard or measure of absolute religion and morality,"[67] a frightening conclusion to the genuinely religious temperament in the orphan Brownson. To locate the *not-me* within the self was to defeat any solution to the feelings of loneliness and inadequacy, the "sense of dependence" on which he and Parker had both originally based people's natural religious inclinations.

From 1841 on, Brownson devoted his philosophical efforts to finding a way to contain thought safely within the self yet at the same time make it possible for thought to place the self in touch with an Other. He desired to contain thought within the self in order to avoid the transcendentalists' impious belief that the human self could think God's thoughts. Therefore he objected, as Channing had, to the romantic cult of genius. Washington Allston's painting of Jeremiah, for instance, sought "to indicate the prophetic character by giving to the prophet the ideas of a maniac. The poet, painter, sculptor, artists of all sorts, it seems to be believed, in order to have genius, to be what their names imply, should be a sort of madmen, doing what they know not, and do not will,—mastered and carried away by a power they are not, and comprehend not." Yet thought, even while contained within the self, must also give people contact with a satisfyingly external authority so as to avoid the error of Parker, who "wished to turn men in utter nakedness out into this bleak and wintry world, . . . to support themselves as best they might from their own native resources."[68]

Brownson believed he had found the appropriate philosophical weapon with which to attack transcendental irreligion in Pierre Leroux's *Refutation d'Eclecticisme*, a rebuttal of Cousin's belief that the me and the not-me are distinct in human consciousness. In Leroux, Brownson found clearly stated the great principle toward which, he said, he had already been heading, "that all life is at once indissolubly subjective and objective." This principle had pro-

---

67. Brownson, Review of Parker, *Matters Pertaining to Religion*, VI, 14.
68. Ibid., VI, 28; Brownson, *Convert*, 346.

found implications for the relationship between religion and reform. All social life is communion with what is not part of the self,
and people can be elevated only by being brought into relation
with an object better than the self. Similarly, it is likely that the
first human being would have degenerated into a sinner and by
doing so debased posterity, for the first human being was "the object by virtue of communion with which his children were enabled
to live. . . . the Church has been right in asserting original sin."
But Leroux's principle had still more fundamental implications for
the question of consciousness: "as there can be no thought without
an object, for it is impossible to think without thinking something,
it follows that the objective element of every thought is really and
truly not-me."[69] In other words, the not-me is part of both reflexive
thought and spontaneous thought, not just the latter, as Cousin,
Ripley, and Parker had thought. Transcendental impiety like Parker's was based on Kant's erroneous assumption that the subject
alone determines the form of the thought of an external object.
This fallacy permitted the notion that spontaneous thought—i.e.,
thought to which the subject does not seem to give form but which
rather seems to flow into the mind from without—is entirely objective and therefore is the voice of divine reason.

A pioneer of the logic of relations in America, Brownson held
that every thought contains both subject and object, and the relation between them is the form of the thought.[70] The mistake of
earlier philosophers lay in the assumption that metaphysics must
begin with either the subject or the object and then attempt the
impossible task of progressing from the one to the other. Doctor
Johnson's reply to Berkeleyan idealists who denied the reality of the
external universe, his kicking a rock, "was not logical, but it was
philosophical." The gesture recognized "that I find myself only in
opposition to that which is not myself." The true point on which to
purchase a beginning in metaphysics is not ESSE or BEING but "in
LIFE [where] according to what we have established, THE SUBJECT

69. Brownson, "Leroux on Humanity," *Works*, IV, 138; Orestes Brownson, *A Letter to The Reverend William Ellery Channing* (Boston, 1842), 23–24; Brownson,
"*Charles Elwood* Reviewed," 346.
70. He had at least one predecessor. See Marsh, *Remains*, 253.

AND OBJECT, ME AND NOT ME, ARE ONE AND INDISSOLUBLE."
Where Locke's error lay in attributing the form of the thought exclusively to the object, Kant's lay in attributing it exclusively to the
subject. Calling the form of a thought *Idea* was well enough, but it
was wrong to make the idea intermediary between subject and object when it is actually the object itself, or rather the object in relation to the perceiving subject. Since the *not-me* is included in every
fact of consciousness, "under the form of every thought . . . lies
always absolute truth." The subject, however, does not perceive absolute truth in its purity but only in its limited relation to the *me*.
Similarly, the *me* is involved in every thought, but the pure *me* is
unfathomable, for the *me* can be conscious of itself only as a subject in relation to an object: "The question, what is the subject?
. . . can never be fully answered, save by one who knows all there is
to be known."[71]

Not only the object and subject but also the thought in which
they were related was impossible to grasp in its purity, a fact which
revealed the fallacy of the New England tradition of claiming to
base philosophy on the evidence of consciousness. A thought—say
an image of an apple—is a fact of consciousness only while the *me*
is thinking the thought. As soon as the *me* attempts to study the
thought as a fact of consciousness, the *me* is of necessity studying a
new thought, not an image of an apple but an apple as an image.
"The fact of consciousness, then, dies the moment we attempt to
seize it, and . . . a new fact is born. Observation of psychological
facts by means of immediate consciousness, is then out of the question." Many so-called facts of consciousness are actually facts of
memory and are therefore *not-me*. Human feelings of inner duality and conflict, the feeling, say, of wishing in conscience to deny
concupiscence, is not a conflict between understanding and willing, reason and passion, soul and body, or any other duality within
the self. Rather, it is a relation between a "Fact of Consciousness"
or a sexual urge of the present instant and a "Fact of Memory" or an
objective "Conscience, the rule of right," established by past
"experience."[72]

71. Brownson, "Synthetic Philosophy," *Works*, I, 64–65, 81.
72. Ibid., 85, 114.

Rejecting the method of "those who seek the principle of philosophy . . . in the fact of consciousness," Brownson observed with unprecedented acuity that "according to this method, the soul studies its own phenomena in itself, by an interior light called consciousness, as it studies the exterior world by the exterior senses. The soul, then, . . . stands face to face with itself, and may be both the subject studying and the object studied. Hence the *me*, as Jouffroy innocently asserts, may be at once both a *me* observing and a *me* observed. Grant this, and what is the evidence that these absolute ideas, though objects of thought, are not nevertheless really subjective?"[73] The method of Kant and Cousin, and indeed of all early nineteenth-century New England moralists, the method of introspective consciousness which the transcendentalists believed gave access to an objective Over-Soul or Reason, instead isolated them in utter subjectivity and mistaken pride.

Brownson was far along toward overcoming the model of thought as internal experience that for more than a century had caused the belief that a desire for holiness must be not only an action but also a self-perception fully known to consciousness: We do not "always clearly and distinctly understand what we are doing. . . . A man's thoughts, feelings, desires, passions, emotions, affections are . . . in the strictest sense his acts." The vaunted evidence of consciousness for human moral ability had long stood in the way of religious humility, but the supposed experience of free will was merely action combined with apperception—"the Subject [acting] . . . with a distinct consciousness of acting."[74]

Longing for the religious humility that a conception of all thought as unconscious might have promoted,[75] Brownson was nevertheless unable to accept it. Unconscious mental activity was objectionable on two counts: it implied moral irresponsibility, and it threatened Brownson's newfound certainty that the *not-me* in every thought is objective. If a thought could be unconsciously present to the mind, then when a thought was obtruded into the

---

73. Brownson, *Convert*, 327; Brownson, "*Charles Elwood* Reviewed," 346.
74. Brownson, "Synthetic Philosophy," 108–10.
75. Arthur M. Schlesinger, Jr., *Orestes A Brownson: A Pilgrim's Progress* (Boston: Little; Brown, 1939), 188–89.

consciousness of the *me*, there would be no guarantee that the apparent element of *not-me* in the thought was a genuinely external reality rather than a creation of the self. Moreover, Brownson was trapped by the nineteenth-century moralistic dogmas that there could be responsibility only where there was freedom and freedom only where there was consciousness. To suggest that people act unconsciously would have been to suggest that "the bulk of mankind are involuntary in their whole conduct" and therefore are not accountable for their actions: "No man is responsible in a moral point of view for what he does involuntarily." People could be held responsible only by rejecting any notion of unconscious action and holding instead that "all actions are in some sense voluntary" because "man is intelligent . . . in his very essence, and therefore must always act with some degree of intelligence."[76]

Torn by his unprecedentedly acute recognition of the contradiction between the two descriptions of the self in the consciousness concept as passive perceiver and active creator of thought, Brownson tried unsuccessfully to reconcile them. On the one hand, he attempted to remain loyal to the notion of thought as an action by the self. Such a view was a guard against the transcendentalists' impious belief that finite human beings could think divinely "other" thoughts. On the other hand he wanted to view thought as conscious "experience" that delivers objective, external knowledge to the self so that human beings would not be trapped in subjectivity. But he also had to deal with what was by then the well-recognized fact that the mind does often perceive without consciously thinking that it perceives. His solution: "While, then, we may say with Locke, that the soul does not always *think,* we must still contend with Leibnitz, that it always *perceives,* and everywhere." Although people were not always self-conscious, they always perceived themselves. The self always "must have a feeble and obscure sense of its own being;—too feeble and obscure, it may be, to give it a clear and distinct consciousness, yet always sufficient to keep alive a faith in its own identity and persistence."[77] There was such a

76. Brownson, "Synthetic Philosophy," 109.
77. Ibid., 92, 94.

thing, Brownson was saying, as a perception insufficiently intense to be known in consciousness but too intense to be unconscious!

In the end, Brownson leaned toward thought. Even after his conversion to Catholicism, he remained a transcendentalist to the extent of believing that universal Reason, though not a human faculty, was the proper object of people's minds and that they could infer the nature of absolute Ideas through analysis of their own thoughts. Although people think particular thoughts, that does not mean, Brownson said, that they know only particulars. People know universals, "and if we did not, we could not even know the individuals."[78] Even though he had exploded the notion that there was such a thing as immediate evidence of consciousness, he still believed that whatever indirect knowledge people had of their own thoughts could be the basis of objective, universal knowledge.

Brownson's heroic but failed effort to base knowledge on an immediate relation between subject and object suggested that the only way to guarantee the objectivity of knowledge was to abandon its subjectivity, to explore the possibility that no knowledge is intuited or perceived within a self. Perhaps all knowledge, including even knowledge of supposed internal states, was external in origin. Perhaps subjective "experience" was only an inference or interpretation. But although such a solution might make it logically possible to believe in the objectivity of thought, it could be achieved only by a thinker willing to accept the corollary that the subject, the self, was contained in thought rather than thought in the self.

78. Ibid., 116–17, 126.

CHAPTER SEVEN

The Thought Sign: Peirce, James, Dewey, Peirce

The Self More Easily Escaped than Perception and Experience

If the movement from Hopkins to Hall may be characterized as a gradual sacrifice of thought in order to save the self, the movement from Unitarianism to Peirce may be characterized as a gradual sacrifice of the self in order to preserve thought. These victories would have seemed hollow to the original proponents of the consciousness concept. Self and thought were supposed to have been indissolubly linked in the concept of consciousness which was an explanation of human spirituality. The soul or thinking self perceived within itself ideas which were either representations of the material world or reflections of the mind's own operations. The breakdown of the concept was due to its increasingly apparent inconsistency with either physics and physiology on the one hand or moral and mental philosophy on the other.

Yet the consciousness concept was itself a determinant of these changes. The concept was, most basically, a description of human spirituality, and as the description's inadequacies became apparent, the move was toward jettisoning the description but not the belief in spirituality that the concept had helped to perpetuate. Rather than opt for either pure materialism or pure mysticism, each side sought to salvage what it could of human spirituality. Hall found in biology and genetics grounds to distinguish a living, growing, bodily self from the rest of stillborn nature. He did not so much abandon the soul as deprive it of thought as its distinctly spiritual possession. Conversely, the thinkers treated in this chapter attempted to preserve thought as a distinctly spiritual process against the suggestion that it was entirely a sensory or bodily phenomenon.

The most certain way to do that was to locate the self in thought rather than thought in the self.

The pragmatic, instrumentalist challenge to the traditional conception of the person as a perceiver was the most radical result of the breakdown of the concept of consciousness. The conclusion was too extreme for mainstream modernists whose adoption of the notion of some unconscious thought, as I argue in the next chapter, was a conservative stratagem for preserving a role for conscious thought—thought perceived in and by a self. Beyond a small circle of academics, philosophers, social psychologists, and political theorists, the extreme hostility to the substantial self exhibited by the subjects of the present chapter was influential mainly as a warning and a provocation toward more conservative solutions such as Freudianism and other forms of modern depth psychology. Those more conservative psychologies preserved some role for a conscious, transcendent self by reducing merely a part of the mind to unconsciousness. Indeed, among this chapter's principal subjects— Charles Sanders Peirce, William James, and John Dewey—only Peirce faced up to the logical conclusion that if the self is contained in thought rather than vice versa, no thought is consciously intuited or directly perceived. Unlike not only the Freudians but even his fellow pragmatists and instrumentalists, Peirce unflinchingly faced the consequence of his selfless premise—all thought is external; that is, no thought is immediately intuited or "experienced" by a self in the manner described in the seventeenth-century consciousness concept.

William James consistently opposed the notion of a perceiving self as a suitable explanatory device for a scientific psychology, but his basic model of thought remained the perceptual model originally described in the consciousness concept. James was therefore able to dispense with the self only by finding something other than the self to be conscious, something else to do the perceiving— thought itself. But he was thereby forced to sacrifice his early opposition to psychological atomism. For since his model of thought remained perceptual, he could get along without a perceiving self only by accounting for experience as the perception of one atomistic "bit" of thought or experience by another bit of thought.

Similarly, John Dewey could never quite escape from perceptual, experiential, conscious models of thought, though he came closer to doing so than James. More than any other thinker, Dewey translated the triumph of thought above self into the selflessness, the almost pietistic selflessness, of twentieth-century political liberalism. Still, Dewey offered no comprehensive explanation of experience, possibly because he believed that James had resolved the problem through his emphasis on the evidence of consciousness as proving continuity in thought. Lacking a comprehensive metaphysical account of knowledge, of relations among thoughts, Dewey's social philosophy, ostensibly idealistic, tended to lapse into an assumption that knowledge was an effective relationship between an organism and its environment.

The course of Dewey and James suggests the enormous scope of the problem addressed by Peirce. For if he was to avoid both Dewey's tendency to biologize thought and the illogical conclusion forced upon James that one bit of continuous thought is perceived by another, how was he to explain experience or perception at all? Peirce's answer was that thought is not experienced or perceived but only inferred from signs. But that answer raised additional questions. What is a thought-sign made of? And in the absence of a perceiving self, how are particular signs related in a general thought?

Not Ideas but Signs

In his lifetime Charles Sanders Peirce (1839–1914) was usually considered a more difficult than rewarding man, a judgment unsustainable in the light of the voluminous if poorly organized writings that he left behind. Rather, he was the most rewarding, as well as the most difficult, thinker with which this study has to deal. Contemptuous of authority in his privileged youth, he was later unfaithful to employers—Johns Hopkins University and the United States Coast Survey—and ultimately dismissed by both of them. Arrogant, rude, and demanding of friends, he was, by the middle-class sexual mores of his time, ostentatiously immoral. Even admiring students and friends judged him mad in his late middle age, a period when his correspondence was filled with deluded money-making schemes whose failures he excused with paranoid fantasies of persecution. Both of his wives accused him of beatings. Three times brought to court and at least once convicted for assault and battery upon other women, Peirce undoubtedly deserved his wives' recriminations. Tales of his lesser misdeeds and self-destructive carelessness occupy many sad pages of his only, unpublished biography.[1]

A mystery to others, he was perhaps equally mysterious to himself and therefore well equipped to explode the consciousness concept and its impious affirmation of human self-knowledge. His deep religiosity seemed a hypocritical facade to many of his contemporaries, but by old age his great sinfulness had not only humbled him but had taught him, like pietists of old, to love humility. So impoverished that he could not warm his house, on Christmas Day, 1909, in his seventy-first year, he wrote to William James: "I know but too bitterly,—and it is a bitterness that I love,—that I fall further short than any man if possible of deserving any good at all; and I cannot protest any condemnation that may be visited upon me."[2]

Physically and intellectually, Peirce resembled his almost equally gifted father, Benjamin, professor of mathematics at Harvard and a notoriously uncooperative teacher who sometimes said not a single word during his classes but merely worked out on the chalkboard equations of interest and comprehension to himself alone. Benjamin Peirce was a lay philosopher and theologian, a Unitarian and a metaphysical dualist, who attempted to reconcile Biblical creation with evolutionary science and who staunchly denied that mind or spirit could be accounted for by the laws of matter. The most prominent American mathematician of his day, he was elected to European learned societies, and he served for a time as superintendent of the United States Coast and Geodetic Survey, one of the most important government-sponsored scientific projects in the nineteenth century. In this last position he was able to employ Charles, who made lasting contributions to geodesy and thus received the most intense and practical scientific experience of

1. Joseph Lancaster Brent, III, "A Study of the Life of Charles Sanders Peirce" (Ph.D. diss., University of California at Los Angeles, 1960).
2. Quoted in ibid., 175.

any major American philosopher in an era when scientific method was becoming a dominant interest of philosophers.

In addition to his father and his scientific experience, Peirce was influenced, as is well known, by Scotus, Darwin, and Kant, and more obscurely by the pietist tradition of New England religiosity. Some of the romantic strain in Peirce may be owing to his reading in Hegel and Schelling, but his fragmentary references to his childhood also indicate a rebellion against his father's rational Unitarianism: "I abominate the unitarians myself, because all through my boyhood I heard in our unitarian family nothing but angry squabbles between Calvinists and Unitarians, and though the latter were less absurd than the former, I thought their church was based on mere denial."[3] It is tempting to read this as expressing at least a temperamental preference for "Concord transcendentalism," of which Peirce himself thought it "probable that some . . . benignant form of the disease was implanted in my soul, unawares." But while Peirce's commitment to the notion of human mentality as part of a yet larger mental universe would have been welcomed in Concord, he was also animated by a different, humbler spirit than the Transcendentalists' confidence in the untapped capacity of the human soul to join with the One. In part this was simply due to Peirce's philosophical acuteness and scientific training, which led him to address questions of thought and self with a rigor unknown in Concord. But pietist lamentation of the untrustworthiness of self-knowledge was entirely consistent with Peircean pragmatism. In support of his pragmatic view that thoughts cannot be made clear by introspection, Peirce cited "all the sages of human nature . . . who from time immemorial have testified to their conviction that man possess[es] no infallible introspective power into the secrets of his own heart, to know just what he believes and what he doubts."[4]

---

3. Quoted in Murray Murphey, *The Development of Peirce's Philosophy* (Cambridge: Harvard University Press, 1961), 15.

4. Charles Sanders Peirce, "The Law of Mind," *Collected Papers of Charles Sanders Peirce* (hereafter *CP*), Vols. I–VI ed. Charles Hartshorne and Paul Weiss; Vols. VII–VIII ed. Arthur Burks (Cambridge: Harvard University Press, 1931–58), VI. 102; *idem*, "Pragmaticism and Critical Common-Sensism," *CP*, V, 498. All citations to Peirce's *Collected Papers* are to numbered paragraphs rather than pages.

In New England Peirce was the most profound speculator since Edwards on the relation of heart and thought, but at age nineteen Peirce denied the conclusion Edwards had drawn from the distinction between "ideal apprehension" and "speculative knowledge," between ideas and signs. This distinction had provided the basis of Edwards's defense of traditional heart religion by basing knowledge of conversion on ideas actually possessed in the mind rather than mere words or doctrines, mere signs instead of experience. Peirce, however, held that signs could be a source of real knowledge, for it was possible to "discuss that which has no existence in nature or the imagination." For example, if a person told you of a four-sided triangle, "You would proceed to show that he had no such conception. . . . You would reason upon that which you could not conceive of." As opposed to what Edwards had thought, religious knowledge was not the privilege of a select few but was freely available to all. For even if people cannot conceive an idea of holiness, "we can reason upon the nature of God" or indeed of any other unthinkable thought such as infinity or nothing.[5]

Signs, in Peirce's view, were the only source of knowledge, for he did not believe that there was such a thing as an idea in the sense in which Edwards, Locke, and Descartes had used the word, the sense of the consciousness concept. It is easy to miss Peirce's rejection of the "way of ideas," for he used the word "idea" throughout his life and not only to suggest the meaning of a conception but also in the empiricist's sense of an "impression . . . on the soul."[6] But if in youth Peirce allowed for such a thing as an impression on the soul, it was an unconscious impression rather than an idea immediately intuited within the self in the manner described in the consciousness concept. His rejection of the way of ideas was based on his youthful revision of what he supposed to be Kant's commonly accepted and "erroneous"[7] view of the relation between thought and its object, which he illustrated (see fig. 1). Whether or not the fig-

---

5. Charles Sanders Peirce, "An Essay on the Limits of Religious Thought Written to Prove that We Can Reason upon the Nature of God," *Writings of Charles Sanders Peirce* (hereafter *W*), ed. Max H. Fisch et al. (Bloomington: Indiana University Press, 1982–), I, 37.

6. Peirce, "A Treatise on Metaphysics," *W*, I, 61.

7. Peirce, "An Essay on the Limits of Religious Thought," 39.

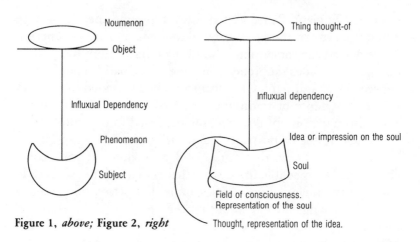

Figure 1, *above;* **Figure 2,** *right*

ure does justice to Kant's view of the relation between noumenon and object, it does accurately suggest that, as Kant said, "Intuitions . . . do not in the least concern us if they cannot be taken up into consciousness."[8] Peirce objected that "while the phenomenon alone is what we are conscious of, mental elements enter into all but the noumenon,"[9] and he believed the correct view could be represented in figure 2. The advantage of this figure is its indicating that conceptualization or "Thought, representation of the idea," unconsciously intervenes between the initial "Idea or impression on the soul" and the "Field of consciousness." Whatever impressions were made on the soul would be raw, unorganized stimuli if they were not somehow organized by the mind *before* being consciously perceived. No conscious thought is an idea but only a sign.

Peirce attacked Kant's attempt to find a warrant for consciousness in consciousness itself. Transcendentalists thought it "necessary to prove that the normal representations of truth within us are really correct," that is, that they correspond to something external. Recognizing that such a demand could not be answered "from external studies" since thought alone was known, transcendentalism

8. Immanuel Kant, *Critique of Pure Reason,* trans. Norman Kemp Smith (London: Macmillan, 1953), A116.
9. Peirce, "An Essay on the Limits of Religious Thought," 40.

or "criticism" of the Kantian sort analyzed thoughts into two broad groups: (1) those that were inferential and consequently uncertain since inference may err; and (2) those that were "particular expressions" of the "I think" or subject in which the manifold of intuition was found. These latter—time (the form of the internal sense), space (external sense), and Kant's twelve conceptions of the understanding—were not inferential. Kant therefore concluded that they were certain and objectively valid. But Peirce held that since Kant applied his concepts of pure reason *a priori* to objects, he had not demonstrated the validity of the concepts but had actually accepted them on faith. Unlike Kant, Peirce saw nothing wrong with resting on faith, and he believed that his analysis of "The Uselessness of Transcendentalism" established the appropriateness of doing so: "A part of his [Kant's] argument is that nothing which rests only on what is inferential can be certain. This is not axiomatic or demonstrable. He therefore leaves hope of proving the contrary which establishes the validity of faith."[10]

Peirce was an "uncritical" transcendentalist. He refused to ask the "critical" question whether thought truthfully signifies reality because he believed on faith that it does so. But he still asked what it was in the nature of the universe that made truth attainable by thinking. Truth being the agreement of a sign with its object, Peirce identified three kinds of true signs. Some signs—*icons*—are true by virtue of resembling their objects. But a resemblance, by its very nature, is only partly true and therefore is also partly false. And since Peirce believed on faith that true thoughts are entirely true, he concluded that the thought sign must represent reality in some other way than resemblance. Some partially true signs—*symbols*—become almost all true by virtue of usually accompanying the things they signify. But entirely true thoughts, Peirce faithfully believed, must be true even the first time they are thought, so they do not *become* true. But suppose a sign's signhood was founded "upon the very nature of things and what have we?" Such a sign, an *index*, would always agree with its object, even the first time it was thought. "Derivation not in time is the relation of accident to substance," which explains how a sign may share predicates with its

10. Peirce, "A Treatise on Metaphysics," 72, 76.

object. Since the sign and its object possess "unity of substance" and since the sign is thought, the object is also thought.[11] The world is constituted of thought, which explains why thinking is so effective a way of dealing with the world. This reasoning was the basis of Peirce's "idealism," as it is sometimes called, but it is more accurately described as "semiotic realism."

To assert that all thought is in signs was implicitly to deny the possibility of introspection, so the next logical step was explicitly to deny it, which Peirce did in 1868 in one of his earliest published essays, "Questions Concerning Certain Faculties Claimed for Man." Others, such as Brownson, had years earlier also denied the possibility of introspection, but Brownson had nevertheless assumed that there was such a thing as subject-object duality. Peirce attacked the whole notion of the existence of two distinct realms of inner and outer, subjective and objective fact. Rather, all facts were external, and what seemed to be internal or subjective was actually inferred from external fact. Peirce pointed to previous instances where supposedly undeniable evidence of consciousness had been demonstrated to be the result of inference. Until Berkeley published his book on vision nothing seemed more obvious than that the third dimension of space is intuited. The history of thought was replete with successful rebellions against the evidence of consciousness. Although Peirce would continue to use the word "consciousness" as a synonym for "thought," he was done altogether with the traditional concept of consciousness, the notion of directly intuited experience within the self: "our whole knowledge of the internal world is derived from the observation of external facts."[12]

Peirce's notion that all thought is in signs seemed to imply an infinite regress. In order of time a sign must be preceded by the thing it signifies. If thoughts are signs rather than ideas, those signs must signify previous thoughts. And if those previous thoughts were also signs, they must have had predecessors. And so on *ad*

11. Ibid., 79–80; Peirce, "Views of Chemistry: Sketched for Young Ladies," *W*, I, 50–56.

12. Peirce added the important qualification that he did not "assume the reality of the external world" but was only questioning the distinction between external and internal. Peirce, "Questions Concerning Certain Faculties Claimed for Man," *CP*, V, 243–44.

infinitum, unless allowance was made for an intuited idea or first impression that was not a sign. But Peirce's mathematical training offered a way of delimiting an infinite regress. Drawing on the concept of infinitesimal numbers—more than zero but less than any finite quantity—Peirce insisted that the fact that human consciousness was finite did not imply of it, any more than finitude did of a physical process, that it had to have a specifiable beginning. For instance, if a person were asked what point on a pen dipped in ink was first immersed, he or she might say the tip. But "tip" would only identify the limit of the body of the pen rather than specifying a point on it. If the person answered instead that the point one inch above the tip first touched the ink, he or she would obviously be wrong; the point one-half inch above the tip was immersed earlier; and the point one-quarter inch above the tip still earlier. The attempt to specify a first point of contact with the ink would clearly be impossible and would lead to an infinite process of specifying points infinitely nearer the tip. Yet the dipping itself was a finite process, for there was at one time no contact between pen and ink. The fact that human thought, like the dipping of the pen, is a finite process does not mean that there must be a pure intuition or first impression: "cognition arises by a continuous process."[13]

If there are no ideas and all thought is in signs, how can thought be general enough to constitute reality? Signs signify particulars, whereas reality constrains particulars and is therefore evidently general. This difficulty, Peirce eventually held, was owing to a naive, nominalistic conception of the meaning of "real." The concept "real" was an inference from the existence of error, which implied an "*ens* such as would stand in the long run," an *ens* independent of what "I" think. The naïvete lay in believing that because the real must be independent of what "I" think, it must be independent of all thought. Peirce believed that the history of science showed that people will reach agreement on any disputed question provided only that they have enough information and enough time to study it: "human opinion universally tends in the long run to a definite form, which is the truth."[14] This final opinion is independent of

13. Peirce, "Some Consequences of Four Incapacities," *CP*, V, 267.
14. Ibid., 311; Peirce, "Fraser's Edition of *The Works of George Berkeley*," *CP*, VIII, 12.

what "I" now erroneously think, and it therefore conforms just as well with the concept "real," as does the more prevalent view that the real is some enduring, nonmental substance.

If reality is constituted of a future thought, it evidently does not exist in the present. Since the phenomenological basis of the concept of the real is constraint, the question arises how a real that will exist only in future thought can exert a constraining influence on the present. Peirce maintained, again, that the difficulty is due to a simplistic nominalism in thinking of cause and effect. For example, an insomniac believes that a soporific power presently exists in opium because he believes that the opium will soon put him to sleep. Clearly, what is dearest to the insomniac's heart is not the present existence of a soporific power in opium but certainty of sleep after ingesting the drug—that is, not a present "power" but merely "a regularity in future events." Therefore, the nominalist's belief in a *ding an sich,* a thing existing independently of knowledge of it, "is a fiction of metaphysics." By abandoning nominalism and all its attendant dangers of skepticism in favor of phenomenalism, Peirce said, it is possible to preserve the reasonable notion that thoughts are signs of external realities. But "the realities which they represent would not be the unknowable cause of sensation, but *noumena,* or intelligible conceptions" to whose truth all people would eventually subscribe, provided only that the process of inquiry went on to infinity.[15] That the process of inquiry would go on forever and that people would be constrained by an infinitely future reality were among the arguments Peirce made in a famous series of essays in 1877–78 in *Popular Science Monthly* under the general title "Illustrations of the Logic of Science."

Two of these essays, "The Fixation of Belief" and "How to Make Our Ideas Clear," are Peirce's most widely read writings, but they have often been misread owing to their having been too seldom studied in the context of Peirce's semiotic realism. A standard interpretation of these essays is that they proclaim logic to be a a social process, a notion tending toward the success orientation Peirce later deplored in popular versions of pragmatism—the test of truth is the ability of a proposition to stand in the long run. Peirce be-

15. Peirce, "Fraser's Edition of *The Works of George Berkeley,*" 12–13.

lieved the exact opposite—a proposition is more likely to stand in the long run if it passes the test of truth, if it is agreeable to logic. "The Fixation of Belief" and "How to Make Our Ideas Clear" are often read as if they were Peirce's major statements, but they were merely coda to his essay of the previous decade, "Questions Concerning Certain Faculties Claimed for Man." Denying in that earlier essay the possibility of introspection, ideas, and intuitive consciousness, Peirce marked out the basis of his semiotic by insisting that thought is a relation of external signs. By asserting in "The Fixation of Belief" and "How to Make Our Ideas Clear" that the best thinking—scientific thinking—tested hypotheses against external fact rather than internal reason, Peirce was merely confirming his decade-old opposition to the consciousness concept. Like human beings, society is contained in thought rather than vice versa. Logic is not a social process, but social processes are logical, are governed by the laws of thought.

Another misreading of these essays holds that in them Peirce described thought as a material, physiological process. Peirce did begin "The Fixation of Belief" with a statement of his eventually famous doubt-belief theory of inquiry—that is, that inquiry results from an organism's struggle to move from the "uneasy" condition of doubt to the "calm and satisfactory state" of belief, to which the organism then clings in a desperate struggle against any renewed irritation of doubt.[16] But this physiological, evolutionary emphasis in Peirce's theory of inquiry was meant only to explain why rather than how people think, and it was therefore preliminary to the basic purpose of the essay, which was a historical survey of methods by which people do think, the methods by which they resolve doubt and fix belief.

Peirce listed four methods of fixing belief in what he believed had been their historical order of discovery, though all four were still practiced. TENACITY was the method of choosing whatever belief suits one's fancy and holding stubbornly to it in the face of contrary experience. But tenacity fails to prevent doubt: "The social impulse is against it." Some tenacious believers are forced toward doubt because they are too logical to ignore the fact that other

16. Peirce, "The Fixation of Belief," CP, V, 372.

people think differently from themselves. Hence humanity advanced to the superior method of AUTHORITY, the fixation of belief by oppression. But the state can not attempt to fix all opinion, only the most important, so that on some issues, albeit minor ones, people's thoughts are left to their natural devices. And since one opinion logically influences another, some people will put two and two together and doubt authority. Let opinion be fixed then by the force that toppled authority, the light of REASON. But this is the *a priori* method of Descartes and other modern system builders. The logical inadequacy of believing whatever is "agreeable to reason" is manifest whenever some newly discovered "external permanency" contradicts it.[17] Hence people were driven logically to SCIENCE, to induction from external signs. The point of "The Fixation of Belief" was to show that human beings are, or at least have been, constrained by logical inference. Although people have always preferred belief, they have been forced to abandon both mistaken beliefs and erroneous methods out of logical necessity. The triumph of scientific method was not accidental but had been forced upon human beings by its logical superiority to all other methods of fixing belief.

Similarly, Peirce's essay "How to Make Our Ideas Clear" has often been misinterpreted as suggesting that the purpose of thought was effective action when he was only attempting to compensate for the deficit in self-understanding created by his denial that the self possesses the "clear and distinct ideas" on which Descartes and Western philosophers after him had staked so much. Thoughts were not distinct, and they had to be *made* clear. Since all thought was inference from external signs, the way to make a thought clear was to consider its external implications. In making these, for him, familiar points Peirce described belief as a "habit" or "rule of action"—expressions which were to cause much misunderstanding.

17. Ibid., 378, 384. Some commentators have suggested that Peirce's emphasis on "external permanency" contradicted his view that reality is constituted of thought. But the only evidence of this is his assertion that "there are Real things, whose characters are entirely independent of our opinion of them" (V, 384). If the "our" is read in the narrow sense of "yours and mine" as opposed to all inquirers, Peirce's view remains intact that the real is the opinion that would be agreed upon if inquiry went on to infinity.

His purpose was to clarify thought rather than reduce it to a physiological epiphenomenon or make it subservient to action. The famous pragmatic maxim he enunciated in this essay was essentially mentalistic, as he tried to emphasize with his intentionally clumsy use of "conception," "conceive," and "conceivably": "Consider what effects, that might conceivably have practical bearings, we conceive the object of our conception to have. Then, our conception of these effects is the whole of our conception of the object."[18] A good example of Peirce's own use of the pragmatic maxim to make an idea clear was the previously mentioned example of the insomniac's belief in the present existence of a soporific power in opium which, Peirce argued, actually amounted only to the belief that the insomniac would sleep after taking the drug.

Even the self, the *I*, which seems to be known intuitively in consciousness, is an external, semiotic inference. Since all thought is in signs, "When we think, then, we our selves, as we are at that moment, appear as a sign."[19] The self is a sign developing according to logic or the laws of inference. Peirce offered a plausible description of how inference could produce a sense of self. An infant begins with no knowledge of the external world, not even the knowledge that his or her body is distinct from other bodies. The small child is not hot and therefore believes the hot stove is not hot. But if the child touches the stove, he or she learns that there is such a thing as ignorance and so begins to suppose a distinction between outer and inner worlds, begins to suppose "a *self* in which this ignorance can inhere. So testimony gives the first dawning of self-consciousness."[20] Thus the human self develops by the same process as language, or rather "my language is the sum total of myself." True, the "man sign" changes over time by developing new meanings, but so do words. And while people make words, it is only by means of words or other external symbols that people think, so words "might turn round and say, 'You mean nothing which we have not taught you.' "[21]

18. Peirce, "How to Make Our Ideas Clear," *CP*, V, 397, 402.
19. Peirce, "Some Consequences of Four Incapacities," 283.
20. Peirce, "Questions Concerning Certain Faculties Claimed for Man," 233.
21. Peirce, "Some Consequences of Four Incapacities," 314, 313.

To the objection that a human being is conscious whereas a word is not, Peirce answered that consciousness is merely "a part of the *material quality* of the man-sign."[22] Every sign, because it is a sign of another thing rather than the thing itself, must have properties of its own that are unrelated to its meaning, unrelated to the thing signified. Otherwise, a sign could not be a sign of a thing, for it would be the thing itself. These unique properties constitute the "material quality" of any sign. For if both the sign and its object are thought, and if the sign is an entirely true sign, the qualities that distinguish the sign from its object must give the appearance of being something other than thought, must give the appearance of being material. A word, if it is to be distinguished from other words, must be composed of a particular material arrangement, such as a special puff of air against the tongue and teeth or, if written, some arrangement of letters such as G-O-D which differ from arrangements of letters in other words. But it is irrelevant to the meaning of the word whether it is spelled G-O-D or D-O-G. A superhuman person could be signified by D-O-G and a four legged animal by G-O-D. When a word is heard or read, its meaning is determined, not by the particular sound or combination of letters that materially compose it, but by a subsequent, interpretive thought. Similarly, the meaning of the man sign is determined not by consciousness or introspective perception but by an interpretant, a semiotic inference. Consciousness is not meaning but merely a feeling, the material quality out of which human thought is composed.

Peirce's belief that human thought is feeling was a culmination of the long-term trend in Western philosophy toward basing the moral life in the passions and affections. Pietists like Ames had embraced that trend by locating part of conscience in the will, and Edwards had built on it by insisting that the self's feeling or willing was a crucial determinant of its understanding of any particular idea. Peirce completed this line of development by denying that there was any such thing as an idea perceived within a self. Rather, the self sign was constituted of thought signs and thought signs of feelings. He admitted that there was an apparent difference be-

22. Ibid., 313.

tween, on the one hand, sensations and emotions which are obviously feelings and, on the other hand, "thinking" which in the common sense of the word is distinguished from sensation and emotion precisely because it seems to involve little or even no feeling at all. But that is because "thinking" is an inferential process in which one thought determines the next, so the greatest attention is paid to where thought is leading, that is, to meaning, rather than to the feeling that composes the thought. On the other hand, the feeling in sensation and emotion is attended to because, leading nowhere, sensation and emotion offer no meaning but only feeling itself to which attention can be paid.[23]

By the mid-1870s Peirce was far ahead of most of his contemporaries and even of Brownson, who thirty years earlier had denied the possibility of grasping the fact of consciousness but not the existence of the fact.[24] Peirce denied the concept of consciousness, denied that there was any such thing as a fact of consciousness contained within or by the self. The self, rather than containing thought, was contained in it. Unlike Edwards who had believed that the mind contains both ideas and signs, Peirce held that all thought was in signs and that the self or mind was itself a sign. The scope of Peirce's achievement and the difficulties it created can be best understood by studying the labored thrashing by which great contemporaries similarly, but much more slowly and never so completely, freed themselves from the concept of consciousness.

The Problem of Continuity in the Absence of the Spiritual Self

William James (1844–1910) is known as a radical in philosophy and psychology, but he was also a reactionary in that he attempted to return to the raw introspection that had been abandoned by theological psychologists like Emmons, Burton, and Taylor in the early nineteenth century. James's commitment to empiricism led him to

23. Ibid., 294.
24. Peirce was also at least thirty years ahead of Ferdinand de Saussure (1857–1913) who is often mistakenly called the founder of the science of signs. See, for example, Jonathan Culler, *Ferdinand de Saussure* (New York: Penguin, 1977), xiv, 72, 96–97.

attempt to deny admittance into the house of psychological science anything that was merely inferential, anything that could not be experienced. This empiricism informed his 1890 *Principles of Psychology*, which, were it not for James's happy gift of phrase, would probably be as forgotten as Dewey's *Psychology* or George T. Ladd's *Elements of Physiological Psychology;* both of which were published three years earlier than James's *Principles.* All three books were fundamentally unsuccessful attempts to prevent metaphysical questions and occult entities from hindering psychological empiricism. James, however, was the rawest empiricist of them all, and his views were simplistic, even by late nineteenth-century standards, as Peirce pointed out in his critical review of the *Principles:* "The notion that the natural sciences accept their data *uncritically* we hold to be a serious mistake."[25]

James seems to have come to his empiricism at least partly in reaction to the Swedenborgianism of his father, Henry James, Senior, who was Emerson's friend and critic. Emerson, said the elder James, "had no adequate doctrine of consciousness." Emerson recognized no difference in kind between consciousness of finite selfhood and participation in the divine self. Henry James, however, followed Swedenborg in believing that sin was synonymous with conscious personhood. A person who believes his life and his self coterminous "cannot possibly feel any true peace or repose in the divine name, . . . for the poor creature is always logically bound to drag his own unsavory corpse about with him" and must therefore feel himself repugnant to the almighty, who "is the most humble or lowly being conceivable, utterly destitute of conscious life or selfhood, and having absolutely no acquaintance with it, save in the person of his worthless creature man." Human salvation required an escape, not as the Transcendentalists believed, into a

---

25. Peirce, "William James, *The Principles of Psychology,*" *CP,* VIII, 61; cf. G. Stanley Hall's review, which, though tinged with jealousy and resentment, was essentially accurate: "abhorring . . . the words unconsciousness, unknowable, if not even unknown, in all their applications, his gnostic passion will not be put off with any appeal to an higher and future synthesis." *American Journal of Psychology* (February 1891): 589.

higher self but rather from a person's natural belief that his life "inheres in himself."[26]

So intensively studied has been the James family that it is unnecessary to establish either the deep ambivalence or the great love between William and his father, but the intellectual continuity and difference between them does need attention. Howard Feinstein asserts that the difference was due to William's misunderstanding of his father's terminology. But there is no evidence that William failed to understand either that Henry located reality in the spiritual realm or that he meant to allow for human independence from God and thus moral freedom by describing natural existence as "phenomenal," an "illusion" of separation between God and humanity. And in any case, William's understanding of his father's terminology is irrelevant. Whether reality is spiritual or natural, William's riposte was logically devastating and, as he well knew, impugned his father's lifework in theology: "You posit [that] . . . from this effected alienation a real movement of return [and redemption] follows. But how can the real movement have its rise in the phenomenal?"[27] Whether the world is material or ideal, a real return cannot originate in an unreal alienation.

The difference between William and his father was a difference of self-interpretation owing to the influence of the consciousness concept upon William. Both men passed through crises of selfhood as profound as that of any seventeenth-century pietist, and Henry responded to his crisis in classic pietist fashion, with still more self-loathing, aimed at self-destruction, and the construction of a theology of selflessness.[28] William's years of youthful depression climaxed in his recalling the sight of an inert idiot in an asylum and the panic that such might be his own fate: "I became a mass of

26. Henry James, *The Literary Remains of Henry James,* ed. William James (Boston, 1884), 266–72.

27. Quoted in Howard Feinstein, *Becoming William James* (Ithaca, N.Y.: Cornell University Press, 1984), 237.

28. Henry James, *Society the Redeemed Form of Man, and the Earnest of God's Omnipotence in Human Nature: Affirmed in Letters to a Friend* (Boston, 1879), 70–80.

quivering fear."[29] William found salvation, not in selflessness as his father had, but in self-confidence inspired by the consciousness concept. Although James cited as his source the French philosopher Charles Renouvier, what inspired his new confidence in human freedom and ability was merely the, by now, traditional mainstay of New England moralists, the evidence of consciousness: "I . . . see no reason why his [Renouvier's] definition of Free Will—'the sustaining of a thought *because I choose* to when I might have other thoughts'—need be the definition of an illusion. . . . My first act of free will shall be to believe in free will."[30] James was to become the most respectable Victorian proponent of the evidence of consciousness for moral freedom. Believing that he owed his moral well-being to the consciousness concept, James never quite escaped it.

Committed to the feeling of selfhood, William would neverthe-less eventually doubt the existence of the substantial self, and ex-cept for the word "universal," the following quotation from Henry perfectly summarizes William's final position on selfhood: "*I* exist only to consciousness only in so far as I feel myself in *universal* rela-tions."[31] William took half a lifetime to arrive at the position that the self consists of relations, and his doing so was the central drama of his intellectual life. In 1904, when he portentously denied that consciousness exists "as an entity," his good friend Charles Peirce

29. William James, *The Varieties of Religious Experience* (Cambridge: Harvard University Press, 1985), 134.

30. William James, *The Letters of William James,* ed. Henry James (Boston: At-lantic Monthly Press, 1920), I, 147. Feinstein attempts to revise the usual acceptance of James's declaration that reading Renouvier marked a turning point in his life by show-ing, convincingly, that James used Renouvier moralistically, to enjoin himself to work willfully at science. The difficulty is that Feinstein assumes that there was a later James who was not willfully directed toward science and that the smooth maneuvering by which James transformed his Harvard appointment in physiology into a professorship in philosophy marked the triumphant liberation of that later, unscientific James (*Be-coming William James,* 331–40). But James conceived of his philosophical work as mental science in a more or less traditional nineteenth-century sense. Introspection was considered empirical and scientific by those nineteenth-century psychologists, includ-ing both Renouvier and James, who remained loyal to the notion of thought as imme-diate experience.

31. Henry James, *Christianity the Logic of Creation* (New York: D. Appleton, 1857), 55.

was astonished: "But your paper floors me . . . by saying that consciousness is often regarded as an 'entity.' . . . Now I do not think
anybody has any such opinions."[32] Perhaps by 1904 no one of any
importance did regard consciousness as an entity, but James had so
regarded it in his 1890 *Principles of Psychology,* which, on just this
point, was subjected to a withering examination at the 1893 meeting of the American Psychological Association. James was nevertheless elected to head the association, and in his presidential address the next year he responded to the criticism of his peers with
typical generosity by admitting that he had "failed" to explain how
complex mental states are possible.[33]

The irony of his failure was that, like the associationists whom he
attacked, James was not consistent in his introspective empiricism.
He criticized associationism because the association of ideas could
not be observed introspectively. No one had ever seen two ideas
fused into one—say, "red" and "sweet" into "plum." All that people know from introspection is that there are thoughts like "plum"
that involve both "red" and "sweet." Introspective empiricism,
James asserted, showed that thought was continuous rather than
atomistic. But no less than the associationists did James lapse into
inference whenever introspection did not support his argument for
continuity, as, for instance, when a clap of thunder interrupts a silence. James said that the notion that a startled reaction to thunder
is due to its discontinuity with the mind's previous thoughts was
based "on a superficial introspective view" and proceeded to argue,
unempirically, against accepting the evidence of consciousness at
face value. People do not hear "thunder *pure,* but thunder-break-
ing-upon-silence-and-contrasting-with-it." Unempirically, James
inferred that "the *feeling* of the thunder is also a feeling of the
silence as just gone." And in order to explain how a present feeling
could include a previous feeling, James added still another inference: in consciousness the past silence flows into and is mixed with

32. William James, "Does Consciousness Exist?" *Essays in Radical Empiricism*
(Cambridge: Harvard University Press, 1976), 4; Peirce, *CP,* VIII, 279.
33. George Stuart Fullerton, "The Psychological Standpoint," *Psychological Review* 1 (March 1894); 124–32; William James, "The Knowing of Things Together," *Psychological Review* 2 (March 1895): 124.

the present thunder: "*In talking of it hereafter, let us call it the stream of thought, of consciousness, or of subjective life.*"[34]

Even James, however, had to admit that in some cases—for instance, sleep—"consciousness is, *for itself*, . . . interrupted and discontinuous." Refusing now, however, to have anything to do with the supposedly empirical evidence of consciousness, he held that these frequent feelings that consciousness is interrupted and discontinuous are "in the mere time-sense of the words." There is, he said, another "sense of continuity, the sense of the parts of a common whole, the consciousness remains sensibly continuous and one. What now is the common whole? The natural name for it is *myself, I,* or *me.*"[35] The continuity of consciousness lay not in an introspected, flowing stream of thought but rather in the feeling of selfhood or personal identity.

The heart of the *Principles*, then, is not the famous chapter "The Stream of Thought" but the subsequent chapter "The Consciousness of Self," in which James was forced to admit the impossibility of basing personal identity on introspective empiricism. The feeling of personal identity is nothing if not an appearance of self-continuity, but by James's time such appearances were frequently challenged. James, a physician as well as a psychologist, was well aware of the whole body of nineteenth-century clinical evidence from treatment of hysteria, amnesia, somnambulance, and other mental disorders, as well as experiments with drugs and hypnosis, which indicated that "*in certain persons, at least, the total possible consciousness may be split into parts which coexist but mutually ignore each other,* and share the objects of knowledge between them. . . . what the upper self knows the under self is ignorant of, and *vice versa.*" He cited, especially, Pierre Janet's hypnotic experiments on "Lucie," whose two selves were capable of receiving contradictory instructions simultaneously. These experiments offered grounds for inferring, as James here did, that consciousness was not a continuous "whole," that it was sometimes "split," that "we thus have, within the bounds of healthy mental life, an approach to an

34. William James, *The Principles of Psychology* (Cambridge: Harvard University Press, 1981), 233–34.
35. Ibid., 232.

alternation of *me's*."[36] In short, consciousness was not a "common whole" whether it appeared so to itself or not.

James therefore admitted in the chapter "The Consciousness of Self" what he had denied in the previous chapter "The Stream of Thought"—the "sense" of selfhood as a "common whole" was an inference or "judgment." The admission enabled him to rise to the more general question of how all judgments of sameness or identity are made—"there is nothing more remarkable in making a judgment of sameness in the first person than in the second or third"— and thus to bring in through the back door the stream of consciousness and his debate with the associationists. Admitting that by making personal identity a mere judgment of the sameness or belonging together of thoughts he was offering an explanation similar to the associationists', he added that they could not explain what fuses formerly discrete ideas in a judgment of sameness. In his account, on the other hand, "the medium is fully assigned . . . in the shape of . . . the real, present onlooking, remembering, 'judging thought' or identifying 'section' of the stream."[37] In other words, one current in the continuous stream of consciousness distinguishes between the other currents and infers, judges, or identifies some of them as belonging with remembered thoughts, thus providing a "sense" of a continuing self.

Aside from the fact that this explanation did not rest on empirical evidence, it hypostatized thought into a substance or entity. James tried unsuccessfully to fend off this consequence in a series of rearguard maneuvers. As he saw, to suppose that each thought appropriates its predecessors would require the thought to exist before its content: "How is this possible unless the Thought have a *substantial* identity with a former owner,—not a mere continuity or a resemblance, as in our account, but a *real unity*?" He answered this possible challenge with a typically homely metaphor: "We can imagine a long succession of herdsmen coming rapidly into possession of the same cattle by transmission of an original title by bequest. May not the 'title' of a collective self be passed from one Thought to another in some analogous way?" But no more than a

36. Ibid., 204, 353.
37. Ibid., 315, 320–21.

cow can a thought take title to itself: "it is itself." If a thought is the appropriator, its appropriations must be to something other than itself: "Its appropriations are therefore . . . to the most intimately felt *part of its present Object, the body, and the central adjustments,* which accompany the act of thinking, in the head."[38] Consciousness, or thought, was no longer a function but an entity, or, rather, a series of appropriating entities rather than a flowing unity.

James's problem was that, like the associationists, he was guided by an unempirical, preconceived notion that thought is a process analogous to sensation and therefore best described in an introspective, perceptual model. There were other possible models, Peirce's notion, for instance, that basic mental processes are inferential with one thought related logically to the next. Surprisingly, James seems either to have forgotten or else never to have understood that Peirce's model of thought as interpretation of signs was based on an argument against the possibility of introspection. After James's death, Josiah Royce reported that "those ideas of Charles Peirce about Interpretation to which I shall here refer, never, so far as I know, attracted William James's personal attention at any time."[39] By 1892, when James revised his two volume *Principles* into a popular, one-volume textbook, he was beginning to doubt, if not the reliability of introspection, at least the distinction between objective and subjective knowledge. But James seems to have thought this insight original on his part rather than Peirce's: "The outer world, but never the inner world has been denied. . . . Yet I must confess that for my part I cannot feel sure of this conclusion."[40]

James wrestled with the questions of selfhood and of relations between thoughts for the rest of his life, with an ever greater willingness to distinguish between "parts"[41] of consciousness. By 1902, when he published *The Varieties of Religious Experience,* he was

38. Ibid., 321–23.
39. Josiah Royce, *The Problem of Christianity,* ed. John E. Smith (Chicago: University of Chicago Press, 1968), 276.
40. William James, *Psychology: Briefer Course* (Cambridge: Harvard University Press, 1984), 400.
41. James, "Knowing of Things Together," 124.

distinguishing between the "field of consciousness" and a "sub-field" which was the self or "me." In fact, James explained religious converts' glorious sense of unification with the One as owing to the bridging of this gap in consciousness between the self and its object. But James went beyond division of consciousness into senses of self and nonself; he spoke now of a "divided self."[42]

Influenced not only by contemporary conversion accounts and clinical evidence but by traditional Christian laments beginning with St. Paul's "What I would, that do I not," James had ceased to identify consciousness with selfhood. James was neither a great scientist nor a great philosopher, but he was great in human sympathy. The consciousness concept had led many to question conversion, but his fellows' conversions led James to question the consciousness concept and its description of thought as experience within a self. He admitted that all people experience contradictory impulses that differ from those of Janet's "Lucie" only in awareness of the contradiction. The question remained, or rather became all the stronger for James, from where do these impulses emerge into consciousness?

Religious considerations, experiments with hypnotism and drugs, and clinical studies like Janet's had begun to convince many turn-of-the-century thinkers of the existence of unconscious mental activity, but they did not do so for James. This was the one point in the *Principles* on which he remained true to his avowed empiricism. Since human beings could not be conscious of what was unconscious, the existence of unconscious mental states could not be verified empirically and was, he said, merely an irresponsible inference, "the sovereign means for believing what one likes in psychology, and of turning what might become a science into a tumbling-ground for whimsies."[43] By the time of *The Varieties of Religious Experience* he was reduced to semantic quibbling: "Unconscious cerebration," James wrote, is "almost certainly a misnomer, [and] is

42. James, *Varieties of Religious Experience*, 385.
43. James, *Principles of Psychology*, 166. Such passages have not been taken into account by those who wish to make James a prophet of "the unconscious." See Robert C. Fuller, *Americans and the Unconscious* (New York: Oxford University Press, 1986), chap. 4.

better replaced by the vaguer term 'subconscious' or 'sub-liminal.' "[44]

James's opposition to unconscious cerebration lay in his well-placed fear that the brain, rather than a soul or self, might thereby become the location of both thought and identity. The danger was clear, for instance, in the work of one of James's graduate students, Edwin D. Starbuck, whose research supplied much of the data for James's *Varieties*. Starbuck also interpreted conversion as a rising into consciousness of processes occurring beneath the "threshold," and he possibly meant to defer to his professor by calling them "subconscious" rather than "unconscious." But all the same, Starbuck wrote that although it cannot be known for certain what passes beneath the threshold of consciousness, "it tends to fill in the chasm in our knowledge, however, to explain it in terms of the nervous system and its functionings." James, on the other hand, continued in the line of Brownson by using "subconscious" to denote thought of which its subject is conscious but not conscious: "in certain subjects at least, there is . . . a set of memories, thoughts, and feelings which are extra-marginal and outside of the primary consciousness altogether but yet must be classed as conscious facts of some sort."[45]

This contradiction, these thoughts of which people were conscious but not conscious, led James finally to repudiate any preexisting self in which consciousness was supposedly contained. In his 1904 essay, "Does Consciousness Exist?" the word "consciousness" was a confusing misnomer, for he questioned only the existence of the occult soul substance, or self, that Edwards had attacked a century and a half earlier: "There is, I mean, no aboriginal stuff or quality of being, contrasted with that of which material objects are made, out of which our thoughts of them are made." Spiritual substance had been posited in order to explain subject–object relations, that is, knowledge. A soul or mind was supposed necessary in order to do the knowing, in order to know the thing known. Soul

44. James, *Varieties of Religious Experience*, 170.
45. Edwin D. Starbuck, *The Psychology of Religion: An Empirical Study of the Growth of Religious Consciousness* (London: W. Scott, 1906), 107; James, *Varieties of Religious Experience*, 161–62, 139.

and mind had often been acknowledged as occult, but their existence seemed supported by the undeniable experience of consciousness. Not so, said James. Consciousness was merely the "logical correlative of 'content' in an Experience of which the peculiarity is . . . *that awareness of content* takes place." Consciousness "is entirely impersonal" and has no implications for the existence of a soul or "self."[46] Subjective "experience" implies that some knowledge is known to be known but not that it is known by a self.

In the absence of a self, what is it that does the knowing? Unlike Edwards, James could not answer "God," for a divine self seemed to James just as occult and unempirical as the human soul. Unlike Peirce, James did not answer that all thought was inference or interpretation rather than experience, for even after abandoning any notion of a perceiving self James conceived of thought as perception. So James decided that thought did the perceiving, decided that "Experience" did the experiencing. The universe was composed of "pure experience."[47] Since people cannot get beyond phenomena, cannot get beyond sharpness, heaviness, or sweetness, or whatever other phenomena they encounter, James decided that those phenomena themselves were the basic realities in the universe. And knowledge, or consciousness, was merely the relation between two phenomena or bits of experience, one known by the other. This way of looking at the universe would solve, James believed, the epistemological issue that had dominated modern philosophy, the question of how a thing can both exist externally and be perceived "in" consciousness, how a thing can be both objective and subjective, how "I" can be in the room while the room is in my mind. The room as a bit of experience contains no duplicity but is merely the intersection of two processes related retrospectively in a new experience—the room-in-relation-to-the-house related to the room-in-relation-to-me.

This was a universe perfectly suited to James's antinomian personality. The multifarious compounding of relations promised immense adventure: "nature is but a name for excess." If consciousness was merely a relation between experiences, it was not merely

---

46. James, "Does Consciousness Exist?" 4–5.
47. Ibid., 4.

God but gods who were possible, as James's resort to the plural form implied when he insisted that it was more likely than not that "superhuman unities of consciousness exist."[48] But while God, or, rather, a god might only be "one of the eaches," there were possibilities of intimacy and warmth far transcending the God-human dichotomy of Christianity. For in the "numerous facts of divided or split human personality which the genius of certain medical men, as Janet, Freud, Prince, Sidis, and others have unearthed . . . I find . . . the strongest suggestions in favor of a superior co-consciousness being possible."[49] Consciousness was only one form of many possible relations between experiences, so without being conscious of it human personalities might possess as intimate a relation with some divine self as the two selves of Janet's "Lucie" did with each other.

But all this failed to answer the question that had troubled James for much of his life, the question of how any relation could be established between two seemingly discrete bits of consciousness or experience, whether between "Lucie's" two selves, between the "room" and "I," or between a past thought and a present one. Janet, Freud, Prince, and Sidis would of course have located "Lucie's" basic identity in her body, especially her brain. James, however, was put off not only by the materialist implications of the medical point of view but also by its implying that a relation between two things requires a third thing to do the relating. Just as he had in the *Principles,* James pointed out in *A Pluralistic Universe* (1909) that the self-compounding of consciousness involved the problem of infinite regress, the problem of how a third term could relate two others without being related to each of them by another set of mediates, and so on *ad infinitum.*[50] Peirce had long since published his solution to this problem in an essay entitled "The Law of Mind," which James considered Peirce's finest contribution to philosophy.[51] Yet James was not good at mathematics, and he

48. William James, *A Pluralistic Universe* (Cambridge: Harvard University Press, 1977), 129, 134.

49. Ibid., 26, 134.

50. Ibid., 37.

51. In "The Continuum," Peirce reports this to have been James's opinion (Peirce, *CP,* VI, 182). For an analysis of "The Law of Mind," see the last section of this chapter.

was apparently impressed only by Peirce's commitment to continuity, not his explanation of it by infinitesimals. Not understanding Peirce's solution, James could find no way to relate thoughts except an infinitely regressive relation of terms or an occult soul. The infinite regression was unacceptable because of its infinity and the occult soul because of its occultness. "Soul," after all, was only a word that did not let one see any "deeper into the fact that a hundred sensations get compounded."[52] Science must be empirical.

It was best, James decided in old age, to *"give up the logic"* that seemed to him to require occult entities. While logic has its proper use, "that use is not to make us theoretically acquainted with the nature of reality." It was best to give up the logical idea that relations between experiences are "internal," the idea that one thought can be remembered by another only if they are both contained in a third. Instead, James said, relations may be "external," may occur by two experiences more or less bumping up against each other. He cited the experiential or commonsense interpretation of his manuscript's being "on" the desk.[53] Gravity or any other theory of physical law was all well and good, but as far as empirical observation goes the relation is external, the manuscript touches the surface of the desk and vice versa, with neither of them participating in the inner structure or meaning of the other. Through sheer intellectual defeat, James had nearly arrived at a conclusion years ahead of its time, for he was on the verge of overcoming what Charles Hartshorne has called the "pre-quantam bias against discreteness."[54]

But if the relations between experiences were external, what was to become of James's long-cherished insistence that introspection reveals thought to be a stream, reveals consciousness to be continuous? One of the advantages of abandoning logic was that he could take at face value what he still considered to be the empirically known experience of continuity in consciousness and not confuse himself "with abstract talk." By insisting on continuity of thought as *"immediately experienced,"* he felt justified, empirically, in

52. James, *Pluralistic Universe*, 95.
53. Ibid., 96, 41.
54. Charles Hartshorne, Review of *Writings of Charles Sanders Peirce*, *Transactions of the Charles S. Peirce Society* 19 (Winter 1983): 64.

clinging to continuity.[55] Yet he frankly admitted that it was impossible, logically, to reconcile continuity with his description of thought as "bits" of experience. The latter view bore a strong resemblance to the atomistic ideas of the associationists, which his emphasis on continuity was supposed to overthrow. But in the absence of a substantial self he needed those "bits" of experience, perceiving each other, in order to remain true to the perceptual model of thought that he had never questioned.

James's abandonment of logic as a basic quality of thought indicates how deeply important he believed empiricism was. Unless continuity could be consciously perceived through "direct perceptual experiences," the only recourse seemed to him to be to the occult entities that his excessively empirical conscience loathed. A thinker could be saved from "artificiality" only by radical empiricism, by taking conscious "experiences at their face value" even if it was illogical to do so.[56]

The Tendency Toward Biologism in the Absence of the Spiritual Self

John Dewey (1859–1952) was born into the liberal Congregationalist milieu in which faith was a conscious perception rather than a holy self-interpretation born of humiliation, and like many other young people of the era he may have had some of Catharine Beecher's problem with the notion of religious "experience." When Dewey was growing up in Burlington, Vermont in the post–Civil War years, his devout, gentle mother wrote out for him his boyhood application for church membership, and a more tentative, less experiential confession of faith could scarcely be imagined: "I think I love Christ and . . . I should like to remember Him at the Communion." His mother may have had a habit of asking if the boy was "right with Jesus," but within the context of liberal Congregationalism such queries were supposed to find ready answers rather than provoke tortured self-interpretation of David Brainerd's sort. Yet the liberals had never given up on the possibil-

---

55. James, "Does Consciousness Exist?" 25.
56. Ibid., 26.

ity that religious "experience" could be dramatic, and as a young teacher in Oil City, Pennsylvania, Dewey had an epiphany. Troubled, as he prayed one night, by the question "whether he really meant business," he received assurance of his oneness with the universe and insisted all his life that he kept the faith that came to him that night.[57]

As a graduate student at Johns Hopkins, Dewey embraced a "psychological standpoint" that, like Jonathan Edwards's, attacked Lockean empiricism by constituting the universe of consciousness contained in a universal self. The crucial influence on Dewey at Hopkins was George Sylvester Morris's version of Hegelian idealism. Morris's complaint against British empiricism, repeated by Dewey in a youthful essay, was that it was not consistently empirical. The British had discovered the psychological standpoint—the insistence that all that people know is experience—and then promptly deserted it. Locke, rejecting Cartesian innate ideas on the basis of the psychological standpoint, had then abandoned that standpoint by assuming that objects exist independently of consciousness, exist as things in themselves. This was unjustified, said Dewey in an argument reminiscent of Edwards's, for "as soon as I imagine an external world, I imagine a consciousness in relation to which it exists." Therefore consciousness "can never have become [begun] at all. That for which all origin and change exists, can never have originated or changed." Human consciousness thus "knows that . . . the universal self never has become."[58] It always was. Metaphysical idealism remained as supportive of traditional theism as it had been in Edwards's time.

The young Dewey found tremendous personal release in these ideas. They reconciled his work as a philosopher with his religious upbringing and justified the involvement in Christian student organizations important to the academic career of a young professor in the 1880s. And while keeping the universal self as safely vague as the God of liberal Christians, Hegelian idealism nevertheless of-

57. George Dykhuizen, *The Life and Mind of John Dewey* (Carbondale: Southern Illinois University Press, 1973), 6–7, 22.

58. John Dewey, "The Psychological Standpoint," *Early Works* (Carbondale: Southern Illinois University Press, 1969), I, 141, 129, 142.

fered much greater intimacy between human and divine consciousness.

Yet so much of the old New England moral individualism remained in Dewey the young Hegelian that he partly abandoned the psychological standpoint and poorly delineated the relations between individual and absolute consciousness. On the one hand, he denied the Lockean identification of mind with consciousness and cited the sheer fact of memory in support of his view that people possess "an indefinite amount of knowledge of which we are not conscious."[59] On the other hand, in his 1887 *Psychology*, he questioned the possibility of "unconscious cerebrations." He admitted that individuals take many actions of which they are not conscious, such as walking while thinking of something else. But Dewey easily dismissed such behavior as non-mental by attributing it to "habit," of which he then offered a purely neural account. Habit was passive association or "unconscious action" within the brain but not within the mind. Mentality involved "active association," or "attention," which in turn was "identical" with consciousness.[60] Despite his criticism of Locke for identifying mind and consciousness, Dewey did the same thing.

The same inconsistent dualism marred Dewey's analysis of the self's activities, which he listed "under the three heads of Knowledge, Will, and Feeling." Instead of hypostatizing these three faculties as his fellow Vermonter, Asa Burton, had done, Dewey took a unified view of the mind that made the faculties merely different ways of regarding the same phenomena. For Burton "taste" was distinct from and superior to the other faculties, a kind of soul within the soul. But for Dewey feeling was merely *"one side of all mental phenomena."* This departure from Burton made no difference from a Hegelian, idealistic viewpoint. But from the viewpoint of physiological psychology, it left no function for a soul or mind. Knowledge was sensation, feeling a neural quality, and will nothing other than *"the body, so far as this is organized so as to be capable of performing certain specific and complex acts."* Dewey

59. John Dewey, *Leibniz's New Essays Concerning the Human Understanding: A Critical Exposition, Early Works*, I, 311.

60. Dewey, *Psychology, Early Works*, II, 104, 103, 117.

quickly tacked on a role for the soul in willing: "the soul through its impulses is already feeling towards an end." But this was to abandon, again, the psychological standpoint; even if people have immediate experience of consciousness, they do not know that it is caused by a soul. As Dewey was to say much later, experience is only experience rather than "immediate knowledge of its cause."[61]

A crucial influence in Dewey's abandonment of this philosophical halfway house was James's 1890 *Principles of Psychology* and especially its argument as to the possibility of the stream of consciousness sustaining itself. Dewey, in fact, believed that James had not been sufficiently thorough and consistent, for whereas he had dispensed with the self as a sustainer or perceiver of thought, he had upheld the need for a self as regards willful conduct. James's lapse, Dewey said, was due to his mistaken notion that the only alternative to a self capable of free will was "theological predeterminism."[62] But there was another alternative—experimental idealism, as Dewey came to call it—in which what is decided *now* is one of the determining elements in the historical process. The future is indeed determined, but determined not eons ago by the ideas of a world soul realizing itself in time and space but by the activity of thought constituting the self here and now. Since the self was not a preexisting "ideal store" attempting to swallow up experience but rather a "specific activity" in the present, it was possible, Dewey believed, to avoid the logical fallacies of traditional arguments for free will while preserving the moral advantage of indeterminism, its emphasis that individual human thought does matter: "Surely the determinist as well as the libertarian may recognize facts of uncertainty, of hesitation, of tentative action, of first trying on this and then that. And it is difficult to see why uncertainty will not do everything in giving zest and sting to life, that James thinks can be given only by sheer liberty."[63]

Considering the self as act resolved the old, troubling ethical

---

61. Ibid., 11, 215, 329, 330; John Dewey, *A Common Faith* (New Haven: Yale University Press, 1934), 37.

62. Dewey, "The Ego as Cause," *Early Works*, IV, 94n; cf. Dewey, "The Theory of Emotion," *Early Works*, IV, 171.

63. Dewey, "Self-Realization as the Moral Ideal," *Early Works*, IV, 43; *idem*, "Ego as Cause," 94n.

problems that had so long dogged New England thought. Dewey saw that moralists like Nathaniel Taylor who based free will on the actions of an occult self might discourage rather than encourage acceptance of responsibility. The "I" that human beings experience is concrete impulse and desire, not an abstract self or occult perceiver of experience. So long as the self was believed to be an occult entity, it would be easy to insist that evil actions had nothing to do with the moral quality of the self but were attributable to circumstance: "it is none of my doing." No such escape from the feeling of moral responsibility would be possible if the self genuinely identified with action: "The deed is . . . what the self, at the time, is," wrote Dewey in a sentence worthy of Edwards. It may be that the person could have done no differently than he did, but that fact has no moral significance so long as the process of determination proceeds *now*, within the person. Despite the necessitarianism of Dewey's system, thought had significance in it because it was included in the process of mediating evil action. A moral person "does not try to escape himself in his deeds; when they are bad, he does not 'lay it off' on circumstances, but stands up to the reckoning, and in the very identification of himself with the evil deed in its consequences gets beyond it."[64]

Just as Christian self-renewal involved a measure of selflessness, so did experimental idealism but with a much clearer political and social thrust. Dewey was about to drop his church membership in 1894 when he wrote that the individual did not need to participate in church ritual or wait on divine assistance for self-renewal when he was "free to enjoy the feeling of his freedom in his common every-day acts." Precisely because the individual was a series of acts rather than a transcendental self, the rise of individual consciousness did not preclude the development of social consciousness. The self was not a distinct entity inevitably isolated from external objects or other people but a by-product of activity in nature. In order to relate nature, individual, and society, it was important that the

64. John Dewey, *The Study of Ethics: A Syllabus, Early Works*, IV, 345, 338, 344.

new psychology be extended into an interpretation of the mind "as a fact developing with reference to its social utilities."[65]

Although Dewey was a rather fierce reviewer of social psychologists such as Frank Lester Ward and James Mark Baldwin, he took heart from their evolutionary perspective on the development of intelligence. Like Peirce, the social psychologists emphasized the resolution of tension within the organism as the primary motive for thought. The organism's attempt to slake desire by brute force must often encounter insurmountable physical obstacles which check its outward action while simultaneously increasing its inner activity and tension, its unrelieved desire. This heightened inner tension causes the organism to attempt to get around the obstacle by a less direct attack, and if this indirect approach works often enough it will become a habit, the habit of intelligence: "Intelligence is thus indirection—checking the natural, direct action, and taking a circuitous course." In the struggle with other organisms for a mate or food, intelligence functions egoistically, but in relation to physical nature intelligence is "objective, impersonal, disinterested." A savage may make a bow and arrow because of a personal desire to kill his enemy. But he will be able to slake his egoistic desire to kill only by focusing objectively on getting the right relation of head to shaft and bow to string: "In this way intelligence gradually, through the mediation of invention, works free from subjection to the demands of personal desire. It sets up its own interest, its own desire, which is comprehension of relations as they are."[66] Fundamentally unselfish, intelligence was, at least potentially, a social consciousness.

Dewey's admiration of selflessness was moderate, not utopian. His flinty realism emerged in his criticism of Ward's belief "that intellectual progress can now cut loose from the conditions under which it originated, namely preferential advantage in the struggle for existence." Ward's socialism was psychologically unrealistic, for in the absence of struggle there would be a lapse of intelligence and

65. John Dewey, "Reconstruction," *Early Works*, IV, 99; *idem*, Review of Lester Frank Ward, *The Psychic Factors of Civilization*, *Early Works*, IV, 210.

66. Dewey, Review of Ward, *Psychic Factors of Civilization*, 207–08.

progress. The purpose of government was not to get rid of struggle but to minimize its waste. This was not socialism but simply the application to society of the method of individual intelligence: "Let society do as the individual does—do what seems best after detailed study of the relevant facts." Yet even this much concerted social action sacrificed some individual interests to progress, a progress from which no individual benefits very much in view of human mortality. The individual must naturally ask why struggle should not be eliminated altogether in order to improve the present at the expense of the future? "This is the psychological basis of socialism. . . . It proposes to put a stop to the suffering which struggle inflicts on individuals; though this implies a brake on progress." Human beings need a measure of selflessness not in order to achieve socialism but in order to reject it: "The sociological function of religion is to cultivate in the individual passive resignation to or even active co-operation in his sacrifice to the good of future generations."[67]

As with James, Dewey's basic model of thinking remained experiential, a model that made it difficult to explain how, in the absence of a perceiving self or at least a biological self, one thought could be related to another in an act of intelligence. Unlike Peirce, Dewey was not even an "uncritical" transcendentalist. He did not ask what in the nature of the universe made truth possible but was content to assert that the success of thought in dealing with the world proved that there was no boundary between mind and matter: "experience is *of* as well as *in* nature. . . . Things interacting in certain ways are experience."[68] Although Dewey remained emotionally committed to idealism, his failure to address the question of relations at the metaphysical level caused him, often, to employ biological expressions. So too did Peirce, but in his metaphysics he treated biological processes as logical relations involving semiosis or thought. In Dewey's writings, however, biological naturalism seemed the last word.

Dewey had tacitly identified thought and neurological activity in his 1896 "Reflex Arc" essay. By 1903 he was ready to assert that

67. Ibid., 210, 208, 211.
68. John Dewey, *Experience and Nature* (New York: Norton, 1929), 4a.

"it is biology which enforces the idea that sensation . . . is a characteristic function of reconstruction in experience," the concept around which he later organized, after the First World War, his *Reconstruction in Philosophy* (1920): "Experience carries principles of connection and organization within itself. These principles are none the worse because they are vital and practical rather than epistemological. . . . Even an amoeba must have some continuity in time in its activity, and some adaptation to its environment in space."[69]

Far more than Peirce, Dewey narrowed the meaning of "knowledge" by his radical insistence that knowledge was merely an unexpected result of the organism's active relation to its environment: "As a *conscious* element, a sensation marks an interruption in a course of action previously entered upon." A passive organism could not have useful experience, Dewey held, because nothing that happened to it would suggest different behavior. No passage better suggests Dewey's belief that the purpose of thought is to modify future behavior than the following: "Suppose fire encroaches upon a man when he is asleep. Part of his body is burned away. The burn does not perceptibly result from what he has done. There is nothing which in any instructive way can be named experience."[70] Because the sleeper was passive, his being burned taught him no way to avoid being burned, no way to act better in the future, and therefore his pain and anguish were not "instructive." But there was a strange self-contradiction in Dewey's argument. By suggesting the possibility of an entirely passive, uninstructive experience, Dewey showed that he had not entirely escaped the dualism he ostensibly opposed. Was it really possible for the burned sleeper to separate his pain from all of his past action and draw no conclusion for better action in the future? Might he not wish that he had slept elsewhere and consequently nap in different circumstances next time?

A recent, superbly spirited defense of progressive liberalism and social democracy has reminded us that Dewey and thinkers like

---

69. John Dewey, *Studies in Logical Theory* (Chicago: University of Chicago Press, 1903), 58; *idem, Reconstruction in Philosophy* (New York: Henry Holt, 1920), 90–91.
70. Dewey, *Reconstruction in Philosophy*, 87–88, 86.

him promised no absolute knowledge, no certain victory, but only new experiences, new sensory disturbances that would require more thought. The promise of uncertainty has certainly been fulfilled. Liberalism has proved to be a way of going forward but a messy way, as messy as Dewey's conception of life itself. But it does not follow that it is a "naive view that the source of the problems plaguing the welfare state can be traced to the inadequacy of the ideas that inspired it rather than the particular historical forces—economic, political, and social as well as intellectual—that shaped it. . . . Intellectuals may help to make changes possible by articulating different visions of society, but between idea and reality there falls much more than a shadow."[71] Instrumentalism may not have promised certainty, but it promised much more than a "vision." It was supposed to be a method of thinking that dealt with the actuality of "historical forces." Liberalism has hardly failed the test, but it has not been an A student either. Its record can only make us wish that there was, in addition to unexpected sensation or "experience," some other logic to guide thought.

The Spiritual Self Constituted in the Continuity of Thought

Isolated and alone, the greatest philosopher of the era, who had early denied that there was such a thing as immediate experience of consciousness, sought a true *via media*. Charles Peirce, unlike James, did not subscribe to a perceptualism that would force him back toward atomistic ideas. Unlike Dewey, he would not constitute the continuity of experience in the activity of a biological organism whose strife with its environment was its only reason and guide for thinking. Peirce's desire to make ideas clear had led him to "look to the upshot of our concepts," a line of thought which became misinterpreted as a suggestion that the beginning and the end of thought is action: "If it be admitted, on the contrary, that action wants an end, and that that end must be something of a general description, then the spirit of the [pragmatic] maxim . . .

71. James T. Kloppenberg, *Uncertain Victory: Social Democracy and Progressivism in European and American Thought, 1870–1920* (New York: Oxford University Press, 1986), 353.

would direct us towards something different from practical facts, namely, to general ideas as the true interpreters of our thought. . . . so that the meaning of the concept does not lie in any individual reactions at all."[72] But how, in a universe devoid of a substantial self or preexisting mind, and without recourse to Dewey's naturalism, could a particular thought be related to another in a "general idea"?

For several years after the 1877–78 *Popular Science Monthly* series Peirce was preoccupied with teaching at Johns Hopkins, with recriminations against the university following its dismissal of him, and with scientific work at the Coast Survey. Then, in 1887, he inherited some money and retired to Milford, Pennsylvania, a resort town on the Delaware River. There he spent and speculated himself into an impoverished old age and returned with great intellectual vigor to metaphysics. Unlike Dewey, Peirce would not recur to the biological organism to answer the question how the continuity of thought was constituted. Unlike James, he was too deeply in love with logic to think illogically about the question. He had to find an answer, and the result of his search was the most sophisticated and comprehensive metaphysics to take cognizance of the state of scientific knowledge at the end of the nineteenth century.

Peirce took heart from the breakdown of the mechanical view of the universe that, in the late nineteenth century, led some, like Henry Adams, to despair of order and to conclude that nothing existed save chaos in which "mind could gain nothing by flight or by fight; it must merge in its supersensual multiverse, or succumb to it." But Adams's despair depended on a view of mind as properly separate from nature, a view that Peirce had long since abandoned. To him, the breakdown of the mechanical view merely confirmed his long held belief that the universe was basically mental rather than material. Peirce was persuaded of the mechanical view's inaccuracy not only by his knowledge of mental philosophy and physics but also by nature's appearance of enormous variation and by "the great fact of growth, of evolution."[73] The degree of variation in the

---

72. Peirce, "A Definition of Pragmatic and Pragmatism," *CP,* V, 2.

73. Henry Adams, *The Education of Henry Adams,* ed. Ernest Samuels (Boston: Houghton Mifflin, 1973), 461; Peirce, "Science and Immortality," *CP,* VI, 554.

natural world could not have originated, Peirce asserted, out of uniformity and law. It must have been the other way round; the small quantity of uniformity and law that existed by the end of the nineteenth century must have evolved, by chance, out of chaos. If evolution produced a chancy universe, evolution was chancy and irregular—qualities consistent not with mechanics and matter but with thought and spirit. Therefore the evolution of regularity in the universe can be conceived of as analogous to the process by which the mind learns to behave regularly, the process of habit formation.

It might be objected that if the regularity of mechanical law cannot comprise the imprecision of mind, neither can mind comprise matter. But while mechanical law operates with at least near invariability, it does so in a universe that cannot be precisely measured. Drawing on the pioneering geometry of the Czech mathematician G. F. B. Riemann, who had boldly posited the curvature of space and helped prepare the way for Einstein, Peirce pointed out that the sum of the angles of a triangle inscribed in curved space rather than a flat plane could not be exactly 180 degrees, as had been taught since Euclid, but must be either a little more or a little less, depending on whether human beings view space in its convex or concave aspect. Similarly, Peirce returned to infinitesimals to show as he had in earlier writings that it is impossible to specify a precise beginning for any continuous entity such as a line. It was evident, therefore, "that we can have no reason to think that every phenomenon in all its minutest details is precisely determined." The immense variety of the universe, the variety even of apparently lawful motion, "must be attributed to spontaneity in some form." Although it was not possible that a law or habit produced spontaneity, the reverse was plausible: "The one intelligible theory of the universe is that of objective idealism, that matter is effete mind, inveterate habits becoming physical laws." The regular, lawful universe is a "crystallized" habit evolved according to "The Law of Mind," which is logic.[74]

A habit is a general conception that guides the process of

---

74. Peirce, "The Architecture of Theories," *CP*, VI, 30, 25, 33; *idem*, "Law of Mind," 102.

thought. Peirce of course rejected in old age, just as he did in youth, the notion that formal logic was a literal duplication of human cognition let alone of the process by which the universe evolved.[75] But he also insisted that the science of logic was the study of relations among signs and that physiological psychology was therefore not the only or even the best key to logic.[76] For if the universe was thought, signs might just as well be mechanical as organic relations. Peirce pointed to calculating machines as an example and said that if it were denied that such machines could think, "in like manner, a man may be regarded as a machine which turns out . . . a conclusion." In other words, if machines cannot reason, neither can people, who, as Hobbes had said, are evidently not spiritual beings but machines. Conversely, if people can reason, so can machines. A steam engine, at every stroke of its piston, works out "its problem in thermodynamics."[77] In 1886 Peirce drew the world's first known design for an "electric switching circuit machine for performing logical and mathematical operations," that is, a computer.[78]

But the parallelism between Hobbes and Peirce was only superficial, for Peirce believed people to be spiritual beings and fundamentally different from machines. The difference, however, lay not in people's ability to reason, which machines can also do, but in the material quality—feeling or consciousness—that constitutes the man sign. Whereas from the point of view of logic it makes no difference whether a conclusion is evolved by the sign system of a machine or a brain, from the point of view of metaphysics, it can only be feelings that create machines and never vice versa. Machines are effete mind or thinking so routinized that, as in the case of the steam engine's repetitive solving of its problem in thermodynamics, there is virtually no creativity, no spontaneity in it. Only feelings could evolve new general signs through a process of habit formation: "Feelings, by being excited, become more easily ex-

75. Peirce, "Grounds of Validity of the Laws of Logic," *CP,* V, 329.
76. Peirce, "Pragmatism: The Normative Sciences," *CP,* V, 28.
77. Peirce, "Critical Analysis of Logic," *CP,* II, 59, 58.
78. Quoted in Max Fisch, *Peirce, Semeiotic, and Pragmatism: Essays by Max Fisch,* ed. Kenneth Laine Ketner and Christian J. W. Kloesel (Bloomington: Indiana University Press, 1986), 425.

cited, especially in the ways in which they have previously been excited." Suppose that "in the beginning" (a continuous process of course rather than a point in time) there was "a chaos of unpersonalized feeling . . . sporting here and there in pure arbitrariness." Then chance repetition "would have started the germ of a generalizing tendency."[79] Thus evolution—habit formation—would have begun to develop regularities and laws amid the chaos.

But how, in the absence of either a physiological or spiritual self to contain them, did two feelings come into repetitious contact with each other in order to form a habit? Believing that a feeling is a continuum in time, Peirce also believed that there is no boundary between a present and past feeling. A past feeling does not influence the present feeling but rather is contained to some degree in the present feeling. At first inspection such a supposition seems preposterous. If present consciousness includes a feeling from a moment ago, that momentarily past feeling must include its predecessor and so on back to infinity so that a present feeling would have to include every feeling since the beginning of time. But the material quality of consciousness half a second ago cannot be present now, and the same goes for a quarter second ago, an eighth of a second ago, or any finite measure of past time, no matter how short. Since the quality of consciousness at any *finite* interval of time in the past, no matter how short, is irretrievably gone, consciousness must span continuous, *infinitesimal* intervals of time. For the purpose of illustration, we may picture the unpicturable (see fig. 3). The third interval contains some of the first, and so would a fourth and a fifth so that however long thought proceeds, "the last moment will contain objectively the whole series."[80]

The first interval in the figure contains some part of the second, so any present, infinitesimal interval of time contains the future as well as the past. A future feeling affects and is affected by the present feeling: "In fact, this is habit, by virtue of which an idea is brought up into present consciousness by a bond that had already been established between it and another idea while it was still *in futuro*." Of course the present does not contain all the future in the

79. Peirce, "The Architecture of Theories," 21, 33.
80. Peirce, "Law of Mind," 111.

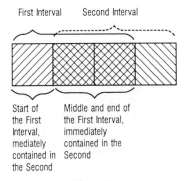

Figure 3

sense that it contains all the past, for the unconscious coordination of the present thought with one among many possible future thoughts is partly a matter of chance or spontaneity. Yet whatever future thought is coordinated with the present, that thought will be a "logical predicate" of the present thought. As thoughts spread in space as well as time, they weaken in intensity and "power of affecting others, but gain generality and become welded with other ideas."[81] Evolution is therefore governed by a "Law of Mind," namely, that thoughts "spread continuously" and stand to other thoughts "in a particular relation of affectibility," which is the logic of sign relations but which Peirce also beautifully denominated "evolutionary love."[82]

Relation of thoughts, Peirce held, amounted to the development of personality, a notion which shows how greatly Peirce differed from both Edwards and Dewey. Edwards's system was subjective in that a person—God—creates thoughts. Dewey's system was subjective in that organisms, including human beings, think or, better, feel their way toward adaptive behavior. Peirce's system was objective in that feelings—thoughts—create persons. Personality, like any other thought, cannot be grasped in an instant or by introspection. In his youth Peirce had brilliantly said that "the word or sign which man uses is the man himself,"[83] and in his maturity he

81. Ibid., 141, 142, 133, 104.
82. Peirce, "Evolutionary Love," *CP,* VI, 287.
83. Peirce, "Some Consequences of Four Incapacities," 314.

added that "every general idea has the unified living feeling of a person." Group spirit, nationalism, and Christian fellowship "are no mere metaphors. None of us can fully realize what the minds of corporations are, any more than one of my brain cells can know what the whole brain is thinking. But the law of mind clearly points to the existence of such personalities."[84] Individual human personality is incorporated not only within present groups but also within groups across time. Or in language more reminiscent of religious tradition, personality is taken up by and contained in the future: "a genuine evolutionary philosophy . . . is so far from being antagonistic to the idea of a personal creator that it is really inseparable from that idea."[85]

Peirce's view that all thoughts—feelings—are external (constitutive *of* rather than constituted *by* a self or general idea) and inferred from signs thus supported the New England religious tradition of emphasizing the difficulty of self-knowledge. Personal character, said Peirce, "is already determinative of acts in the future to an extent to which it is not now conscious." This statement, however, was merely in apparent agreement with Calvinist determinism, for Peirce's was a "developmental teleology." Personality contains a teleological element only because it is a thought, and present thoughts are to some extent affected by future thoughts. But the "mere carrying out of predetermined purposes is mechanical . . . and hostile to all hopes of personal relations to God."[86] The present also affects the future so that Peirce was able to support, more basically even than Dewey, the coexistence of freedom and determinism. Peirce did not spell out but surely understood the crucial, pantheistic implication of this view, which was that the divine self is created in the same thought process that creates human selves.

This "synechism," as Peirce called it, meant that all people are, all of the time, in personal communication with God, which raises the question why they are not all conscious that they have such a relationship with him? Having abandoned the consciousness con-

84. Peirce, "Man's Glassy Essence," *CP*, VI, 270, 271; cf. Francis Ellingwood Abbott, *The Way Out of Agnosticism* (Boston, 1890), 70.
85. Peirce, "Law of Mind," 157.
86. Ibid., 156–57.

cept, Peirce could answer in the tradition not only of pragmatism but of Puritan humility. Those facts that "stand before our eyes and stare us in the face are far from being, in all cases, the ones most easily discerned."[87] No more than human selves is the divine self capable of introspective consciousness or able to obtain self-knowledge any other way than through an interpretive act. God is an idea that must be *made* clear.

Peirce's notion that neither God nor human beings are transcendental selves has exerted little influence in the modern world. The consciousness concept has remained intact to a degree, for thought is still usually described as the creation rather than the creator of the self. But Peirce's description of thought as interpretation did help make it possible for psychologists loyal to the self to distinguish between two kinds of thought, which they labeled "conscious" and "unconscious." Peirce thus inadvertently helped create a middle path between, on the one hand, the insistence in the consciousness concept that all thought is immediate experience and, on the other hand, radical proponents of the self sign like Hall who had been driven to the conclusion that unconsciousness should be humanity's normative ideal.

87. Ibid., 162.

✳

CHAPTER EIGHT

The Self Sign:
Prince, Royce, Putnam

"Conscious" and "Unconscious" Redefined

Two physicians and a philosopher of the Absolute worked out the modern compromise whereby the self retains a tenuous upper hand over thought. Under the terms of this compromise thought is viewed, if not always as immediately known experience within the self, at least as an action by the self. If the self has thereby lost the privileged inner life it was once accorded by the consciousness concept, the self has at least retained its transcendental and even spiritual superiority to thought. The self found its practical defenders in physicians, who, situated at the critical juncture where speculative hypotheses must satisfy the needs of suffering human beings, would probably not have liked, had they known of it, Peirce's view that the self was a sign. And knowing of James's progress toward his final notion that while there is such a thing as experience there is no self to contain it, physicians distanced themselves from his conclusions as well. It was interesting for philosophic pluralists to suggest that selfhood was a relation of thoughts, but a patient suffering from dissociation wanted as firm a self as possible and might have seen, albeit wrongly, a contradiction between mental health and new concepts of the self. Siding with patients, physicians insisted that every person is a transcendental self.

Morton Prince's theory of multiple personality was an initial, unsuccessful defense of the consciousness concept. Attempting to develop a materialist perspective like Holmes's while avoiding Hall's preference for unconsciousness, Prince asserted that consciousness was the actuality of brain activity. This scheme enabled Prince to argue that there was no such thing as unconscious thought. All thought was conscious. If a patient seemed to suffer

234

from unknown thoughts, those thoughts were not unconscious but were known to a second, dissociated self or personality within the patient. But Prince's solution was purely semantic. From the point of view of a patient who thought of himself or herself as a single human being, Prince actually offered not multiple personalities but a divided self. John Owen King has described a three-century transformation in self-interpretation: "Puritan authors described symptoms of melancholy that they read as signs of salvation," as signs of rejected temptation. "By the end of the nineteenth century the meaning attached to such obsessional ideation had precisely reversed: a horrid thought indicated that one might become morally insane," indicated a self divided between sick thoughts and a healthy but not necessarily permanent abhorrence of those thoughts.[1] Worse, Prince's proposed cure—obliteration of unwanted personalities—amounted in practice to lopping off part of the patient.

The alternative to Prince's argument for the consciousness of all thought was to accept, as Josiah Royce did, Peirce's description of all thought as external, as an inferential process of sign interpretation rather than immediate experience of ideas within the human self. But unlike Peirce, Royce did not so much reject as greatly modify the consciousness concept. Royce still believed that all thought was immediately experienced, if not within the human self, within the Absolute Self, or God. And even as regards human beings Royce salvaged a vestige of the consciousness concept that Peirce had discarded by viewing thought, if not as immediate experience within the self, at least as action by the self.

Above all, Royce continued to allow for a distinction between two different kinds of thought, which he labeled "conscious" and "unconscious," though he used these terms in senses that would have been unrecognizable to seventeenth-century adherents of the consciousness concept. "Conscious" thought, rather than being immediate experience within the self, was simply thought that the self had already retrospectively discovered in a further act of

1. John Owen King, *The Iron of Melancholy: Structures of Spiritual Conversion in America from the Puritan Conscience to Victorian Neurosis* (Middletown, Conn.: Wesleyan University Press, 1983), 10.

thought or interpretation. "Unconscious" thought, on the other hand, was an action by the self that the self had not yet discovered.

This view of thought as interpretation or inference rather than experience was never understood by Freud or most psychoanalysts since. Influenced more deeply than they know by now rather antique aspects of the consciousness concept, psychoanalysts usually conceive of both conscious and unconscious thought as experience within a self. So conventional has become the phrase "unconscious thought" that most of those who use it are oblivious to the fact that it contradicts their notion of thought as experience. But it was only because there was available an alternative notion of thought as inference or interpretation that Freudianism won its most important early adherent in America. Having already abandoned the traditional notion of thought as experience, James Jackson Putnam differed from other proponents of the self such as Hall and Prince in that he found no semantic inconsistency in a distinction between "conscious" and "unconscious" thought.

It was not Freud's notion of the unconscious that attracted Putnam but rather Freud's seeming to be a more or less traditional defender of the self and of consciousness. Indeed, by New England standards Freud was so traditional, even so simplistic, in his notion of the self as a subject of experience that Putnam could accept psychoanalysis only by grafting on to it Royce's description of thought as inferential interpretation of signs. That done, Putnam could view Freud as offering patients the possibility of conscious control over unconscious thoughts. The self's division was a division not of substance but of activity, a division between conscious and unconscious thought. Some degree of unification and health could be achieved by making the unconscious conscious, by extending the dominion of consciousness. This description of human beings as interiorly divided was in some respects a retreat to faculty psychology but with crucial differences, including a great deal more room for conscious activism by the self.

Whereas the concept of consciousness was so largely modified that it would have been unrecognizable to John Locke, neither did faculty psychology survive unscathed. For in the practical realm of therapy, consciousness became one of the modern faculties and also defined, negatively, the other modern faculty—unconscious mentality. Unlike most psychologists of his time and indeed many scholars since, Charles Peirce had the acuteness to recognize and approve the survival of faculties in modern psychology. He objected to the concept of consciousness and its doctrine of a unitary self when he attacked "the old psychology which identified the soul with the ego, declared its absolute simplicity, and held that its faculties were mere names for logical divisons of human activity. This was all unadulterated fancy. . . . The observation of facts has now taught us that the ego is a mere wave in the soul [which] . . . may contain several personalities . . . , and that the faculties, while not exactly definable and not absolutely fixed, are as real as the different convolutions of the cortex."[2] Peirce's view was reflected in the physicians' new functional therapy that eventually divided the self into conscious and unconscious functions. But the consciousness concept had emphasized the unity of the soul's thoughts as well as the unity of the soul. If the consciousness concept was defeated on the unity of the soul, it was victorious on the unity of thought. Modern, functional psychology does not include the ancient division of labor whereby the understanding of a thought is an action distinct from willing or nilling it. Whether a thought is conscious or unconscious, it is believed, as James insisted, to be simultaneously understood and felt or, as Dewey said, understood because it is felt.

Both Prince's and Putnam's careers offer a caveat against what has become the standard interpretation of the coming of psychoanalysis to the United States—a move from a "somatic" to a "functional" style of therapy.[3] "Somatic" to "functional" to "somatic" would be an exaggeration, but it would get one thing straight—the commitment of early New England psychotherapists to a bodily constitution of the self. Prince's willingness to engage in functional therapy was based not on a rejection of the soma's importance but

---

2. Charles Sanders Peirce, "Lessons from the History of Science," *Collected Papers of Charles Sanders Peirce* (hereafter *CP*), Vols. I–VI ed. Charles Hartshorne and Paul Weiss; Vols. VII–VIII ed. Arthur Burks (Cambridge: Harvard University Press, 1931–1958), I, 112. All citations to Peirce's *Collected Papers* are to numbered paragraphs rather than pages.

3. Nathan Hale, *Freud and the Americans: The Beginnings of Psychoanalysis in the United States* (New York: Oxford University Press, 1971), chaps. 4 and 5.

in his confidence that to treat consciousness was to treat directly the operations of the brain. Putnam went even farther in his somatic bias. Rather than limiting brain operations to conscious states as Prince had done, Putnam believed the brain could think even when there was no mental phenomenon, no awareness of thought. "Somatic to functional" is true enough so long as it is remembered that the early psychotherapists were able to make the transition precisely because they never lost confidence that "body" and "mind" were two names for the same thing.

Whereas Prince described described his monism as "material-ism," Putnam called himself an "idealist"—a difference that re-flected Putnam's basically spiritual approach to the problem of consciousness. Influenced by Royce, Putnam was willing to allow the body to think unconsciously because the body in turn could be ideally constituted in the mind of the Absolute. This spiritual sub-strate for the bodily person was crucial to a transitional figure like Putnam who mediated between older, religious concerns and new secular therapies.

Although popular self lore has, since Putnam's day, surrendered any specifically religious concerns, faith in a partly unconscious "self" meets one of the needs of modernists that "soul" met for earlier times: "Self" provides grounds for the continuity of life in this world if not the next by providing a presumedly unitary subject for diverse experiences over time. But because modern secular psy-chology tacitly assumes an organic, bodily basis for the self, mod-ernists conceive of the problem of identity as a subjective and emo-tional rather than ontological question. The fashionable rhetoric of the "fragmented self" expresses only an "alienation" of one part of the self from another part, an alienation among parts of the self, as it were, rather than any question as to the existence of the self in some basically unified form. In the popular phrase, we must get "in touch with our selves" so as not to flounder helplessly and un-happily over the question of what the self really wants. Our self-preoccupied age views as a basic statement of the problem of iden-tity what many nineteenth-century theologians, philosophers, and physicians, considered its solution—conflict within the self.

Multiple Personality Theory as a Device for Preserving the
Consciousness Concept

Morton Prince (1854–1929) was the most prominent member, both socially and professionally, of the "Boston School" of psychotherapy. Descended from Puritans who had fled Laud, Prince was a crusader in his profession and in civic affairs. In recognition of his progressive activism in working for utilities regulation and a new city charter, he was once offered the mayoral nomination of the Boston Good Government Association. His father had been mayor of the city as well as the unsuccessful gubernatorial candidate of the gold Democrats in 1896. The same combination of social activism and intellectual conservatism that characterized his father's politics carried Prince to the top of the medical establishment but left him unprepared for the psychoanalysts' heterodoxies. A graduate of Harvard College, where he helped found the Football Club, he went on to Harvard Medical School, where he gave special attention to the physiological basis of thought. Almost from the beginning of his practice in the early 1880s he specialized in nervous illness. Eventually he taught neurology at Harvard, then Tufts, and he became president of the American Neurological Association.[4] Prince lived the comfortable life of the Brahmin establishment, and a bit of smugness mars his many writings. Nevertheless, he was kind and intellectually active, though not sufficiently acute to prevent the consciousness concept from isolating him from new schools and directions in psychotherapy.

When Prince began to practice medicine, the treatment for nervous illness was governed by what Nathan Hale has aptly called the "somatic style" of S. Weir Mitchell, a Philadelphia physician.[5] Prince's mother was both a nervous invalid and a member of a prominent Philadelphia family, which may explain why Prince seems early in his career to have been in personal contact with Mitchell, who, like Prince, would become a contemptuous oppo-

---

4. Merrill Moore, "Morton Prince," *The Journal of Nervous and Mental Disease* (June 1938): 701–16.
5. Hale, *Freud and the Americans*, 47.

nent of what he once described as Freud's "filth."[6] Mitchell owed his specialty in neurology to the Civil War and the numerous gunshot wounds and other injuries it inflicted on the nerve tissues of combatants. Having directed a hospital for soldiers suffering from nervous disorders, he carried his expertise into postwar civilian practice, where the nervously ill turned out principally to be women. Meanwhile, the psychiatric hospitals established in the antebellum era fell on hard times. They had practiced a "moral" treatment based on the patient's self-examination—a clinical application of the confidence in self-knowledge born of the consciousness concept. But these hospitals' claims to high cure rates were shown to rest on misleading record-keeping techniques.[7] Pessimism about moral therapy presented an opportunity for a somatic approach such as Mitchell had developed out of his Civil War experiences, so by the 1880s he was famous for his somewhat inappropriately named "rest cure." Mitchell did prescribe rest but only in support of his primary therapy, which was to "make" fat and blood, the deficiency of which, he believed, accounted for weak nerves.[8]

Yet just as the moral style had left room for somatic therapy by suggesting that the mind could derange the brain, so the somatic style in turn contained the seeds of its own destruction by functional psychotherapy. The theories of George M. Beard, another famous neurologist who early influenced Prince, were a case in point. In 1868 Beard, a New Yorker, created the term "neurasthenia" (from Greek roots for "nerve," "privative," and "strength") for what he considered to be the want of "nerve force," or, more clearly, exhaustion of nerves. Completely confident that the illness was physiological, Beard believed that it could be manifested in any function of the nervous system, and he listed more than a hundred symptoms, ranging from "excessive gaping" to "exhaustion

6. S. Weir Mitchell, quoted in C. P. Oberndorf, *A History of Psychoanalysis in America* (New York: Grune and Stratton, 1953), 52.

7. Gerald Grob, *The State and the Mentally Ill: A History of Worcester State Hospital in Massachusetts* (Chapel Hill: University of North Carolina Press, 1966), 231–32; Albert Deutsch, *The Mentally Ill in America: A History of Their Care and Treatment from Colonial Times* (New York: Columbia University Press, 1949), 155–57.

8. S. Weir Mitchell, *Fat and Blood: And How to Make Them* (Philadelphia: Lippincott, 1877), 25.

after defecation." But despite his commitment to a physiological basis for neurasthenia, Beard described its cause functionally; the advancement of civilization excited and exhausted the nerves. Small wonder, then, that neurasthenia was originally peculiar to the United States, for that nation had made the most rapid advances in "steam-power, the periodical press, the telegraph, the sciences, and the mental activity of women." If neurologists believed that neurasthenia had a somatic etiology, they offered a preventive measure that was functional; Mitchell, in a famous address to Radcliffe women, urged them to think less.[9] From such functional prophylaxis it was only a short step to psychotherapy.

Among American neurologists, Prince made one of the first and most rapid transitions from the somatic style to a psychological therapy for nervous illness because of his commitment to the concept of consciousness. Although he was a physician, Prince was also an amateur moral philosopher. His medical school thesis on *The Nature of Mind and Human Automatism* bore a strong resemblance to the determinism of Holmes Senior but went far more deeply into the metaphysical issues, including the concept of spiritual substance, which Prince opposed. But while his position was materialistic, it was also so thoroughly monistic that he believed that "the spiritualist will probably find little herein to disconcert him." Indeed one would have thought not, since by the second chapter Prince declared that *"there is one substance, mind."*[10] The important part of his thinking was not his ostensible materialism but his monism, which let him remain loyal to the notion of consciousness as experience within a self.

Consciousness, said Prince, was neither opposed to matter nor collateral with it but, rather, "the essence of physical change in cerebral protoplasm." Accepting Descartes's notion that every change in the mind is accompanied by molecular change in the brain, Prince nevertheless rejected the Cartesian view that brain states run

9. George M. Beard, "Neurasthenia, or Nervous Exhaustion," *Boston Medical and Surgical Journal* (April 29, 1869): 217; *idem,* Beard, *American Nervousness: Its Causes and Consequences* (New York, 1881), 7–8, vi; Silas Weir Mitchell, *Address to the Students of Radcliffe College* (Cambridge, Mass., 1896), 13.

10. Morton Prince, *The Nature of Mind and Human Automatism* (Philadelphia: Lippincott, 1885), 7, 29.

parallel to mental events. Neither did he argue, as many had begun to do, that brain states cause mental events. Rather, he held that mental events *are* changes in brain states. His argument did not oppose but rather rested on the impassable gap between sensory perception of an object's qualities and knowledge of the thing-in-itself. Just as redness and roundness are, in Lockean theory, ideal representations rather than the apple's real substance, so too would molecular changes in the brain, if viewed objectively by another person, be understood to be mere representations of the actuality of thought. If human senses were fine enough to perceive the molecular changes in another person's brain, the sense of sight would perceive those changes as undulations; hearing as noise, and so on. But those perceptions would no more be of the substance of the brain than redness is the substance of the apple. Therefore nothing in a materialist approach prevented the subjective experience of thought or consciousness from being viewed as the thing-in-itself of the brain's molecular activity: "*A feeling is NOT accompanied by a molecular change in the same brain; it is 'the reality itself of that change.'* "[11]

Prince believed that his monism, as opposed to psycho-physical parallelism, strengthened traditional moral views, especially confidence in conscious willing as a determinant of behavior. If consciousness was not perception by a supernatural soul but rather the actuality of the brain's physiological activity, then the "evidence of our own consciousness" for free will and self-determination was as conclusive as earlier moralists had thought. Metaphysical dualism mistakenly made mental events "collateral" rather than essential to bodily actions. Dualism thus led "to the denial of the truth of that conviction possessed by each one of us, that our feelings have something to do with the production of our actions." But the free will established by Prince's monism was the free will of the body, not of any agent or soul existing apart from the body and able to overrule its desires. Being a natural process, volition was also, in Prince's view, utterly mechanical and "determined by the strongest motive," which was why he called his system "human automatism." Nevertheless, his system showed "that matter is not what it is sup-

11. Ibid., 55, 66.

posed to be by the vulgar and ignorant" and "elevated" matter "to a higher rank." If consciousness was the actuality of the brain's activity, "consciousness is just as much the cause of the 'working of the body' as these molecular disturbances."[12]

This monistic view of thought and matter helped inspire Prince's eventual confidence that in using psychological methods of treatment he was not ignoring material reality but rather dealing directly with the actuality of the brain's workings. The same may have been true of many other contemporary neurologists, including Freud, Charcot, Bernheim, Janet, and Breuer, all of whom were in the vanguard of physicians moving toward functional treatment of nervous illness. Freud's commitment, for example, to a "material substrate"[13] of consciousness allowed him to commit himself from the beginning of his career to, in Peter Amacher's words, "a therapy that involved mental phenomena."[14] Like these others, Prince, confident that the subjective experience of consciousness was the actuality of the brain's physiological action, was in advance of many of his fellow neurologists in his willingness to view nervous illness as psychological in origin.

Prince displayed his functional and psychological approach in his attitude toward one of the most publicized nervous disorders of the late nineteenth century, "railway spine." Railroad accidents then attracted much the sort of public interest and newspaper coverage that airplane disasters do today and for about the same reasons. Hundreds of private citizens traveling at what in living memory would once have been unthinkable speeds, were subjected to killing and crippling derailings, collisions, and bridge collapses. Railroads, as some of the largest corporations of their time, made inviting targets for large damage claims and lawsuits, which required expert testimony by physicians. Thus sprang into being a new illness, railway spine, by which was meant "hysteria" suddenly following an accident and manifested in neuralgia, tremors, narrowing of the field of vision, ataxia, and so on. There were two

12. Ibid., 132, 26, 141, 151, 155, 108.
13. Freud, quoted in Peter Amacher, *Freud's Neurological Education and Its Influence on Psychoanalytic Theory* (New York: International Universities Press, 1965), 59.
14. Amacher, *Freud's Neurological Education*, 56.

different theories of the etiology and prognosis of railway spine. One school maintained that the illness was entirely somatic, that it originated in a lesion in the central nervous system (hence the name "railway spine"), and was permanently disabling. Prince subscribed to the other school, which was led by the great French neurologist J.-M. Charcot and which held that the illness was merely functional and tended toward recovery.[15] This division of opinion within the medical profession was uncomfortably public owing to physicians' appearances in court as expert witnesses on opposing sides in damage suits. Functionalists like Prince offered a more optimistic prognosis and were favored by railroads attempting to limit damage awards. The controversy played an important role in leading not only Americans like Prince but also some European neurologists, including Freud and Ernest Jones, toward less somatic emphasis in their approach to hysteria.[16]

Believing that railroad spine was functional, Prince consequently concluded that it contained a "mental factor"[17] and that by "association"[18] it might persist after any somatic lesion was healed. He cited statistics showing that a smaller percentage of railway workers than of passengers suffered traumatic neuroses following accidents. The reason, he believed, was that the public approached rail travel with greater fear than the workers so that the accident itself found them predisposed toward terror and psychical shock. Physical trauma was less likely to produce mental trauma in persons with a positive attitude at the moment of the event, as was the case, Prince thought, with football players and military person-

15. Morton Prince, "The Present Method of Giving Expert Testimony in Medico-Legal Cases," *Boston Medical and Surgical Journal* (January 16, 1890): 76–77.

16. Frank Sulloway, *Freud, Biologist of the Mind: Beyond the Psychoanalytic Legend* (New York: Basic Books, 1979), 37–39; Ernest Jones, *Free Associations: Memories of a Psycho-Analyst* (London: Hogarth, 1959), 157.

17. Prince's remark was reported as part of the discussion following Philip Coombs Knapp's paper, "Nervous Affections Following Injury; 'Concussion of Spine.' 'Railway Spine.' 'Railway Brain.'" *Boston Medical and Surgical Journal* (August 9, 1888): 134.

18. Morton Prince, "A Study of the Pathology of Hysterical Joint Affections, Neurasthenia and Allied Forms of Neuro-Mimesis." This paper was written many years before its publication in Prince's collection entitled *Clinical and Experimental Studies in Personality* (Cambridge, Mass.: Sci-Art Publishers, 1929), 66. In the context of Prince's materialism, "association" did not imply a relation of ideas in the soul but habit formation in the brain.

nel.[19] On the other hand, once psychological trauma had occurred as the result of a physical shock, Prince thought it likely that further harm could result from merely psychological causes, such as participating in a court case for damages.[20]

In the same early years of his medical career, when Prince was thinking of railway spine as at least partly psychological in etiology, he was becoming interested in hypnosis. Well acquainted with European and especially French medicine because his mother had been treated for nervous illness by Charcot in Paris,[21] Prince kept abreast of the uses of hypnosis by Charcot, A. A. Liebault, Hippolyte Bernheim, and especially Pierre Janet. Like Prince, Janet was committed to a notion of consciousness as the actuality of brain activity,[22] yet employed functional therapy and associationist terminology. He argued that hysteria was a reaction to trauma, with the hysteric's consciousness narrowed and dominated by a few obsessions. The rest of the thoughts that had previously populated the hysteric's consciousness became centered in another personality that possessed its own individual consciousness even though it inhabited the same brain.[23]

Janet's theories enjoyed great cachet because of his clinical success. One occasional symptom of hysteria had long puzzled neurologists—anesthesia or lack of sensation, especially of pain. In a famous case Janet had used hypnotism to treat an anesthetic hysteric—"Lucie"—and had found a second personality, which he designated "Adrienne." When Lucie was anesthetic, Adrienne received her sensations.[24] Anesthetic hysterics, it turned out, were not genuinely anesthetic but merely possessed a second self that

19. Morton Prince, "Accident Neuroses and Foot-Ball Playing," *Boston Medical and Surgical Journal* (April 28, 1898): 393.

20. Morton Prince, "Remarks on the Probable Effect of Expert Testimony in Prolonging Traumatic Neuroses," *Boston Medical and Surgical Journal* (April 30, 1896): 433–34.

21. Moore, "Morton Prince," 707.

22. Henry F. Ellenberger, *The Discovery of the Unconscious: The History and Evolution of Dynamic Psychiatry* (New York: Basic Books, 1970), 358.

23. Pierre Janet, *The Mental State of Hystericals: A Study of Mental Stigmata and Mental Accidents*, trans. C. R. Corsan (New York: Putnam's, 1901), passim but especially 484–528.

24. Ibid., 256.

received the sensations. Using hypnotic suggestion, Janet rid Lucie of Adrienne, or, rather, united the two selves into one.

Prince responded enthusiastically to the Europeans' reports of success with hypnosis and used it to treat Clara Fowler, some of whose experiences were described at the beginning of this book. In 1906 Prince told the tale of Clara's seven years of therapy in a big, popular book, *The Dissociation of a Personality,* that made hers the most famous case of multiple personality in America.[25] To understand why Clara Fowler was discussed in popular magazines and made the subject of a Broadway play—*The Case of Becky* (1913)— one must know something of Prince's still fairly gripping book, which had the ingredients of a popular thriller—acute detective work, surprise twists of plot, and an unjust death sentence narrowly averted when the true criminal admits guilt and kills herself.

Using hypnosis, Prince discovered two other personalities besides "Clara," who was a neurasthenic college student, self-critical, serious, and bookish along the lines of the New England stereotype. "Sally," the second personality, longed to travel unchaperoned with male companions and was responsible for the drinking and smoking that embarrassed the prim Clara. Sally herself named the third placidly conventional personality, "The Idiot." Prince, following the lead of William James,[26] cautioned that the first personality observed in order of time was not necessarily the true one. He considered using hypnosis to obliterate Clara in favor of the Idiot, who evidently came closest to his ideal of womanhood. Poor Clara, "whom we had protected and cared for, must no longer be allowed to live. . . . Every friendly association must be broken as through physical death." But Clara was saved at the last minute by Sally, who suggested to Prince that when Clara was hypnotized she was subsumed within the personality of the Idiot. Although Prince admired Sally's liveliness, he now decided that she was the unwanted demon and persuaded her to commit mental "suicide." He

25. William James's "Ansel Bourne," discussed in *The Principles of Psychology* (Cambridge: Harvard University Press, 1981), was a close second. See Michael G. Kenny, *The Passion of Ansel Bourne: Multiple Personality in American Culture* (Washington, D.C.: Smithsonian Institution Press, 1986), chaps. 2 and 4 for accounts of the Bourne and Fowler cases.

26. James, *Principles of Psychology,* 363.

then united Clara and the Idiot into one conscious personality by
telling the hypnotic state in which they were joined "*to awaken
with all her memories.*" Prince believed he had effected a cure by
finding Clara's "Real" self.[27]

Under cover of his intentionally melodramatic narrative, Prince
preached to his popular audience a theory of multiple personality
disorder that was deeply informed by the consciousness concept's
traditional notion of thought as experience within a self and only
one self. James and many other psychologists held that none of the
many possible selves that might be formed from "the mass of consciousness" was more real or normal than the others. Disagreeing,
Prince argued that "the psychological point of view is too limited.
What test have we of adaptation?" Anguished patients, at odds
with their circumstances, could not afford the broad tolerance of
philosophers. To a patient and her physician, symptoms of dissociation were signs of "a sick self. Common experience shows that, phi-
losophize as you will, there is an empirical self which may be designated the real normal self."[28]

It has been suggested that Clara manipulated Prince,[29] but he in
turn channeled her behavior within the confines of the concept of
consciousness as he communicated it to her. Although one cannot
but be suspicious of the alacrity with which "Sally" confessed when
Prince was on the verge of doing in Clara, the latter seems readily to
have accepted Prince's dismissal of her religious conversion as the
result of a trance accidentally induced by staring too fixedly at a
brass lamp in church.[30] In the hands of an earlier counselor, say
Thomas Shepard, such an event might have been made the central
moment of her life. But instead she accepted Prince's view that her
religious conversion had nothing to do with her, that her feeling of
great change and new health in church was a mere physiological
residue of her unconscious, hypnotic state. Interpreted either way,
the change would not have proved permanent, but Shepard would

27. Morton Prince, *The Dissociation of a Personality: A Biographical Study in Abnormal Psychology* (London: Longmans, Green, 1906), 240–41, 499, 516, 524.
28. Ibid., 233.
29. Otto Marx, "Morton Prince and *The Dissociation of a Personality*," *Journal of
the History of the Behavioral Sciences* (April 1970): 126.
30. Prince, *Dissociation of a Personality*, 348.

have interpreted subsequent backsliding and accusing conscience as evidence not only of the continuation of sin in her heart but also of divine favor. In Prince's view, however, any subsequent lapse into old ways after her cure had nothing to do with her true self.[31]

Prince's book had scarcely made its popular splash before his theory of dissociation was challenged by the arrival in this country of the Freudian theory of repression and unconscious thought. Although Prince would become a lifelong opponent of the notion of a sexual etiology for the neuroses, he invited to Boston the first Freudian analyst to visit the city—Ernest Jones, who had begun to practice psychoanalysis in England in 1906. For attempting to discuss sexual topics with a child patient in London, Jones had been more or less banished to a psychiatric post at the University of Toronto. Detesting that city's provincialism, he reached out in correspondence to American psychotherapists including Prince. In December 1908 Jones visited Boston and spoke to a small group of psychotherapists and psychologists at Prince's luxurious Beacon Street home.[32] But Jones's relations with Prince deteriorated as respect for psychoanalysis increased.

Freud's influence in New England grew rapidly after September of 1909 when the Viennese analyst lectured successfully at Clark University in Worcester at the invitation of a fellow believer in biologism, G. Stanley Hall. Summarizing the whole range of his theory as he had developed it by then, Freud laced his lectures with homely illustrations and delivered them in a modest tone calculated to appeal to a learned New England audience. Crediting Josef Breuer with the creation of psychoanalysis, Freud presented himself as a mere reporter and developer of his colleague's great discoveries. Invoking scientific conscience, he compared those who refused to try his method to a histologist who refused to use a microscope. Defending his emphasis on sex, he credited a Clark psychologist, Sanford Bell, with discovering infantile sexuality and added the disclaimer that "I didn't arrange the whole affair. But

31. Although Sally subsequently returned at least once and "implied a persistent existence as a subconsciousness," Prince still insisted that she was dead (ibid., 524).

32. Hale, *Freud and the Americans*, 205; Jones, *Free Associations*, 187.

the fact remains. . . ."[33] Shrewdly assuaging cultural and ethical fears, Freud assured his audience that forbidden and repressed impulses lose their power on being brought to consciousness.

It is difficult now to appreciate how revolutionary the notion of repression seemed to turn-of-the-century thinkers like Prince, accustomed to conceiving of thought as immediately known experience within a self. In order to repress an unwanted thought, the self must not only be able to think the thought without knowing it but must still know enough of its unpleasantness to repress it. There was a great deal less difficulty in Prince's theory of multiple personality than in Freud's theory of the unconscious. In the opening salvo of Prince's counterattack, his 1910 essay "The Mechanism and Interpretation of Dreams," Prince paid tribute to Freud's "brilliant stroke of genius" in recognizing that dreams were "orderly determined phenomena, capable of logical interpretation." But he challenged the notion that dreams symbolized repressed or unconscious thought. Prince, an agnostic, compared dreaming to the "hallucinatory symbolism" in religious conversions which betrayed no evidence, he thought, of resistance or disguise: "it is preposterous logic to assume that the hallucinatory words, 'Saul, Saul, why persecutest thou me?' were a disguisement of the true thought and intended not to be understood by Saul."[34]

Jones, outraged, sprang to Freud's defense and easily poked holes in Prince's argument. Since Prince himself engaged in symbolic interpretation of dreams, his therapeutic practice, contrary to his avowed theory, suggested the presence of "thoughts not accessible to introspection." As for religious epiphanies, since even Prince called them hallucinatory, they were evidence that, contrary to Prince, people are unaware of the "true state of their own mental processes."[35]

33. These words, reported in Ernest Jones, *The Life and Work of Sigmund Freud* (New York: Basic Books, 1955), II, 213, were omitted from the printed version of the lectures. See Sigmund Freud, *Five Lectures on Psycho-Analysis*, trans. James Strachey (New York: Norton, 1977), 42–43.

34. Morton Prince, "The Mechanism and Interpretation of Dreams," *Journal of Abnormal Psychology* (October–November 1910): 158–59, 186.

35. Ernest Jones, "Remarks on Dr. Morton Prince's Article: 'The Mechanism and Interpretation of Dreams,' " *Journal of Abnormal Psychology* (February–March 1911): 334.

Jones and Freud himself soon became contemptuous of Prince and moved efficiently to isolate him. They organized the American Psychoanalytic Association, which succeeded, against Prince's protests, in monopolizing the term "psychoanalysis" for Freudianism and in claiming the high ground of science for their views.

Prince's case against unconscious thought rested on the same introspection, the same supposedly empirical evidence of consciousness, that had been employed in New England for more than a century: "I do not find that my conscious activity appeals to 'anything else' but my own conscious processes."[36] Because he considered thought to be known experience within the self, the "conception of an idea continuing to exist as such without being a state of consciousness" was as literally "unthinkable" to him as it had been to Jonathan Edwards. Ideas "out of mind," ideas not consciously experienced within the self, "do not exist as ideas at all."[37] Influenced by philosophical approaches to consciousness since the time of his medical school thesis on *Human Automatism*, Prince insisted that all mentality was conscious.[38] His early use of the word "subconscious" is as misleading as William James's use of the same word. To Prince the prefix "sub" did not signify thought beneath the threshold of consciousness but a *sub*ordinate self with its own fully conscious thought processes. Eventually, he dropped "subconscious" in favor of "co-conscious" because the latter term suggested multiple personalities, an interpretation consistent with his traditional view that all thought must be consciously experienced within a self. If a thought was not experienced within one's self, one evidently had a second, dissociated self that experienced the

36. Prince, "Some Problems of Abnormal Psychology," a paper written in 1904 but first printed in his *Clinical and Experimental Studies in Personality*, 291.

37. Morton Prince, "The Unconscious: A. Dormant Consciousness (Physiological Residua). B. Physiological Memories," *Journal of Abnormal Psychology* (October–November 1908): 261.

38. Even today, a leading philosopher tells us, "no other part of the culture . . . [but] *only* philosophers remain perplexed about how one can have unconscious motives and desires." Richard Rorty, *Philosophy and the Mirror of Nature* (Princeton, N.J.: Princeton University Press, 1979), 123; cf. Paul Ricoeur, *Freud and Philosophy: An Essay on Interpretation*, trans. Denis Savage (New Haven: Yale University Press, 1970), 358–374.

thought, for "the only alternative explanation [unconscious thought] is more difficult of credence."[39]

In an answer to Prince that Freud called the first "clever word" about the "unconscious," the British psychologist Bernard Hart challenged Prince's empiricism. Hart admitted that the "unconscious," as employed in Freudian theory, "cannot even be conceived as having a phenomenal existence." But Hart was not willing to dispense with a concept just because it was a phenomenal impossibility, just because it could be known only in signs rather than empirically. Even though human beings cannot imagine such things as unconscious ideas and complexes, "if we ascribe certain properties to these entities, and assume them to act according to certain laws—then we shall find that the results thus deduced will coincide with the phenomena which occur in actual human experience. This train of thought is the analogue of that underlying all the great conceptual constructions of physical science—the atomic theory, the wave theory of light, the law of gravity, and the modern theory of mendelian heredity." The essential method of science is neither semantic consistency nor raw empiricism but rather "the construction of a conceptual model which will enable us to resume our experience."[40]

It is possible to sympathize with Prince's response that whereas science might depend on concepts, the Freudians treated concepts like facts,[41] but his was the weaker argument, as he eventually admitted. After the First World War had brought Prince respite from warfare with psychoanalysts, he finally gave up the identification of consciousness and selfhood. During the war he recovered his sense of self-importance by contributing *The Psychology of the Kaiser* (1915) to the Allies' propaganda effort, and he also brought some of his old work on railway spine to bear on the problem of shell shock. Confident in 1929, the year of his death, that "the Freudian

39. Prince, Preface to B.C.A., "My Life as a Dissociated Personality," *Clinical and Experimental Studies in Personality*, 23.

40. Freud, quoted in Jones, *The Life and Work of Sigmund Freud*, II, 64; Bernard Hart, "The Conception of the Unconscious," *Journal of Abnormal Psychology* (February–March 1910): 366.

41. Prince, "Mechanism and Interpretation of Dreams," 351.

tide is slowly receding," Prince could acknowledge that some of his early work was chiefly of historical interest, an example of "how far we have traveled in reaching our modern conceptions . . . of the subconscious as a part of the mind, . . . not split-off and dissociated."[42] He insisted, though, that "we have no mental conflicts between our opposing desires and impulses which we cannot satisfactorily adjust or control" and that therefore human beings were unified selves.[43] But the discrediting by the Freudians of the notion that human beings enjoy complete knowledge of their thoughts had made Prince's original views untenable. Consciousness was evidently not the actuality of brain activity if some of that activity was unconscious. If conservative adherents of the self were to continue to constitute the self in the body, must they also surrender all hope of preserving a role for conscious thought and revert to the biologism of Hall and Freud?

Thought an Action by but Not in the Self

Josiah Royce (1855–1916) mediated between pragmatism and psychotherapy by combining a philosophically old-fashioned adherence to the self with an interest in Peirce's symbolic logic. Born and raised in a remote California mining town and having done his undergraduate work at Berkeley when the young university had no philosophy department, Royce owed much of his now underestimated importance and influence to William James, who may have seen an affinity between Royce's philosophic zeal, on the one hand, and that of Henry James, Senior, on the other. As William James embarked on his empirical, pragmatic philosophy that largely rejected his father's spiritual teachings, he may have found it comforting to shepherd a young absolutist who argued that human consciousness would be impossible in the absence of a higher self. Charmed when the callow Californian first visited Cambridge in 1875, James was also a part-time instructor at Johns Hopkins in 1877–78 when Royce wrote his doctoral thesis, which took as its governing question, "What kind of a mode of consciousness is that

42. Prince, *Clinical and Experimental Studies in Personality,* ix, 285–86.
43. Morton Prince, *Psychotherapy and Multiple Personality: Selected Essays,* ed. Nathan G. Hale, Jr. (Cambridge: Harvard University Press, 1975), 210.

which we call knowledge?" Royce answered that knowledge is existence and that the existence of human error showed that knowledge is relative: "Individual consciousness is but a shadow; what is
permanent is the World."[44]

The "World" of Royce's dissertation evolved into the "Absolute
Self" in an 1883 series of Lowell lectures at Harvard that became
The Religious Aspect of Philosophy (1885). After four years of
teaching English at Berkeley, Royce had seized the opportunity
James offered him of serving as the latter's sabbatical replacement
at Harvard in 1882–83. Rough mannered but intelligent and ener-
getic, the young instructor so impressed Harvard believers with
what they believed to be an original argument for the existence of
God that his appointment was eventually made permanent. In his
doctoral thesis Royce had inferred the relativity of knowledge from
the existence of error, and in his Lowell Lectures he extended the
inference into an argument for the existence of an Absolute Self.
Although this emphasis on error gave a surface originality to
Royce's argument for the Absolute, he was relying on the same infinite regress implied by a relation of thoughts that already be-
devilled his pluralistic opponents like William James. Recognition
of an error about an object implies recognition of the truth about
an object: "But two judgments cannot have the same object save as
they are both present to one thought. . . . Only as present to an
including thought are they either true or false. Thus then we are
driven to assume an infinite thought, judging truth and error."
This infinitely inclusive thought was an Absolute Self, not a "mere
aggregate of truths" but a "rational unity" self-consciously known
"as forming in their wholeness one single thought."[45]

Soon after publication of *The Religious Aspect of Philosophy*,
Royce suffered a collapse that, after his recovery, led him to criticize
somatic theories of nervous illness and to insist that neurasthenic
suffering had a positive, ethical aspect. Beyond vague suggestions
of suicidal impulses, few details of Royce's illness are now known,
but he initially accepted a somatic, neurological explanation of it:

44. Josiah Royce, "Of the Interdependence of the Principles of Knowledge"
(Ph.D. diss., Johns Hopkins University, 1878), 1, 152.

45. Josiah Royce, *The Religious Aspect of Philosophy* (Boston: Houghton Mifflin,
1885), 425.

"The break-down is nervous of course," he wrote to Daniel Coit Gilman, "and needs nothing, I am assured, but a long sea voyage" to rest his exhausted nerves. During that voyage he described one of his symptoms, in a letter to William James, as "a certain (not exactly 'fearful') looking-for of judgment and fiery indignation," a sense of damnation, as it were, that he would in time defend as psychologically useful. Royce seems to have attributed his later, famous emphases on loyalty and community at least partly to his illness. In his essay "The Case of John Bunyan" he argued that the great poet's spiritual crisis had taught him "to forsake henceforth his solitude, to join himself 'unto the people of God.'" Preaching to his fellow men was as therapeutic to Bunyan as was Royce's loquaciousness—a trial to all who knew him—and immense labors in philosophy: "The motor speech-functions, whose inhibition had led to such disastrously rebellious insistent habits, were never again suffered to remain without absorbing and productive exercise."[46]

Royce presented his paper on Bunyan to the American Psychological Association in 1893 in order to challenge the notion that "mental processes of a morbid type" indicate a strictly somatic illness, a mere "'degeneracy' of constitution." Rather, the "symptomatic value" of a sufferer's thoughts lay in their "*relation*" to the patient's "organized mental life." Doubt was one thing in relation to the mind of a nineteenth-century agnostic and quite another in relation to the mind of a seventeenth-century Puritan, for whom it could lead to despair. Such was Bunyan's case, but his conviction of doom also "led the way over to recovery." Out of complete hopelessness was born his interpretation of his own soul as untemptable, so that he could interpret further temptations as coming from the devil and not reflecting upon his own moral quality. The recognition that further evil was alien to his soul depended on a feeling of total guilt, but it also provided a rest from guilt. In principle, therefore, Bunyan's spiritual treatment and cure did not differ greatly from the associationist-dissociationist orientation of Janet's and Prince's therapy of suggestion and substitution: "A better device than this for the 'segmentation' of insistent questionings could

46. Josiah Royce, *The Letters of Josiah Royce,* ed. John Clendenning (Chicago: University of Chicago Press, 1970), 211, 215; Josiah Royce, "The Case of John Bunyan," *Studies in Good and Evil* (New York: D. Appleton, 1898), 73.

not have been imagined by any physician learned in the cure of souls." But as opposed to Prince's attempt to obliterate the unwanted thoughts, Bunyan's spiritual cure was continous and ethically enriching. It taught him to "watch and be sober," to be "objective in his whole attitude towards life." Like other Puritan converts, Bunyan could draw comfort from subsequent trials by interpreting them as signs of regeneration: "His deeper consciousness is beset but never overwhelmed."[47]

Royce's doctrine of a "deeper" or Absolute Self made it easy for him to accept the notion of unconscious thought. For an individual human being to be influenced by a thought of which he was not conscious did not imply, in Royce's scheme, any violation of the consciousness concept. Even though the thought was unconscious in the individual, it was conscious in the Absolute Self. In *The Spirit of Modern Philosophy* (1892) Royce said that absolute idealism revealed the "deeper self" to be "*the self that knows in unity all thought.*" Thanks to the Absolute Self's containment of all thought, Royce was in one respect a much more thorough pragmatist than James, who never abandoned the notion of thought as immediately, empirically known, if not by a self, then at least by another "bit" of thought. On this question Royce came much closer to the spirit of Peirce by denying to human beings (but not to the Absolute) the possibility of introspection or intuitive consciousness: "The inner life . . . is an outer life." Rejecting the notion of "consciousness as . . . an inner affair," Royce held that the human self finds itself not through privileged or immediate access to its own thoughts but "only in so far as I am known and reflected upon by my subsequent life. . . . And if you talk of one's secret heart, what is it but just that inner brooding . . . which . . . illustrates . . . the very impossibility of knowing myself except by looking back on my past self."[48]

But if positing an Absolute Self resolved the problem of the relation of human thoughts, it left open the question of how thought was related in the Absolute, which Royce had after all described as an infinite relation of thoughts. Did not the infinite regress im-

47. Royce, "Case of John Bunyan," 31, 61–62, 67–69, 72–73.

48. Josiah Royce, *The Spirit of Modern Philosophy* (Boston: Houghton Mifflin, 1892), 374, 208.

plied by the relation of thought render self-contradictory the notion that a self could either create thought or be created by it, so that the self, whether human or Absolute, was only an appearance rather than a reality? This was the position of F. H. Bradley, whose *Appearance and Reality* (1893) was one of Royce's principal targets in *The World and the Individual* (1899).

Royce believed that he found a way to defend the self in 1898 when he heard Peirce's lecture in Cambridge entitled "Reasoning and the Logic of Things." Greatly impressed, Royce would become the first prominent philosopher to call public attention, not merely to Peirce's pragmatism as James had done, but to the logical and semiotic writings that were Peirce's main achievement in philosophy. In Royce's view, Peirce's notion of thought as a logical, inferential process of sign interpretation made it possible for the mind to achieve a positive conception of infinity and thus to vindicate "the concept of the actual Infinite against the charge of self-contradiction. I am minded, also, to attempt the closely related task of defending the concept of the Self against a like charge." Royce's strategy was to show that an infinite, self-inclusive process did not have to be conceived negatively as a process without end. Rather, infinity could be conceived positively as a process whose every step required an additional step. Such, for example, would be the process of a mapmaker charged with making, on part of the surface of England, a perfectly accurate map of England. The map, to be perfectly accurate, would have to include a representation of the map, and the representation, if perfectly accurate, would include a representation of itself, and so on: "We should see, namely, why the one purpose, *if* it could be carried out, would involve the endless series of maps." Royce therefore did not "accept the view that to be self-representative is, as such, to be self-contradictory," for a positive concept of such a process was possible.[49]

Although Royce may have scored a hit on the notion of the self as self-contradictory, he did not explain how the infinite process of self-representation progressed in thought, did not explain how one thought was related to the next. At about the time that Royce was

49. Josiah Royce, *The World and the Individual* (New York: Macmillan, 1899), I, 476, 506, 542.

writing *The World and the Individual* Peirce was embarking on his
late metaphysics, aimed at showing that a universe of pure thought
or feeling could evolve selves. Royce, however, seems at this time to
have believed that the map of England and the numerous other
examples that he offered of self-representative systems established
the primacy of the self: "I hold that any world of self-representative
Being must be of such nature as to partake of the constitution of a
Self, either because it is a Self, or because it is dependent for its
form upon the Self whose work or image it is." Peirce's criticism of
The World and the Individual was vague, both in the letter of qualified praise he sent to Royce and in his franker comment to James
that Royce's logic was "execrable."[50] But he may have had in mind
among other possible criticisms the fact that Royce, initially conceiving of the Absolute as a *creation* of infinite thought, had defended the conception by depicting the Absolute as a *creator* of
thought. Royce saw the problem more clearly in *The Problem of
Christianity* (1913): the Beloved Community "cannot win the love
of the lost soul who is to be saved, unless it already consists of those
who have been saved by their love of it. One moves thus in a
circle."[51]

Like many previous defenders of the self, Royce tried to convert
the weak spots in his philosophy into evidence for the symbolic
truth of the doctrine of new birth: "Only some miracle of grace (as
it would seem) can initiate the new life, either in the individuals
who are to love communities, or in the communities that are to be
worthy of their love." Royce's philosophy of loyalty, like the Christian doctrine of salvation, taught the necessity of the "utter transformation of the primal core of the social self." Royce asserted that
this philosophizing of regeneration did not render Christianity
"mere morality, any more than it is a mere mysticism."[52]

No historical understanding can be gained by debating or judging the question whether Royce's system was "genuinely" religious, but it was not, as it has been called, a recovery of "the Puritans' sense of this psychomachy," a return like that of "Hooker,

50. Ibid., I, 542; Peirce, *CP,* VIII, 217.
51. Josiah Royce, *The Problem of Christianity,* ed. John E. Smith (Chicago: University of Chicago Press, 1968), 130.
52. Ibid., 130, 194, 220.

Shepard, the Mathers, and Edwards . . . to Paul and the psychology of the irrational he found therein."[53] Royce differed not only from a neurologist like Prince but also from Puritans like Shepard and Hooker in the ethical significance he attached to personal crises of self-interpretation. For Royce was still hemmed in to a significant degree by the consciousness concept. As a philosopher of the Absolute, he was able to go farther than Prince in acknowledging the possibility of unconscious thought, but even unconscious thought was, for Royce, thought by a self. What was other for the Puritans was not other for Royce but lay within. Puritans recognized an element of self in the conversion process, but the new self-interpretation they sought included an interpretation of the old self as dead. The new self-interpretation Royce sought was not the Puritan interpretation of the self destroyed but the modern interpretation of the self possessed, of the unconscious brought to consciousness.

To view Royce as rebelling in the spirit of the Puritans against "a theologically liberal and Progressive America" that reduced spiritual crises to "an unfortunate episode of the mind breaking down" is to miss not only the nature of the change in self-interpretation from the seventeenth through the nineteenth centuries but also a principal cause of that change. The Puritans' emphasis on conscience had helped propel the focus on the inner life that produced the seventeenth-century consciousness concept, and theologians were crucial discussants and shapers of changes in self-interpretation down almost to the end of the nineteenth century. It may be true that the Puritans' notion of temptation from without was "far more comforting" to sufferers than the modern view that "neurosis was part of their self."[54] But religious theorists, beginning with the Puritans, had helped bring on the change, which was produced at least in part by the logic of the consciousness concept that they had helped create and nourish. For the notion of the seventeenth-century consciousness concept that all thought was immediate, privileged experience created by and in the self had made it increasingly

53. King, *Iron of Melancholy*, 235, 251.
54. Ibid., 220, 225.

difficult to view feelings of temptation as the work of an other. By the end of the nineteenth century the only alternative to including neuroses and psychoses in the self was the equally heterodox solution of the proponents of the thought sign, who proposed to do away altogether with the transcendental self or soul. Royce followed in the line of earlier thinkers who attempted to preserve the transcendental self against originally unforeseen consequences of the consciousness concept by modifying rather than, as Peirce did, entirely rejecting the concept.

Royce played a crucial role in mediating between advocates of the self sign and advocates of the thought sign, especially Peirce. Unlike G. Stanley Hall, Royce would not limit the self to an organic body. Unlike Morton Prince, Royce was not so hamstrung by the consciousness concept as to insist that all thought is known in and by a self and that therefore unconscious thought implied multiple selves, implied that a thought unknown by one self must be known by another. Earlier advocates of the self had allowed for a self that was not entirely self-conscious, but it was from an advocate of the thought sign that Royce learned most thoroughly that "there is no royal road to self-knowledge. Charles Peirce . . . maintained (quite rightly, I think) that there is no direct intuition or perception of the self." Since the self is not self-conscious, it can be known only by "inference" or interpretation of signs. But unlike Peirce, Royce never extended this insight into an attack on a preexistent or transcendental self. He called the self a sign, but he never went so far as to assert that thought could somehow have existed apart from and prior to its organization into a self. The interpretive methodology invented by Peirce, a doubter of the self's pre-existence, was interpreted by Royce as "the will to be self-possessed," the will of the self to make conscious what was unconscious.[55] Consciousness might be symbolic interpretation rather than immediate experience within a self, but it was still an action by the self, an indication that the individual human being still possessed a measure of spiritual autonomy and superiority to his or her thoughts.

55. Royce, *Problem of Christianity*, 285, 308.

Psychoanalytic Theory Interpreted as a Defense of the Conscious Self

James Jackson Putnam (1846–1918) never doubted the existence of the transcendental self in some basically unified form, but thanks in part to the influence of Royce, who was his patient as well as his philosophic guide, Putnam became willing to allow a symbolic basis for unconscious thought. A son and grandson of prominent physicians, Putnam became in his turn a leader in medicine. Eight years older than Prince, Putnam proceeded earlier along a similar success track, through Harvard College, the Medical School, European study, and eventually a professorship in neurology at Harvard. He participated energetically in the somatic style of nineteenth-century therapy for nervous illness and only in the 1890s, a decade later than Prince, did Putnam go over to a functional, psychological orientation. Raised a reasonable Unitarian, Putnam did not initially share the monism that had made Prince willing to assume that in using psychological treatment he was dealing directly with brain matter. Yet when Putnam went over to psychotherapy, he was, thanks in part to Royce, much less reluctant than Prince to modify the concept of consciousness.

One stimulus that seems to have helped drive Putnam toward psychotherapy was the popular and practical success of the "mind cure" movement in its "new thought" and Christian Science variants. Gail Thain Parker has described the way in which mind cure stepped into the void left by the optimistic sunbeams of the mainstream churches and offered badly needed help to troubled spirits. Like many other scholars, however, she derides the curists' mental philosophy as old-fashioned because it depended on the traditional faculties.[56] But modern views of the mind—whether Freudian analysis or Peircean semiotics—do nothing if not divide mental functions into something like traditional faculties. If Parker is right in her claim that the mind curists helped prepare the American people to accept Freud,[57] it was because they helped break down

---

56. Gail Thain Parker, *Mind Cure in New England: From the Civil War to World War I* (Hanover, N.H.: University Press of New England, 1973), 164–65.
57. Ibid., 4, 146–49.

the concept of consciousness as total self-knowledge. The curists' psychological theory at least allowed that human beings may have trouble understanding themselves, and troubled souls often obtained more solace from the curists than from liberal clergy espousing self-control or from physicians practicing the somatic style.

As a defensive measure against the curists, a few members of the clerical and medical professions—including Putnam and Prince—combined forces for a time in the Emmanuel Movement, which was doomed to failure by its proposed division of labor. Physicians were supposed to restrict themselves to physiological problems and, for "simply functional" treatment, pass the sufferer "on into the Rector's study."[58] But by the early twentieth century Boston physicians like Prince and Putnam had long been moving toward a functional, psychotherapeutic approach themselves. Indeed, Putnam thought that the psychology of suggestion might explain the success of the mind curists, for if the patient one day found himself or herself better, whether owing to the curist or not, he or she might attribute the improvement to the curist's treatment: "The seeds of hopefulness and confidence which are thus implanted so regulate the subconscious forces of the mind that the gain becomes steady and progressive."[59]

Still another important influence that helped move Putnam away from spinal and nerve fatigue theories of neurasthenia was William James's 1890 *Principles of Psychology*. Putnam's training at the Harvard Medical School had overlapped with James's, and the two men had become lifelong friends. Putnam drew on and expanded James's stream metaphor when he informed neurologists that the mind was "a deep and swiftly flowing river," whereas "personal or habitual consciousness" was "an eddy beneath the bank, which forever seeks to change its shape and draw in water from without, yet never wholly loses its identity." Putnam exploited James's view that attention and will are the same thing. The neur-

58. Lyman Powell, *The Emmanuel Movement in a New England Town: A Systematic Account of Experiment and Reflections Designed to Determine the Proper Relationship between the Minister and the Doctor in the Light of Modern Needs* (New York: Putnam's, 1909), 7, 12.

59. James Jackson Putnam, "Remarks on the Psychical Treatment of Neurasthenia," *Boston Medical and Surgical Journal* (May 23, 1895): 511.

asthenic felt weak, lacking in will, and without self-control because his "consciousness is no longer permitted to focus itself exclusively upon the main object of his attention, but unrelated ideas and emotions intrude themselves." Initially attentive to an object, the neurasthenic felt weak willed and unable to follow up because of a lapse of attention. The vast river of the mind swept away the eddy of personal consciousness so that one idea succeeded another with no apparent relation to its predecessor and without regard to the neurasthenic's effort to attend to a consistent line of thought. The result was a loss of identity: "The patient is a puzzle to himself and his struggles often seem to carry him deeper into the mire."[60]

The principal therapy Putnam could offer in the 1890s was suggestion. If words or other stimuli "can arouse *within* the realm of consciousness, thoughts and sentiments—or, in physiological language, nerve currents—favorable to the physical and mental health, it is equally conceivable that, by similar stimuli, we should be able to arouse similar images or currents in the regions of the mind lying *outside* the ordinary realm of consciousness." Just as the mind curist planted seeds of hopefulness which might take root and grow by chance association with feelings of well-being, so should the physician help the patient "to really conceive of himself as capable of being a different person."[61] Good bodily health, attractive clothes, and cheerful surroundings were also important, he said, and pointed to the fact that religious converts often bore witness to their feeling of being new persons by adopting new habits, new friends, and new clothes.

Putnam's pointing this early to religious conversion as "the sort of change in temperament which the physician tries to bring about" lends weight to John Owen King's view that in moving from the somatic style to the psychology of suggestion to psychoanalysis (and self-analysis), Putnam drew on the New England tradition of conversion narratives and spiritual autobiography.[62] But it is easy to extend too far this illuminating point that psychoanalysis is a conversion process. To Putnam, psychoanalysis was not the

60. Ibid., 506.
61. Ibid., 506, 507.
62. Ibid., 507; King, *Iron of Melancholy*, 275.

same sort of conversion for which the Puritans had longed. The difference was profound. Where Puritan conversion diminished the self in favor of the Other, Putnam, like Royce, intended to extend the dominion of the conscious self. The name of Freud is so rightly attached to a legacy of cultural radicalism that it is easy to forget that psychoanalysis could and did appeal to conservative thinkers through its promise of a triumph of the conscious self over the unconscious other.[63]

When Putnam first heard of Freudian analysis he believed that it differed from the hypnotic therapy of Janet and Prince mainly in placing an emphasis on consciousness and introspection. Freud's method, Putnam said, "does not differ much in principle, from the other methods which I have characterized as 'substitutive.'" Putnam's model of the mind remained the associationist view. Ill minds resulted from dissociation of consciousness in which separate clusters of thoughts produced conflicting and therefore troubling impulses. "Substitutive" therapies, such as hypnotism and even James's method of building habits of discipline and facility in "conscious effort," were actually repressive.[64] In these therapies, enhanced control by the self or principal consciousness was not so much achieved by reassociation as by obliteration, as in Prince's decision in favor of Clara over Sally. Putnam eagerly engaged in clinical trials of psychoanalysis years before he had even met another psychoanalyst because he was committed to resolving psychological conflict at the highest possible level of consciousness: "The aim then ought to be to bring back the hidden experience into the clear light of consciousness, so that its real significance can be estimated, after which the reorganization of the disordered forces of the mind is likely to take place of itself."[65]

63. For an excellent discussion of this question, see Fred Matthews, "The Americanization of Sigmund Freud: Adaptations of Psychoanalysis before 1917," *Journal of American Studies* (April 1967), 46–60.

64. James Jackson Putnam, "Recent Experiences in the Study and Treatment of Hysteria at the Massachusetts General Hospital; With Remarks on Freud's Method of Treatment by 'Psycho-Analysis'," *Journal of Abnormal Psychology* (April 1906): 36; James Jackson Putnam, "Neurasthenia," *American System of Practical Medicine,* ed. A. L. Loomis and W. G. Thompson (New York: Lea Brothers, 1898), IV, 582.

65. James Jackson Putnam, "A Consideration of Mental Therapeutics as Employed by Special Students of the Subject," *Boston Medical and Surgical Journal* (August 18,

Owing to the influence of James and Royce, Putnam disagreed with Freud's view of thought as "experience." Though James, like Freud, viewed thought as experience, he also held that no past mental state ever recurs. And what James had held to be "true of conscious mental states is true of subconscious mental states." Consequently, Putnam rejected Freud's view "that the old unfinished experience is given a chance to work itself out in the process that leads to cure." A memory, Putnam said, is a new mental state containing references to a past mental state rather than an actual repetition of the past state. Therefore Freud did not understand the metaphysical basis of his successful therapy, which rather than being the "working out" of a repressed "experience" was the inducing of a new mental state which, in Roycean fashion, is *accepted by the patient as representing* an ideal 'working-out' of the old and mischievous idea."[66]

Royce's emphasis on social experience helped prepare Putnam to accept Freud's emphasis on relations within the family.[67] Royce's elaboration of Peirce's description of thought as a series of triadic, semiotic relations was interpreted by Putnam as meaning that the individual human being is not entirely self-conscious and that therefore "it is in each man's social relations that his own mental history is mainly written, and it is in his social relations likewise that the causes of disorders that threaten his happiness and his effectiveness and the means for securing his recovery are mainly to be sought." Putnam therefore discounted mechanist analyses of the

1904): 181; cf. John C. Burnham, *Psychoanalysis and American Medicine: 1894–1918* (New York: International Universities Press, 1967), 22.

66. Putnam, "Recent Experiences in the Study and Treatment of Hysteria," 37–38.

67. Other influences of this sort on Putnam were Henri Bergson, whom he frequently cited, and Susan Blow. The latter was his patient as well as a pioneer kindergarten teacher and author of *Symbolic Education* (1894). She may have introduced Putnam to William Torrey Harris's *Hegel's Logic* (1890), which he once recommended to Freud (*James Jackson Putnam and Psychoanalysis: Letters between Putnam and Sigmund Freud, Ernest Jones, William James, Sandor Ferenczi, and Morton Prince*, ed. Nathan G. Hale [Cambridge: Harvard University Press, 1971], 135). But her influence is hard to gauge and is indicated more by the quantity than the content of her correspondence with Putnam. See the Putnam Papers, Francis A. Countway Library of Medicine, Boston.

brain, such as Prince's, as not "pragmatic" in the absence of knowledge of the social relations that caused the problem in the first place.[68]

It is not surprising, then, that Ernest Jones found Putnam sympathetic when the two analysts met at Prince's house in December 1908. The legend that Putnam's attitude underwent something like a conversion in the months following their meeting is due mainly to Jones's egocentrism and love of the dramatic. Accustomed to hostility, the prickly psychoanalyst was charmed by Putnam's fair-mindedness and openness to new ideas. Putnam's personality combined, beneath a better-mannered exterior, the same search for truth and willingness to fight for it as did Jones's. Putnam promised Jones that he would take a new look at Freudianism and reevaluate his notion that it did not differ in principle from "substitutive" therapies such as hypnotism.[69]

Putnam kept his promise to reconsider his opinions, but he changed them very little. By May 1909 he was convinced that Freudianism was therapeutically superior to the substitutive method of Janet and Prince, but this was merely a reformulation of his previously expressed preference for resolving psychological conflict at the highest possible level of consciousness. In substitutive therapies like hypnotism, "the former traits of character are, as it were, sidetracked by the formation of . . . a new personality." But Freud's method allowed, in Roycean fashion, for the absorption of the old character by the new, "as when a person utilizes, more or less consciously, all the influences, painful as well as pleasurable, which have been brought to bear upon him." Royce's influence on Putnam was clear in Putnam's statement that Freud's method was that of "self-conscious persons of the type of Bunyan." Therapeutic suggestion resulted in adaptation to "a definite environment," whereas the Freudian method of consciousness and introspection adapted people for environments of many sorts. "The memories of

68. James Jackson Putnam, "The Treatment of Psychasthenia from the Standpoint of the Social Consciousness," *American Journal of the Medical Sciences* (January 1908): 77; James Jackson Putnam, "The Bearing of Philosophy on Psychiatry, with Special Reference on the Treatment of Psychasthenia," *British Medical Journal* (October 1906): 1023.

69. Jones, *Free Associations*, 187.

the experiences through which a person has passed, under these circumstances, come to his aid in the way of enriching his perceptions and his thoughts, to an extent which would otherwise be impossible."[70] The therapeutic superiority of Freudian analysis was actually a moral superiority owing, in Putnam's view, to its enhancement of the patient's consciousness and self-understanding. This view that psychoanalysis was a moral therapy had been Putnam's opinion all along, and it would eventually be the principal disagreement in his friendship with Freud.

Not Freudian analysis but rather Roycean philosophy, by revealing the spiritual basis of matter, permitted Putnam to move comfortably toward a somatic interpretation of the unconscious, one that would let him accept, as Morton Prince and William James had been unable to do, the semantic contradiction in the notion of unconscious thought. "For matter," he eventually wrote, "is not the truth itself, but only a symbol of the truth." Since Freud's approach to the mind had been somatic and biological from the start, he had never been hindered by the concept of consciousness that Putnam worked hard to modify. The triumph of Freudianism in American psychotherapy did not depend on a total abandonment of somatic bias. Locating the unconscious in soma, in bodily habit, offered conservatives like Putnam a way of remaining loyal to an active role for the conscious self. A somatic interpretation of the unconscious helped Putnam put aside his Jamesean objections to the notion that a thought could be repeated and thus, in Freudian terminology, "worked through." Indeed, a somatic basis for the unconscious lent all the more importance to James's famous emphasis on habit: "The habits that we seek to alter," wrote Putnam, "reside in the psychological mechanism of our bodies, and these, just because they live, are more or less susceptible of change." That these habits began in childhood was a familiar principle, "but it is to the keenness and the genius of Freud that we owe its working out in ways which must indeed be tested farther, but which are certain to be of great utility."[71]

70. James Jackson Putnam, "The Relation of Character Formation to Psychotherapy," *Psychotherapeutics* (Boston: Badger, 1910), 198–201.
71. James Jackson Putnam, "Presidential Address before the American Pathologi-

Putnam met Freud in Worcester the next September when the creator of psychoanalysis attempted to overcome moral objections to his system by lecturing disarmingly at Clark University. But on one point—psychological determinism—Freud failed to win over his wary audience. New Englanders, influenced by the consciousness concept and accustomed for a century to thinking of free will as necessary for moral responsibility, were disturbed by Freud's insistence that the same principle of cause and effect that physicians applied to their patients' bodily illnesses must be applied to illnesses of the mind as well. After one of the lectures, Putnam asked Freud if such a view did not render pointless all moral estimates of human actions and character: "To this Freud replied, with impressive earnestness, that it was not moral estimates that were needed for solving the problem of human life and motives, but more *knowledge.*"[72] Putnam was not satisfied with this answer, and he would never abandon the belief in free will that he owed to his Unitarian heritage.[73] But he was sufficiently impressed with Freud's own personal uprightness and with the clinical promise of psychoanalysis to overcome any scruples about its moral implications. The old New England confidence that natural knowledge and spiritual truth could not contradict each other gave Putnam courage: "If our spiritual life is good for anything it can afford to see the truth."[74] These words, which Freud found "particularly fine,"[75] were the result of the two men's having cemented their friendship during three days spent, after the Clark conference, at Putnam's rustic summer home in the Adirondacks. During Freud's visit Putnam agreed to write an article for Prince's *Journal of Ab-*

cal Association," *Journal of Abnormal Psychology* (August 1913): 179; Putnam, "Relation of Character Formation to Psychotherapy," 197, 189.

72. James Jackson Putnam, "Elements of Strength and Elements of Weakness in Psychoanalytic Doctrines," *Addresses on Psycho-Analysis* (London: International Psycho-Analytical Press, 1921), 450.

73. One of Putnam's surviving childhood essays, entitled "Original Sin," (Putnam Papers, Countway Library), espouses free will. Cf. James Jackson Putnam, "A Plea for the Study of Philosophic Methods in Preparation for Psychoanalytic Work," *Journal of Abnormal Psychology* (October 1911): 82.

74. James Jackson Putnam, "Personal Impressions of Sigmund Freud and His Work," *Journal of Abnormal Psychology* (December–January 1909): 307.

75. *James Jackson Putnam and Psychoanalysis*, 92.

normal Psychology that would explain psychoanalysis to American therapists.

In that article Putnam continued his interpretation of Freud as a proponent not of the unconscious but of consciousness. Freud's surprising revelation was of the power of consciousness to recover seemingly lost memories and of how bringing those memories to consciousness effected a cure. The fact that the memories had been forgotten in the first place was itself a testimony to the power of the conscious self; forgetting was repression, even in normal persons, by an intentionally forgetful self. It was to be expected, then, that the strongest and potentially most damaging repression should be centered on sex, for "The pressure which all of us are under to make individual interests subservient to community interests finds its strongest, its most fundamental expression at the . . . intense and varied emotions that cluster round the great instinct and function of reproduction."[76] Freudianism was thus reconcilable with a Roycean emphasis on self-possession.[77]

Thanks to Royce's description of thought as an inferential rather than experiential process, Putnam could insist that all thought, even unconscious thought, was created and contained in only one self. In his article on psychoanalysis Putnam alarmed Freud by citing Morton Prince in support of the notion that "awareness" is not necessary for "consciousness." Reading this as an endorsement of Prince's theory that there was no such thing as "unconscious" thought but only "co-conscious" multiple personalities, Freud protested to Putnam that he could not understand "how you can accept Morton Prince's view." Putnam answered that he had meant only to deny that "'consciousness' contains always an element of 'self-consciousness'." Even though he had irenically cited Prince, Putnam disagreed with Prince's notion that all thought was conscious. Putnam's explanation, Freud replied, "relieved me greatly."[78]

Freud was mistaken in his relief, for the same Roycean notion of thought as inference that led Putnam to oppose Prince's view that

76. James Jackson Putnam, "Personal Impressions of Sigmund Freud and His Work [continued]," *Journal of Abnormal Psychology* (February–March 1910): 376.
77. See Putnam, *James Jackson Putnam and Psychoanalysis*, 172–73.
78. Ibid., 92, 94, 96.

thought was conscious experience within a self would eventually lead Putnam to oppose Freud's notion that some thought was *un*-conscious experience within a material self. Several years later when the differences between them were becoming clearer, Putnam tried to explain his views to Freud: "what we call experiences in analysis are really symbols." In both "logical thought" and "unconscious thinking . . . one proceeds . . . with the aid of inference."[79]

Freud himself thus posed a threat to mentality and even spirit, the values that, ironically, had originally interested Putnam in functional psychology and psychoanalysis. In the months just after the Clark conference the two therapists' friendship had grown via correspondence, but by the summer of 1910 Putnam, in Roycean fashion, was cautioning Freud that "somehow the genetic scheme on which you are working, and which shows that men are elabo-rated forms of the lower and lowest organisms must harmonize with the principle of mental perfection and purpose as the real ba-sis of the universe. . . . I believe . . . that we have something to work towards as well as something to work *out* of." Putnam's fear that this probably seemed like "nonsense" to Freud moved the great analyst to a pious disclaimer: "Although I am resigned to the fact that I am a God forsaken 'incredulous Jew,' I am not proud of it and do not look down on others." He added that if the basic principles of psychoanalysis were so difficult to determine, then "the idealistic truths which you are not willing to give up cannot be so certain." But Putnam was certain. Psychoanalysis as it presently existed, he told Freud, was "too materialistic. . . . It . . . fails to recognize that mind, consciousness, reason, emotion, will, are not merely *products* of evolution but underlying *causes* of evo-lution."[80]

Putnam believed that Freud's failure to perceive the truth was due to his friend's strict adherence to "natural science"[81] and his rejection of metaphysics and philosophy as sources of real knowl-edge. Putnam had learned from Royce what Royce had learned

79. Ibid., 196, 195. "Inference" eventually replaced "thought" as Putnam's ge-neric term for mental processes. See James Jackson Putnam, *Human Motives* (Boston: Little, Brown, 1915), passim.
80. Putnam, *James Jackson Putnam and Psychoanalysis,* 102–3, 105, 118.
81. Ibid., 161.

from Peirce—induction was not the only objective method for science. Deduction or interpretation of signs could lead to the discovery of new facts.[82] Putnam could see that a recently deceased hero had had scientific feet of clay: "I admired William James to the point of adoration. But . . . his very courage and his scientific conscientiousness proved, I think, his enemies. He made them into great block images . . . and could not see the truth because of them."[83] Psychoanalysts, of course, disagreed with James's belief that all thought was immediately, empirically known to its subject through conscious introspection, but psychoanalysts were only slightly less empirical than James. Psychoanalysts, interpreting mental phenomena as symbols of material events, failed to see that the latter were also symbols: "The symbolism which you found in dreams exists in all life," Putnam told Freud. Only through the same interpretive approach to material nature that Freud had applied to mental phenomena could the highest truth and the ultimate well-being be reached. Putnam, however, was a physician of unusual breadth. Freud, with his narrow medical education, admitted that "I comprehend very little of philosophy and with epistemology (with, not before) my interest ceases to function."[84]

Even in regard to their symbolic interpretation of thought, psychoanalysts were, in Putnam's view, too narrow, for they interpreted thought as symbolic of material experience rather than spiritual truth. A religious belief, say God, even if it originated in a father complex, might "represent logical truths."[85] Citing Royce, Putnam urged that the Trinity, though "regarded with derision by most scientific men . . . symbolizes nothing less than the [triadic] structure of every thought." And "in the structure and working of the human mind, the structure and working of the universe finds itself revealed."[86] One could not be a competent scientist, Putnam told Freud, without accepting "by inference, though perhaps un-

82. Royce, *Problem of Christianity*, 309.

83. Putnam, "Presidential Address before the American Pathological Association," 175.

84. Putnam, *James Jackson Putnam and Psychoanalysis*, 95, 170.

85. Ibid., 165.

86. Putnam, "Presidential Address before the American Pathological Association," 177–78, 171.

consciously," principles that led to such conclusions. Putnam may have had not only Royce but also Peirce in mind when he assured Freud that "logic and mathematics have been found recently to coincide in proving certain of these views."[87]

As a believer in moral as well as scientific certainty, Putnam believed psychoanalysts should help patients not only come to terms with their illness but also to achieve "a suitable 'Sublimation.' "[88] This conviction was due in part to observation of his upper-class New England patients with obsessional tendencies that, as John Owen King has said, Putnam himself possessed.[89] Putnam understood how important his moralism was to his own well-being: "I find that many of my patients, and I myself, need all the *motive* that can be secured, and . . . the strongest motive is that which comes from a recognition of our responsibility as self-conscious beings." Psychoanalysis as thus far developed, Putnam told Freud, implied "an incorrect because incomplete, view of human life and motive." Patients needed religious and philosophical truth, for belief gave hope and motives for living. Putnam considered no patient "really cured unless he becomes better and broader morally, and conversely, I believe that a moral regeneration helps towards a removal of the symptoms."[90]

Freud, however, believed that to urge a moral or philosophical view on a patient was "after all only to use violence." After Putnam's death Freud explained his friend's "ethical bias" with the notorious "resistance" formula with which his disciples have often diagnosed opponents rather than answered their arguments: "he was one of those happily compensated people of the obsessional type for whom what is noble is second nature." But this rang false when applied to one who had been so loyal to Freud and who, as a psychoanalyst himself, had both anticipated Freud's charge and effectively dealt with it: "a *part* of my own interest in these

87. Putnam, *James Jackson Putnam and Psychoanalysis,* 169; cf. Putnam, *Human Motives,* 23.
88. Putnam, *James Jackson Putnam and Psychoanalysis,* 106.
89. King, *Iron of Melancholy,* 276.
90. Putnam, *James Jackson Putnam and Psychoanalysis,* 106, 118.

matters is the desire to escape from seeing my own Complexes."[91]

Putnam pressed on with his revisions of psychoanalytic doctrines in the next few years and assembled them in a book, *Human Motives* (1915), that made clear that Royce's Absolute Self and Peirce's view of thought as inference, freedom and human brotherhood, more than Freud's materialism and scientific determinism, constituted Putnam's own motives. Freedom and brotherhood applied "not alone to men themselves, regarded as units, but also to the thoughts and emotions of men, especially those that, having been expelled (through 'repression') from the society of that special group of feelings which we elect to call 'ourselves,' become organized and systematized into 'complexes,'—somewhat as the Miltonic Satan, cast out of heaven, organized himself in hell." Freud was of course right that human beings have an evolutionary history and selfish drives. But like Royce, Putnam believed that "limitation is the necessary condition of effort. . . . Even our ideals would not have their present form were it not that our lot is cast in a world of limitation, in which progress is possible only through conscious effort, compromise, and adaptation." Putnam's basis for these assertions was Peircean "inferences" rather than Scottish common sense, but like the New Divinity men, he had been forced to find some basis for selfhood other than human consciousness. Like Royce, he based the self in "the totality of the expressions and life of the world-will, when considered in its conscious unity."[92]

Human Motives contained a criticism of psychoanalysis that Freud seems to have considered personal: "To accustom ourselves to the study of immaturity and childhood before proceeding to the study of maturity and manhood is often to habituate ourselves to an undesirable limitation of our vision." Freud's reply would have been splendid if he had said no more than that although such was indeed his limitation, it had enabled him "to observe what had been hidden from others. Let that justify my defense." But he added a stinging rebuke. Usually, it is the immoral who publicly call for "religious-ethical conversion. . . . Jung, for example, I found sympathetic so long as he lived blindly, as I did. Then came

91. Ibid., 43, 183.
92. Putnam, *Human Motives,* 12–13, 15, 65, 58.

his religious-ethical crisis with higher morality, 'rebirth,' Bergson and at the very same time, lies, brutality and anti-semitic condescension towards me. It has not been the first or last experience to reinforce my disgust with saintly converts."[93]

Putnam wrote out a long, troubled reply and then sent a shorter draft instead, but the longer letter deftly modified psychoanalysis with pragmatic logic, according to which beliefs were external objects to be discovered rather than known immediately through conscious introspection. Freud had cautioned Putnam that the failure of *Human Motives* to persuade Freud "should not surprise you: you will know how little one can expect of argument." Putnam's pragmatic answer was that "if, however, for the word 'arguments' we substitute the term 'analysis'—that is to say, the interpretation of one's thought and the discovery of opinions really held—the case is very different. Thus, if anything I say leads you to discover that you do at heart believe what I think you believe, and that you do actually recognize the importance of so believing, then the effort on my part will have been worth the making." Freud, no more than any other human being, enjoyed immediate knowledge of his thoughts. If Freud would only examine his actions, he would find that his true beliefs did not contradict Putnam's. Freud would never have made the sacrifices he had in his pursuit of truth if he did not believe his efforts could be effective, if he were not in reality a believer in the mental and spiritual freedom that he denied in theory. Freud was thus at heart a deeply religious man, a believer in a "universal religion because all men feel themselves bound, in some measure, by these ties. . . . In my opinion this bond is the very essence of the social bond, . . . stronger even than the sex bond, though by no means exclusive of it."[94]

The exchange over *Human Motives* marked virtually the end of Putnam's correspondence with Freud. The First World War eventually interrupted the mails. Depressed by the war, Putnam, an anxious man in the best of times, found difficulty in both sleep and work. His practice had declined, evidently because of his adherence to psychoanalysis. He died on November 4, 1918, a week before

93. Ibid., 19–20; Putnam, *James Jackson Putnam and Psychoanalysis*, 188–89.
94. Putnam, *James Jackson Putnam and Psychoanalysis*, 189, 192–93.

the beginning of the postwar period in which the Freudian view of the mind, at least in its rough outlines, became an accepted, even dominant feature of American culture. Putnam had taken satisfaction from seeing psychoanalytic theory begin to penetrate the colleges and universities. The satisfaction he might have drawn from seeing it penetrate the broader culture would scarcely have been personal. He had too much of the Puritan in him for that. But he would have seen beneath the facade of cultural and sexual radicalism. He would have understood the basically conservative thrust of the triumph of psychoanalysis in modern culture, understood that it preserved the self's superiority to thought in a world reluctant to abandon what little remained of the concept of consciousness.

✻

Afterword

At the end of a complicated story, some retrospection is in order. The argument of this book has been that the modern notion of some thought as unconscious is a compromise aimed at preserving as large a role as possible for the self. The compromise preserves something of the original, prideful notion in the consciousness concept that the self not only creates all thought but has complete and immediate knowledge of all its thoughts. If the modern compromise forfeits the consciousness of some thought, it retains the notion that the self is the creator of all thought. In yielding the notion that human beings enjoy complete self-knowledge, the modern compromise amounts to a return to a model of the self that in some ways resembles that of the old faculty psychology in which human beings were also described as conflicted and mysterious to themselves.

New England proponents of the self sign have thus adhered over the course of the three centuries covered in this study to three models of the self: first, the model in faculty psychology that explained self-conflict as the result of a division between the self's faculties of understanding and willing; second, the model in the consciousness concept according to which there should be no self-conflict because the self is asserted to enjoy complete and immediate knowledge of all its thoughts, including its desires; and third, the modern model that explains self-conflict as the result of a division in the self between its conscious and unconscious activity in thinking. These three models of the self might be diagrammed in chronological order from left to right as in figure 4.

The principal difference between the modern and faculty

CONSCIOUSNESS IN NEW ENGLAND

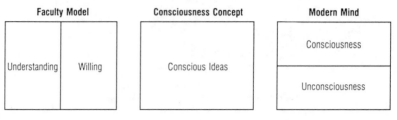

Figure 4

models can be ascertained from the matrix derived by imposing one diagram on the other (see fig. 5). The matrix illustrates the point that the modern word "consciousness" is not synonymous with the ancient word "understanding." "Consciousness" involves both "understanding" and "willing" as those terms were formerly employed. So too does "unconscious." The modern division is not between two fundamentally different qualities of thought, which was the way understanding and willing were conceived in the faculty model. Rather, the modern division is between thoughts that differ only in regard to whether the self is presumed or not presumed to be immediately conscious of them. If the consciousness concept was partially defeated, it nevertheless succeeded in determining its concessions, succeeded in perpetuating consciousness (or its absence) as the fundamental question about the self.

The story told in this book, however, offers reasons for a skeptical view of the modern model of the self as divided between conscious and unconscious thought, at least insofar as the former is viewed as more internal than the latter. Indeed, the rise of an argument for the externality of thought to the self was a fundamental cause of the modern compromise. This line of reasoning reached its nineteenth-century apogee in Charles Sanders Peirce's semiotic re-

Consciousness Understanding	Consciousness Willing
Unconsciousness Understanding	Unconsciousness Willing

Figure 5

alism, according to which all thoughts are external. In this model no thought is "conscious" in the sense of the seventeenth-century consciousness concept; no thought is immediately present in a knowing self. Rather, thoughts can only be known after the fact, by signs. And selves do not create thoughts; the relation of thoughts creates selves.

The story of the demise of the consciousness concept has wide ramifications for American history, but in this book it has been possible to offer only occasional sideways glances at those ramifications. But to follow outward some of the paths radiating from the main line of the story would throw new light on many aspects of the history of the eighteenth and nineteenth centuries. The clearest contribution of this book in that regard is its interpretation of seventeenth-century conversion and the transformation that was effected in nineteenth-century understanding of evangelical religion by Lyman Beecher, Charles Finney, and their like. But a great deal more might be done in exploring how the consciousness concept transformed Christian "fundamentalism" from a religion of pious doubt into one of self-confident religious "experience." The rise of middle-class morality and what has been called the cult of domesticity become a great deal more understandable in view of the rise of the consciousness concept. So do the success myth and the cult of the self-made man. The relationship of middle-class self-control to, in other social contexts, middle-class self-assertion can be seen as not a contradiction or paradox but a consistent response to the consciousness concept and the confidence that it inspired in self-knowledge and free will. Republican political theory, economic theories based on self-interest, the rise of political parties, romantic love, forensic psychiatry, prison reform, insane asylums, education reform, abolitionism, and humanitarian movements of all sorts were deeply affected by the consciousness concept. Indeed, the influence of the consciousness concept can be seen not only in the past but also in the excessive confidence of many present-day historians, derived partly perhaps from the similar confidence of their subjects, that historical processes are "experienced."

I hope to explain elsewhere at greater length than would be appropriate here why I think that it is a much superior method to view history not as a record of human "experience" but as "interpretation." But one of the reasons Peirce's semiotic monism seems to me the most reasonable position, if also the least influential, of all those described in this book, is that it overcomes the self-contradictory notion, widely prevalent among historians and social scientists, that whereas reality may be "experienced" in thought, thought is nevertheless entirely distinct from reality. One need not be committed to any particular detail of Peirce's metaphysics to see that his semiotic monism, which privileges thought, cuts through many of the issues that befoul contemporary discussions of the relation of thought to behavior. But to speak of privileging "thought" arouses in some minds the old metaphysical issues of idealism and materialism that Peirce meant to get past. Those with a materialist cast of mind may find it easier to give a fair hearing to semiotic monism if they substitute for "thought" a word like "form" or "relation."

The limited range of Peirce's influence in American culture is suggested by the fact that in popular lore the self retains a mostly unquestioned upper hand over thought. The prevalence of computers, for instance, has not led to popular acceptance of the notion of thought as an external process of sign relations rather than internal perception within a self. In conveying even fairly sophisticated descriptions of computer design to popular audiences, mass marketers choose book titles that honor the self. The fact that machines can think is most profitably described, not as suggesting that thought is larger than selves but that machines have souls.[1] Despite (perhaps partly because of) the vogue of depth psychology and the plethora of self-help manuals, willful, conscious self-control remains nearly as popular an ideal as it was in the nineteenth century and has found proponents far more banal.[2] The titles of more than five hundred books currently in print begin with the word "Self," whereas only a handful begin with "Thought."

In the natural sciences the story is more mixed. Although descriptions of the genetic process as a "code" in the DNA molecule might suggest to some that it is more reasonable to think of biological processes as thoughts or forms or relations than as self-replica-

1. Tracy Kidder, *The Soul of a New Machine* (Boston: Little, Brown, 1981).
2. G. Gordon Liddy, *Will* (New York: Dell, 1981).

AFTERWORD

tions, many biologists, especially sociobiologists, seem to side with the self sign.[3] On the other hand, physics and especially quantum mechanics lends credence to descriptions of the universe as fundamentally thought.[4] To attempt to outline the contemporary debate in these fields would carry this study improperly beyond its scope.

But this book, dealing with the decline of the consciousness concept, does offer a useful historical background to, and reasons for a cautionary view of, the interpretive revolution presently taking place in the humanities and social sciences. Because the interpretive revolution is founded on the semiotic realism that was one result of the decline of the consciousness concept, this study may correct or at least reveal some of the excesses in current interpretive theory. "Interpretisms" like structuralism and deconstruction so greatly overstate the discontinuity of thought and of history that they can make interpretation seem pointless or impossible. Charles Peirce would never have agreed with Jacques Derrida, the leading deconstructionist, that "*in a certain sense, 'thought' means nothing.*" Peirce did oppose, just as Derrida does, "the metaphysics of Presence," the notion that "the signified is a meaning thinkable in principle within the full presence of an intuitive consciousness."[5] But while Peirce agreed that thought is not immediately intuited within a self, he nevertheless believed that thought has meaning and that its meaning can be known.

Derrida, believing that an attack on the concept of consciousness requires an attack on the concept of meaning, offers mistaken tribute to the greatest semiotician of the nineteenth century: "Peirce goes very far in the direction that I have called the de-construction of the transcendental signified, which at one time or another, would place a reassuring end to the reference from sign to sign." Peirce traveled no distance at all in that direction. While he believed that the signifying process had no reassuring end (or beginning), he was a consistent transcendentalist in the sense that he

3. Richard Dawkins, *The Selfish Gene* (New York: Oxford University Press, 1976).
4. Erwin Schrödinger, *Mind and Matter* (Cambridge, England: Cambridge University Press, 1958).
5. Jacques Derrida, *Of Grammatology* (Baltimore: Johns Hopkins University Press, 1974), 93, 49.

believed that signs have meaning and that that meaning may refer to "Reals" external to the signifying process even though nothing exists but signs.[6]

Derrida's views are a critical extension of Saussure's distinction in linguistics between the *signifie* (the thing signified) and the *signifiant* (the signifier or word) that arbitrarily represents it,[7] but language is far too narrow a field from which to reach general conclusions about thought. In addition to words, there are many kinds of signs, and not all of them are arbitrary. Peirce's typology of signs is *index, icon,* and *symbol.* An *index* is not an arbitrary sign but, rather, possesses a real relation with the thing it signifies, as, for instance, a weather vane's relation with the wind. An *icon* is not arbitrary but resembles the thing it signifies; the meaning of a portrait is established, at least partly, by the portrait's resemblance to its subject. *Symbols* are the only type of sign whose meaning is arbitrary; the octagonal shape of stop signs is symbolic since stop signs could just as well convey their message by a triangular shape if that were the arbitrarily chosen convention. This arbitrariness has been viewed by some, especially those who have come to the study of signs out of a linguistic or literary background, as the essence of signhood, and they therefore assert that the symbol is "the sign proper." Since words seem to be symbols—arbitrary signs—it is easy (but mistaken) to conclude that "literary works" are free to violate "the codes that define them, and this is what makes the semiological investigation of literature such a tantalizing enterprise." Conversely, disciplines like medicine, meteorology, economics, and, presumably, history search for "indexes" or causal relations, "and there is no reason to think that they would gain substantially" from semiotics.[8]

6. Ibid., 49; Charles Sanders Peirce, "The Fixation of Belief," in *Collected Papers of Charles Sanders Peirce* (herafter *CP*), Vols. I–VI ed. Charles Hartshorne and Paul Weiss; Vols. VII–VIII ed. Arthur Burks (Cambridge: Harvard University Press, 1931–1958), V, 384. All citation to Peirce's *Collected Papers* are to numbered paragraphs rather than pages.

7. Ferdinand de Saussure, *Course in General Linguistics* (New York: McGraw-Hill, 1966), 111–37.

8. Jonathan Culler, *Ferdinand de Saussure* (New York: Penguin, 1977), 104, 114, 105. But see also the substantial modifications in Culler's, *The Pursuit of Signs: Semiotics, Literature, Deconstruction* (Ithaca, N.Y.: Cornell University Press, 1981), 22–25.

Peirce's much broader, more useful, and more positive approach to semiotics makes clear that this "parochially glottocentric" view, as Thomas Sebeok has aptly labeled it, mistakenly overestimates both the degree to which literary critics are liberated by the symbolic nature of their subject matter and other scholars enslaved by the indexical nature of theirs. Sebeok calls it a "minor trend, which . . . asserts, sometimes with sophistication but at other times with embarrassing naïvete, that linguistics serves as the model for the rest of semiotics—Saussure's *le patron general*—because of the allegedly arbitrary and conventional character of the verbal sign."[9] Intellectual historians, fortunately, seem not to have been discouraged by literary scholars' assertions that semiotics is useless in disciplines such as history.

Yet intellectual historians do seem well on the way, unfortunately, to accepting the mistaken notions that linguistics is the semiotic master science and that a semiotic approach to language allows for no meaning or reference beyond language itself. A recent review article asserts that new approaches to intellectual history involve "a focused concern on the ways meaning is constituted in and through language. . . . Most [of the intellectual historians discussed in the article] seem ready to concede that language can no longer be construed as simply a medium, relatively or potentially transparent, for the representation or expression of a reality outside itself and are willing to entertain seriously some form of semiological theory in which language is conceived of as a self-contained system of 'signs' whose meanings are determined by their relations to each other, rather than by their relation to some 'transcendental' or extralinguistic object or subject."[10]

In Peirce's view, however, semiotics should be based on objective, scientific study, not merely of language but of the process of thought. Because he considered thought to be a process, Peirce's approach to it was diachronic and had the still useful result of showing that in addition to the "signified" and the "signifier" the

9. Thomas Sebeok, "Ecumenicalism in Semiotics," *A Perfusion of Signs*, ed. Sebeok (Bloomington: Indiana University Press, 1977), 182.

10. John E. Toews, "Intellectual History after the Linguistic Turn: The Autonomy of Meaning and the Irreducibility of Experience," *American Historical Review* (October 1987): 881–82.

signifying process involves a third element, the "interpretant" or thought to which the sign gives rise.[11] The signifier's meaning lies neither in the signified nor in itself but in the thought it provokes. This new thought or interpretant may in turn become a sign, but it may do so only by being interpreted by a subsequent thought, another interpretant. As an apostle of free will, Peirce did not believe any thought to be precisely determined, nor did he think that a thought can strike entirely out of the blue. The sign does not have meaning without the interpretant, but the interpretant is partly determined by the sign. Even symbols, though arbitrarily chosen, are not arbitrarily interpreted. Even if a stop sign's conventional, arbitrarily chosen shape were triangular rather than octagonal, the sign's interpretant would still be the thought of stopping. For two reasons, then, it is possible for historians interested in causality to interpret history as a semiotic process: first, not all signs are arbitrary; and second, even signs arbitrarily chosen are not arbitrarily interpreted.

A recent, ambitious book offers a cautionary example of the danger of approaching history as if it were as arbitrary as, according to some, language is. *The Iron of Melancholy* by John Owen King, III, is one of the most daring of recent works in intellectual history. My study has profited greatly from King's extensive treatment of some of the same material on conversion and psychological theory that is discussed in these pages. But King rejects the assumption that the text represents its time. Almost as if to prove his point, he quotes Marshall Sahlins quoting Mikhail Bakhtin that it is "the other way around—*expression organizes experience.*" King therefore proposes, in the phrase of Michel Foucault, study of "discursive formations," study of the basic structures of meaning imposed by the textual expressions through which people attempt to share their "experiences" with, or impose them on, each other. Discursive formations "determine" and "authorize" some expressions of meaning while forbidding others. "Questions of discourse precede

11. Charles Sanders Peirce, "The Categories in Detail," *CP,* I, 339. Cf. Umberto Eco, "Peirce and the Semiotic Foundations of Openness: Signs as Texts and Texts as Signs," *The Role of the Reader: Explorations in the Semiotics of Texts,* ed. Umberto Eco (Bloomington: Indiana University Press, 1979), 182–83.

arguments that writing acts like a mirror, presenting the virtual image of unseen but real forces elsewhere."[12]

Many troublesome questions are raised by such assertions. Presumably the structures of past discursive formations are ascertained through the study of texts, so must not a representative reading of texts "precede" any knowledge of the discursive formation itself? How do the people of a particular time and place acquire knowledge of the discursive formation that authorizes their expression except through "experiencing" it (or the texts that represent it)? Would it not therefore be as accurate to say that "experience" organizes expression as vice versa? If discursive formations and the expression of them in texts do organize "experience," historical change would occur, as King suggests, because of the failure of one text to imitate another: "The inexactness of a copy constitutes history, for the inability to repeat *is* history."[13] But *why* should one text fail to imitate another? Cannot the same words be strung together in the same order an infinite number of times? The cause of the failure can hardly lie in the words themselves. Some other reality—be it social, cultural, or personal—must have interfered with the desire of the text's creator to organize his or her "experience" by imitating past expressions. And in turn, the only way texts can be agents of change is by interacting with some opposing reality, some other material force, some other text or discursive formation. The text, in and of itself, is fundamentally conservative. Its tendency is toward perpetuation of itself. The text becomes an agent of change only when its tendency toward self-perpetuation is resisted by some reality external to the text.

The extension of change or "inability to repeat" into an absolute by structuralists and deconstructionists, rather than heightening interest in change, ironically dampens interest in change. If change is rendered inevitable by textuality, what needs explanation is not change but persistence and continuity. *The Iron of Melancholy,* while emphasizing *différance* in methodologically self-conscious

---

12. John Owen King, III, *The Iron of Melancholy: Structures of Spiritual Conversion in America from the Puritan Conscience to Victorian Neurosis* (Middletown, Conn.: Wesleyan University Press, 1983), 7, 9, 19.

13. Ibid., 82.

moments, actually describes a persistent tradition of spiritual confession. Uninterested in change, King offers only incidental and
perfunctory suggestions as to why the New England tradition of
personal confession changed from a religious and moral to a secular
and psychological orientation: Edwards had to deal with New England's becoming "industriously improved"; and Josiah Royce was
limited to "the terms imposed by the new discipline of neurology."[14] These causes of change presumably must have originated
outside the tradition of personal confession, for that tradition is the
discursive formation whose function is to explain persistence and
continuity. But it is never explained how such a persisting structure
or frame could exist when the only materials of which it could be
made are texts incapable of repetition. It is as if a weatherman,
reporting drought, lapsed into discussion of a flood.

Understood as study of an exchange of thought between or
among people rather than simply the structure or frame within
which they speak, a history of "discourse" opens the possibility of
texts being viewed as agents of change. Although this study does
not reject other agents of change (and sometimes refers to them as
partial explanations), its focus has been on texts and their responses
to each other. Since words can be repeated and texts are replicable,
failure in mimesis is not inevitable, and texts must account for
change in some other way than native "inability to repeat." Inability to repeat is the result of a conflict between the text and some
other reality, some other text or social situation or personality. A
text's failure to replicate itself indicates the presence of an opposing
context. Whereas the conflicting reality is no doubt often nonver-
bal, the approach of this book has been to examine conflicts between "texts" in the narrow sense—for example, the verbal texts of
conversion and consciousness.

Far from supporting a nihilistic view of history as a series of
meaningless, arbitrary disjunctions, a legitimate semiotic approach
supports rather old-fashioned narrative, interpretive strategies in
which there is assumed to be a logical relationship between events
and their antecedents. If the historical process is a semiotic process,
it is therefore also, in Peirce's view, a logical process. It is not true

14. Ibid., 16, 221.

that "Logic, according to Peirce, is only a semiotic. . . . And logic
. . . occupies in that semiotics only a determined and not a fundamental level."[15] Logic is fundamental because, in Peirce's view,
logic is not "a semiotic" but all semiotic. Again, it is Peirce's insistence on the third element in signification, the interpretant, that
makes his semiotic constructive and positive. Whether the relation
between the signified and the signifier is indexical, iconic, or symbolic, the interpretant of the sign is determined by a process of
thought. And logic, the science of thought, is therefore also the
science of sign interpretation. Peirce's analysis of the possible relations between the signified ("object" in his terminology), signifier
("sign") and "interpretant" might be diagrammed as in figure 6.

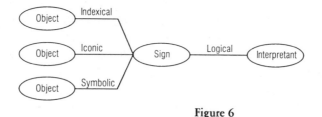

Figure 6

While supporting traditional narrative history, a semiotic approach does suggest one abrupt departure from the traditional conception of intellectual history. A semiotic approach renders untenable the assumption that intellectual historians deal with materials
and problems fundamentally different from those of other historians. Signs are objects. If thinking is in signs, thinking is not the
subjective action described in the consciousness concept. Thinking
is action as objective and external as casting a vote or leading an
army into battle. The common view that it is less historical to be
interested in the history of thought *per se* than in the influence of
thought on "real" events, especially in the political and social
spheres, is founded on the false distinction in the consciousness

15. Derrida, *Of Grammatology,* 48. For a more accurate view, see Max Fisch, "Just
How General Is Peirce's General Theory of Signs?" *Peirce, Semeiotic, and Pragmatism:
Essays by Max Fisch,* ed. Kenneth Laine Kettner and Christian J. W. Kloesel
(Bloomington: Indiana University Press, 1986), 356–61.

concept between subjective thought and objective action. Only by rejecting such views and by keeping in mind a point that Peirce and other late nineteenth-century psychologists established—all human thought is action and all human action is thought—does it become possible to view the developmental logic of a sequence of thoughts as a real force able to constrain and determine human behavior. Some intellectual historians, notably J. G. A. Pocock, have insisted that thought is action, but Pocock describes the history of intellectual activity as the history of "second-order activities"—that is, theory.[16] This may be a fair description of theory, but it is unlikely to rouse social historians from their sleepy conviction that intellectual activity and "reality" are not very intimate acquaintances.

Intellectual history should not address the naive question about the relation of "thought" to "action" that it is usually thought to address. To refuse to address that question is not to cop out but rather to insist on the mistakenness of the question. Thought cannot help but change the world, for thought *is* action. Since the history of thought is the history of action, it is just as "historical"— and in a diachronic sense a good deal more so—to study the impact of thought on thought as to study the impact of thought on action (using "thought" and "action" in their traditional, narrower senses). Only by emphasizing that thought may be appropriately described as *physiological* action will the false dichotomy between intellectual and "real" events be overcome. Peirce, in a typically anomalous statement of his monism, declared that "faith requires us to be materialists without flinching."[17]

16. J. G. A. Pocock, "A New Bark Up an Old Tree," *Intellectual History Newsletter* (April 1986): 4.

17. Peirce, "A Guess at the Riddle," *CP,* I, 354. For a superbly lucid point of entry into recent developments in mathematical theory that provide support for Peirce's semiotic monism, see René Thom, *Mathematical Models of Morphogenesis,* trans. W. M. Brookes and D. Rand (New York: Halstead Press, 1983).

Acknowledgments

For help in securing research grants or in reading manuscript, and in some cases for both, I am grateful to Albert Anderson, Thomas Bender, Stephen Collins, George Cotkin, Norman Fiering, David Hall, David Hollinger, Carol Hoopes, Daniel Walker Howe, Bruce Kuklick, Kenneth Lynn, Fred Matthews, Jean Matthews, Bruce Mazlish, and Jesper Rosenmeier. Diane Collins skillfully prepared the line drawings.

For financial aid and released time from teaching, I am indebted to the American Antiquarian Society, the Babson College Board of Research, the John Simon Guggenheim Foundation, and the National Endowment for the Humanities.

The American Antiquarian Society, the Boston Athenaeum, and the libraries of Babson College, Brandeis University, Harvard University (especially the Divinity School), and Wellesley College provided most of the source materials. Their staff members were generous and helpful.

Quotations from the manuscripts of Charles Morton are published by permission of Houghton Library and the Harvard University Archives. Figures 1 and 2 are published by permission of Indiana University Press.

I could have written this book more quickly if Carol, Johanna, and Benjamin Hoopes had not been or become part of my life while I wrote. It might have been no worse a book, but it would not have been as good a life.

Index

INDEX